MARK TWAIN ABROAD

DEWEY GANZEL

MARK
TWAIN
ABROAD

THE CRUISE OF THE
"QUAKER CITY"

The University of Chicago Press
Chicago and London

Library of Congress Catalog Card Number: 68–16691
The University of Chicago Press, Chicago 60637
The University of Chicago Press, London, W.C. 1
© 1968 by The University of Chicago. All rights reserved
Published 1968. Printed in the United States of America

For C.H.G. *and* F.G.DeF.

ACKNOWLEDGMENTS

The research for this book was encouraged and sustained by several dozen generous people. Many of these are personal friends who would be embarrassed if I should single them out for special thanks. Most are members of the staffs of public libraries—people who are for the most part as anonymous to me as I am to them, those who brought me books, found little-known or long-forgotten items in their collections which I never would have found alone, and, with remarkable patience, gave me advice when I asked for it (and often before I asked). I am particularly indebted to the staffs of the New York Public Library, The Library of Congress, The Western Reserve Historical Society, and the Oberlin College Library.

I am especially grateful to the Trustees of the Mark Twain Estate for permission to use, cite, and quote previously unpublished manuscript materials and for their permission to reprint Clemens' unpublished play about the *Quaker City* voyage as well as the photograph of Clemens and Charles Langdon. Most of Clemens' unpublished manuscripts are in the Mark Twain Papers at the University of California, Berkeley, and as anyone who has used it knows, this collection is a model of efficient organization and availability. I have indicated specific indebtedness to the Papers in my notes, and these, I hope, make clear that without the Mark Twain Papers and their editors, past and present, my task would have been much more difficult, if not impossible. All previously unpublished Clemens' manuscript materials quoted in the text are copyrighted by the Mark Twain Company.

I appreciate the kindness of the Librarian and staff of the Patten Free Library, Bath, Maine, who allowed me to copy Captain Duncan's manuscript log and to reproduce the painting of the *Quaker City*. I am indebted to John E. Duncan for permission to quote from the log of his great-grandfather, Captain Charles Duncan, and for his generosity in allowing me to reproduce the photograph of the captain.

I am grateful to Mr. Severance A. Millikin who allowed me to quote from *The Journal Letters of Emily A. Severance*, a privately printed edition of the letters which his grand-mother wrote on the *Quaker City* journey. I should also like to thank Mr. Howard Henderson for his great assistance in searching out important data and Mrs. Isabel Angus Enscoe for information about her grandfather, Dan Slote, as well as for the photograph which I reproduce of the man who was Clemens' closest friend on the voyage.

I have here and there quoted from previously printed sources. Most of these are ephemera or works now in the public domain, but I have used a number of copyrighted works, the products of a generation of able Clemens schol-ars, and this debt—an enormous one—I have tried to indi-cate in my notes. My research has been supported by grants in aid from Oberlin College. Parts of this book have ap-peared, at various stages of its incubation, in *Modern Philology, Anglia*, and *English Language Notes*.

D. G.

CONTENTS

ILLUSTRATIONS

ABBREVIATIONS

AL *American Literature*

Alta *San Francisco Daily Alta California*

Autobiography *Mark Twain's Autobiography*, ed. Albert Bigelow Paine, 2 vols. (New York: Harper and Brothers, 1924)

BM *Mark Twain, Business Man*, ed. Samuel C. Webster (Boston: Little, Brown and Company, 1946)

Cutter Bloodgood Cutter, *The Long Island Farmer's Poems* (New York: N. Tibbals and Sons, n.d.)

Herald *Cleveland Herald*

IA Samuel Clemens, *The Innocents Abroad; or, The New Pilgrims' Pilgrims' Progress* (Hartford, Conn.: American Publishing Company, 1869)

Journal Letters Emily Severance, *Journal Letters of Emily A. Severance*, ed. Julia S. Millikan (Cleveland: The Gates Press, 1938)

Letters *Mark Twain's Letters*, ed. Albert Bigelow Paine, 2 vols. (New York: Harper and Brothers, 1917)

Log Captain Duncan's log, manuscript in Patten Free Library, Bath, Maine

MF *Mark Twain to Mrs. Fairbanks*, ed. Dixon Wecter (San Marino, California: Huntington Library, 1949)

MTP Mark Twain papers, the University of California Library, Berkeley, California

Notebook *Mark Twain's Notebook*, ed. Albert Bigelow Paine (New York: Harper and Brothers, 1935)

Paine Albert Bigelow Paine, *Mark Twain: A Biography*, 3 vols. (New York: Harper and Brothers, 1912)

Porter Josias Leslie Porter, *A Handbook for Travellers in Syria and Palestine*, 2 vols. (London: John Murray, 1858)

Sun *New York Sun*

TMB *Mark Twain's Travels with Mr. Brown*, ed. Franklin Walker and G. Ezra Dane (New York: Alfred A. Knopf, 1940)

Traveling *Traveling with the Innocents Abroad*, ed. Daniel Morley McKeithan (Norman, Oklahoma: University of Oklahoma Press, 1958)

Woman's Pilgrimage Mrs. Stephen Griswold, *A Woman's Pilgrimage to the Holy Land; or, Pleasant Days Abroad* (Hartford, Conn.: J. B. Burr & Hyde, 1871)

I

NEW YORK CITY

"Isn't it a most attractive scheme?"

The overwhelming desire of the European to emigrate to America has a singular counterpart in his overwhelming desire, once he is established on these shores, to return to Europe as an American tourist. Though immigrants, by and large, have accepted the attitudes and assumptions of their adopted country wholeheartedly and with few misgivings,

A list of abbreviations used for frequently cited sources will be found on p. xiii. All page numbers given within parentheses or brackets in this book refer to *The Innocents Abroad* (Hartford, Conn.: American Publishing Co., 1869).

1

they have maintained, even through several generations, a special interest in revisiting the "old world." The attraction is not solely or perhaps even primarily familial, but rather something more subtle and harder to identify—a need to determine a cultural identity in contrast to other similar but distinct cultures. This "new breed" is most demonstrably American away from home. Immersed in the current of European civilization, the American discovers those cultural attitudes that are distinctively his own; the foreign delineates the familiar; the old divides the borrowed from the new. Whatever his supposed reasons for crossing the Atlantic—provincial curiosity or cultural pilgrimage—the American goes to Europe, as Emerson said, "to be Americanized." What he finds there—whether in Whitman's "old dynastic slaughterhouse" or James's "sublime synthesis"—is something of himself. The European tour, the natural consequence of this appetite, is as old as America itself. Economic depression may restrict it, wars may stop it for a time, but European travel has recurred whenever Americans have had money and leisure.

This phenomenon was never more obvious than in the years immediately following the Civil War. For four years, transatlantic travel had been difficult and incompatible with patriotic sentiment, but with the coming of peace all restrictions disappeared and European tourism returned at a rate which would have been incredible a few years before. America was resuming its love affair with Europe, its prewar diffidence supplanted by a vulgar appetite which seemed irrepressible. For the war had made many Americans rich—very rich—and Europe lay waiting to be bought and, apparently, brought home for a price.

No showcase was more masterfully arranged to satisfy this appetite than the Paris Exhibition of 1867. It was to be a worldwide bazaar: every country with any national pretensions—from Great Britain and the United States to Siam and Loo-choo—was to be represented. It was to be (its advance publicity promised) the most spectacular display of art and industry the world had ever seen—more than 150,000 square yards of exhibition area not counting the enormous park and horticultural garden which was to be erected around it, and thousands of exhibits from almost every field of human endeavor.[1] Most important of all, it was to be set in the most sophisticated city in the world, a city which was itself the epitome of civilization.

The Exhibition was just the sort of lure to attract Americans. "Everybody will go to Paris who can," wrote a newspaper correspondent in 1867, and, although the cost of living was at a nearly all-time high and a collapse of the economy seemed imminent to many, thousands of Americans were going abroad; the U.S. Secretary of the Treasury estimated that Americans would spend $75,000,000 in gold in Paris during the summer of 1867.[2] "We are shipping ten and maybe even twelve thousand persons a month from the port of New York alone," wrote another correspondent, "and if all our other ports together are doing half as much, America will have sent considerably over a hundred thousand persons to Europe, (chiefly to Paris,) this year before the time for travel in that direction is up." [3]

The desire of Americans to go to Europe in 1867 exceeded the capacity of ships to take them, and booking passage for the late spring and early summer was completed far in advance of sailing. The regular carriers could not supply nearly enough berths, and many ships long unused to passengers and some which had never seen them before were pressed into service. In early April, when little space was left, an advertisement appeared in several New York papers:

EXCURSION TO PARIS
ITALY, GREECE, CRIMEA
HOLY LAND, EGYPT, &C.

The Magnificent side-wheel ocean steamship

QUAKER CITY

Will leave with the above excursion (accompanied by Lieut. Gen. Sherman,) on

Saturday, June 8th
At 3 o'clock P.M.

[1] Paris Universal Exhibition 1867, *The Complete Official Catalogue* (Paris, 1867), p. iii.

[2] *The Independent*, April 11, 1867.

[3] The correspondent was Clemens; *San Francisco Daily Alta California*, May 19, 1867; *TMB*, p. 193.

The ship will visit St. Michael's, Gibraltar, Marseilles, Genoa, Leghorn, Caprera, Civita Vecchia, Naples, Palermo, Athens, Corinth, Constantinople, Sebastopol, Smyrna, Holy Land, Egypt, Malta, Cagliara, Palma, Valentia, Madeira and Bermuda, and the party will have ample opportunity to visit Paris, Lyons and all points of interest in Italy, Switzerland and the Holy Land.

Gen. Sherman writes:—"Your programme is all that could be desired, and should be adhered to absolutely."

Applications to join the party (now nearly complete, the number being limited to 110) must be made to the Committee through

C. C. Duncan
117 Wall Street, N.Y.[4]

Even the casual reader could see that this was to be no ordinary voyage. Paris? Of course, but not Paris alone; the entire Mediterranean was to be laid at the feet of these happy excursionists—"Italy, Greece, Crimea, Holy Land, Egypt, &c." As if this were not enough, there was to be on board one of the most famous heroes of the Recent Unpleasantness, General Sherman himself. It was no surprise that one did not merely book passage but, rather, applied to "the Committee" to be among the 110 passengers admitted to such a voyage.

Inquirers were given a brochure which listed even more delicious surprises and details. "The undersigned [Charles C. Duncan] will make an excursion as above during the coming season, and begs to submit to you the following programme," it began. "A first-class steamer, to be under his own command, and capable of accommodating at least one hundred and fifty cabin passengers, will be selected, in which will be taken a select company, numbering not more than three-fourths of the ship's capacity. There is good reason to believe that this company can be easily made up in this immediate vicinity, of mutual friends and acquaintances." (Such intimacy suggested that it was almost indelicate to advertise.) "A middle and pleasant route will be taken across the Atlantic, passing through the group of Azores, . . . a day or two will be spent here, enjoying the

[4] *Brooklyn Daily Eagle*, April 9, 1867.

fruit and wild scenery of these islands," then Gibraltar and "a day or two . . . looking over the wonderful subterraneous fortifications." Along the coast of Spain to Marseilles, where passengers might disembark for the Paris Exhibition and visit besides, "the beautiful city of Lyons, lying intermediate, from the heights of which, on a clear day, Mont Blanc and the Alps can be distinctly seen." To Genoa—overland through Switzerland or on the ship itself—from whence "excursions may be made to Milan, Lakes Como and Maggiore, or to . . . Verona (famous for its extraordinary fortifications), Padua, and Venice." The group would visit Rome, of course, and Naples and "Herculaneum, Pompeii, Vesuvius, Virgil's tomb, and possibly, the ruins of Paestum." Then Palermo and a trip through the Aeolian Isles, in sight of Stromboli and Vulcania ("both active volcanoes"), through the Straits of Messina, "with Scylla on the one hand and Charybdis on the other" to Athens, the Greek Isles, Constantinople, the battlefields at Sebastopol, then to Smyrna, and overland or by sea through the Holy Land— "Jerusalem, the River Jordan, the Sea of Tiberias, Nazareth, Bethany, Bethlehem." To Alexandria—Cairo and the Pyramids!—and then, via Cagliari and Parma ("All magnificent harbors, and charming scenery, and abounding in fruits"), to Spain and, "after spending a short time with our friends the Bermudians," home! Surely no place abounding in historical or cultural interest (to say nothing of fresh fruit) had been omitted from this progress. And the manner of travel was to be the ultimate in ease and style:

A southern track will be taken, and the Atlantic crossed within the latitudes of Northeast trade winds, where mild and pleasant weather, and a smooth sea, can always be expected. . . . The steamer will be provided with every necessary comfort, including library and musical instruments.

There were to be two Mason and Hamlin organs and a Chickering piano, and a printing press from which would issue a daily newspaper throughout the trip. "An experienced physician will be on board. . . . The ship will at all times be a home, where the excursionists, if sick, will be surrounded by kind friends, and have all possible comfort and sympathy." All boating in port would be at the expense of the ship and "articles of interest or curiosity, procured by the passengers during the voyage, may be brought home in the steamer free of charge." Finally, the trip could be extended or the itinerary changed en route by a unanimous vote of the passengers.[5]

With such an attraction, surely the Committee on Applications would have to be stringent! However, another factor helped to keep the company select—the fare was $1,250 and, in addition, a minimum of $750 in gold was suggested for travel expenses away from the ship. This was in sharp contrast to the mere $200 fare of a first-class, round-trip journey to Paris on a Cunard steamship. Considering the length of the cruise, the price was reasonable, but it was, nevertheless, clearly beyond the means of all but the very rich. This was to be a luxury cruise—the *first* luxury cruise—a phenomenon, since become a standard American resort, in which the rich could be rich together.

In one important respect, however, the *Quaker City* cruise was to be different from its successors. The rich would be not only rich but pious too. Word-of-mouth publicity soon made well known what could not be crassly printed in the advertisement or brochure: Henry Ward Beecher, the most famous evangelical minister in America, was planning personally to escort the party through the Holy Land! To the cultural attractions of storming Europe with General Sherman was to be added the spiritual enrichment of exploring Palestine hand in hand, so to speak, with the most dynamic Christian of them all. Beecher, his reputation as yet unsullied by the scandal with Mrs. Tilton, had an enormous national following. His presence on the voyage would assure its success, not only among his own affluent congregation at Plymouth Church, Brooklyn, but also among church groups throughout the country who read his sermons in the *Independent,* a national weekly, and fervently supported his brand of muscular Protestantism. (It is possible that Beecher's interest in writing his life of Christ—published several years after the cruise—first suggested the voyage to Captain Duncan, himself a member of

---

[5] The brochure is reprinted in *IA* pp. 20–23.

Plymouth Church; the Holy Land was the initial goal of the voyage and the Paris Exhibition a supplementary attraction.)

In any case, Beecher's reputation attracted many of those who made application "to join the party." Initially, at least, the largest group was from Plymouth Church, those "mutual friends and acquaintances" whom the brochure had courted, but passengers came from all over—Ohio, Massachusetts, California, Oregon, Pennsylvania, Missouri—everywhere, in fact, that the clarion call was heard by people who had $2,000 to spend and five months' leisure in which to spend it.

It is somewhat ironic, then, that the passenger who ultimately brought fame to the voyage was himself neither rich nor pious, leisured nor genteel. In fact, had the *Quaker City* departed six months earlier, he would not have been aboard at all, for when Samuel Clemens landed in New York on the cold morning of January 12, 1867, he had no plans to leave. It must have seemed to him then, standing on the upper deck and watching the great ice-shrouded steeples of the city come into view, that he was making a hero's return. Thirteen years before, a gawky frontier boy of nineteen, he had left home for the first time, traveled to New York to see the Crystal Palace World's Fair and, "taking a liking to the abominable place," had stayed six months, working as a printer's helper. In 1853 he had had only a dream of success; in 1867 he had begun to taste its first fruits—thousands of newspaper readers in the West knew him as Mark Twain, and it seemed clear that millions throughout the country soon would. For he arrived in New York in 1867 with the kind of newspaper assignment every reporter dreams of. Five years of roughing it with western frontier papers had gained him such a following among San Francisco readers that he was able to demand and receive a roving commission to write occasional letters to the *San Francisco Daily Alta California*. He was to write as often as he liked and about any subject, however casual, which held his imagination, and New York promised to be of inexhaustible interest. In contrast to the lonely boy he had been during his first sojourn, the man of 1867 seemed surrounded by people he had known in the West, many of them old friends who, like himself, had come back to "the States," back East, for national fame and fortune. He had every reason to believe, as his ship moved through the ice-choked harbor, that he would remain, happily, in New York for some time to come.

Six weeks later the ice in the Hudson River had begun to disappear, and so had his satisfaction with the city. "The only trouble about this town is, that it is too large," he wrote the *Alta*. There was something about the distances between places and people in a large city which was foreign to Clemens' imagination. It was as if he were unable to grasp the multiplicity of urban society; it seemed confused and ultimately meaningless to him.

The town is all changed since I was here, thirteen years ago, when I was a pure and sinless sprout. The streets wind in and out, and this way and that way, in the most bewildering fashion, and two of them will suddenly come together and clamp the last house between them so close, and whittle the end of it down so sharp, that it looms up like the bow of a steamship, and you have to shut one eye to see it. The streets are so crooked in the lower end of town that if you take one and follow it faithfully you will eventually fetch up right where you started from.[6]

When he had described the superficial activities of the town—the raciness of the theater, the personalities (Beecher, Anna Dickinson, Ada Isaacs Menken), and the tourist sights—he found he had little else to say. "I have just written myself clear out in letters to the *Alta*," he wrote his mother, "and I think they are the stupidest letters that were ever written from New York. Corresponding has been a perfect drag ever since I got to the States."[7]

The solution, clearly, was to move on. But how? Although he was being well paid for his *Alta* letters, he was as hard pressed by the post–Civil War inflation as any wage earner. His California friend, Charles Henry Webb, in 1867 a New York publisher, agreed to bring out a book of his collected pieces (*The Celebrated Jumping Frog of Calaveras County, and Other Sketches*), but it would bring no royalties until summer, and Clemens did not hope for much even then ("I

---

[6] *Alta*, February 2, 1867, *TMB*, pp. 82, 83.
[7] *Letters*, p. 127.

don't believe it will ever pay anything worth a cent," he wrote home).[8] Even his lectures on Hawaii, so successful on the West Coast, failed to draw. He was at a dead end.

He knew, however, where he wanted to go. Just as his trip to Nevada in 1861 epitomized the surge of Americans westward to new opportunity, so his appetite for European travel in 1867 suggested the counterattraction of a journey east to the supposed source of learning and culture. He wanted to be a part of "the perfect exodus" of Americans he saw going abroad. "It is as much as I can do to scare up an individual who will acknowledge in a calm, unprejudiced manner that he is not going to Paris this year," he wrote,[9] and if that was the way the country's imagination turned, should not his as a journalist's turn that way too? Besides, he was partial to fairs of any kind. The Crystal Palace had attracted him to New York thirteen years before, and now the Paris Exhibition drew him to Europe.

He heard about the *Quaker City* excursion early—nearly a month before the advertisement appeared, and he endorsed it enthusiastically in a letter to the *Alta*:

Prominent Brooklynites are getting up a great European pleasure excursion for the coming summer, which promises a vast amount of enjoyment for a very reasonable outlay. The passenger list is filling up pretty fast. . . . It is essentially a pleasure excursion, and so private caprices will be allowed full scope. Isn't it a most attractive scheme? Five months of utter freedom from care and anxiety of every kind, and in company with a set of people who will go only to enjoy themselves, and will never mention a word about business during the whole voyage. It is very pleasant to contemplate.[10]

He did more than contemplate the pleasure. It was exactly the sort of trip he had been looking for. He liked nothing better than shipboard living, and the excursion promised five months of it, moving past a panorama of scenes and subjects which would give an inexhaustible variety to his letters to the *Alta*. It was not, he was informed, gotten up for speculation either. The sponsors of the cruise did not

[8] *Paine*, p. 320.
[9] *Alta*, May 19, 1867, *TMB*, p. 193.
[10] *Alta*, March 2, 1867, *ibid.*, pp. 111–13.

intend to make money out of it, and this was, in part, the reason such a strict control over the passenger list had to be maintained. Although Clemens appears to have been somewhat fearful that he would not meet the standards of the Committee, he paid his ten per cent deposit for the voyage and took his chances.

They were slim ones. If he were approved, he was told, he had to pay the remainder of his fare, $1,125, by April 15 or lose his deposit and his place. He did not have his fare and there was, apparently, only one place he could get it. Would Fredrick MacCrellish & Company, the proprietors of the *Alta California,* be willing to finance his journey? This seemed uncertain, but he wrote them nevertheless, proposing an arrangement whereby the *Alta* would pay his passage and twenty dollars apiece for fifty letters of a column and a half each, about 2,000 words per letter.[11] "I expect to go on this excursion to the Holy Land and the chief countries of Europe," Clemens wrote, "provided I receive no vetoing orders from the *Alta*—and against all such I fervently protest beforehand." [12]

He knew the scheme would be superficially attractive to the proprietors, for every newspaper of any pretensions had a "Special European Correspondent" in Europe in 1867. Americans were avid for news of Europe and the Exhibition, and unless a newspaper had a staff correspondent on the scene, most news was months old by the time it appeared in provincial newspapers. A paper the size of the *Alta* had several foreign correspondents with part- or full-time status, and it was not inconceivable to Clemens that he might be made one of these. The proprietors, however, regarded his plans with misgivings and probably would have refused him if his good friend Colonel John McComb, an important member of the paper's editorial staff, had not spoken strongly in his favor. At length, the owners agreed and telegraphed the chief of their New York bureau to "ship Mark Twain in the Holy Land Pleasure Excursion & pay his passage." [13]

[11] *Autobiography,* vol. 1: 243.

[12] *Alta,* March 2, 1867, *TMB,* p. 116.

[13] Clemens to his family, April 15, 1867, Waller Collection, photostat in *MTP.* See also *Paine,* vol. 1: 310 n.

Clemens did not hear of their decision immediately, for he had traveled to Missouri to visit his mother and was gone for more than a month. When he returned, he was delighted with the news and called at 117 Wall Street to arrange the details of his passage.

We had to wait awhile, because the Chief manager was not in [he wrote his family later the same day] & we did not make ourselves known. A newspaper man came in & asked how many names were booked & what notabilities were going, & a fellow —(I don't know who he was, but he seemed to be connected with the concern,) said, "Lt. Gen. Sherman, Henry Ward Beecher & Mark Twain are going, & probably Gen. Banks!" I thought that was very good—an exceedingly good joke for a poor ignorant clerk.

It was an unexpected compliment to be billed as an attraction, and he was delighted by it. He did not know then how important he was to be to the list of "notabilities."

When my jolly old Captain came in, [he continued] we squared accounts & then went down to look at the ship (Steamer Quaker City.) She is a right stately-looking vessel.[14]

The *Quaker City* was a good-sized ship for an excursion. Registered at nineteen hundred tons, she was just over thirteen years old in 1867, having served briefly with the Collins (American) line for North Atlantic service between New York and Liverpool and later as a supply ship in the Civil War. Her service speed was ten knots (twelve for short periods), which was fast enough for a cruise, and she had been, as the advance publicity put it, "newly rebuilt, and fitted up in an elegant manner, with handsome saloons, pantries, etc." [15] The "rebuilding" consisted chiefly of repainting, but she was no doubt a handsome sight: a clipper bow gave her black hull a somewhat rakish look, the paddle boxes which covered her two side wheels were a bright red, and the two tall smokestacks were a gleaming black.[16] She

---

[14] *Ibid.*

[15] *New York Tribune,* June 8, 1867.

[16] N. R. P. Bonsor, *North Atlantic Seaway* (Prescot, Lancashire, 1955), p. 58.

was one of the early ocean paddle-wheel steamers, a hybrid that could not rely wholly on steam for long-distance locomotion, and fore and aft she carried fully rigged masts. Her cabins were large, but not luxurious. They had "room to turn around in," Clemens said, "but not to swing a cat in, at least with entire security to the cat" (p. 29). They were, however, "neatly arranged and more spacious than those of the English steamers," wrote another passenger. Her cabin was typical and very comfortable. "It had two berths, wash-stand, and a long seat with a cover, which you could raise and pack away many articles. This had a cushion covered with red velvet forming a sofa. The state-room also contained a mirror, a number of shelves, and the floor was nicely carpeted." [17] All of the lower-deck cabins, such as this one, were connected by a small passage to a "saloon," or lounge, furnished somewhat elaborately with several crimson velvet sofas and easy chairs. There were two such saloons, one forward for ladies and one aft for gentlemen. From each, a flight of polished steps led up to an elegant dining room which had six long tables, a chandelier, and large windows with gilt cornices and heavy damask curtains. It was here that Sunday services were to be held, and the room was furnished with the new piano as well as a cabinet organ to accompany hymns on those occasions. From the dining room, one could exit to the promenade deck, which extended more or less the length of the ship and from which the upper-deck cabins could be reached. Amidships, confined by the paddle boxes on either side and a deckhouse fore and aft, was a large area which could be protected from either sun or showers with tarpaulins; in this gangway was a large bulletin board for posting general notices and the daily reckoning of time change and mileage. Also on the upper deck was the large after cabin, a saloon forty or fifty feet in length which contained tables for writing, comfortable chairs for reading, and another piano. On the forward deck were large pens to hold the cattle—bullocks, sheep, and hogs—which the ship would carry for provisions, and nearby was space for chicken coops which would be lashed to the decks during the voyage. Although

---

[17] *Woman's Pilgrimage,* pp. 135–36.

the *Quaker City* was not the palace afloat which those who organized the cruise believed it to be, it was, as one of the passengers wrote home, "quite as good as I had anticipated." [18]

Clemens himself was delighted. The ship, he said, was being "sumptuously fitted up," and his upper deck stateroom, he declared, was "handsome." He was pleased with the other arrangements for the cruise, too:

Our ship in which we are to sail for the Holy Land, is to be furnished with a battery of guns for firing salutes, by order of the Secretary of the Navy, and Mr. Seward has addressed a letter to all foreign powers, requesting that every attention be shown General Sherman and his party. We have got a piano and a parlor organ in the cabin, and a snare drummer, a base [*sic*] drummer and a fifer, and the passengers are instructed to fetch along all their old guitars, fiddles, flutes and sheet music. . . . I have got . . . a regular brick for a roommate. We have got the pleasantest and jolliest party of passengers that ever sailed out of New York, and among them a good many young ladies and a couple of preachers, but we don't mind them. Young ladies are well enough anywhere, and preachers are always pleasant company when they are off duty. We sail the 8th of June, positively. [19]

Clemens' certainty was ill-founded, however. A week after he wrote the above, the cruise all but collapsed: Henry Ward Beecher was not going after all. Nearly 110 passengers had signed to make the journey, but among them were forty-five members of the Plymouth Church who were not so interested in seeing Europe and the Mediterranean as they were in accompanying their pastor wherever he might be going, and now he was not going anywhere. As one of the passengers told the story afterward:

Mr. Beecher, finding his name made use of for the purpose of bolstering up the enterprise, a position not bargained for and one which is always distasteful to a person of sensitive nature, suddenly remembered that he had engaged to write "Norwood," and would be compelled to forego the pleasure of accompanying the excursion.

[18] *Journal Letters,* p. 4.
[19] *Alta,* April 30, 1867, *TMB,* pp. 165–66.

Here was a damper. What was to be done? A committee of
two, consisting of the manager and a friend, waited upon the
divine and implored him to reconsider and relent. But he was
firm; he must write "Norwood;" very sorry, indeed, but could
not possibly go, and the committee retired, saddened and disheartened.

The forty-five members of Plymouth church, who had only
wished to accompany Mr. Beecher and whose interest in the
excursion had now ceased, also seceded. Their respectability was
so assured that they had not been required, as members of other
churches had been, to prepay a percentage of the passage money,
and there was, consequently, nothing in the way of their change
of mind. It was an unlooked-for and terrible blow.[20]

Beecher's novel, *Norwood*, had already been published (in
May, 1867), so the correspondent was incorrect on that
point, but his irony was justified. It is clear that Beecher
had had little intention of going, and in retrospect it seems
surprising that anyone could have believed he would take a
five-month vacation from his pulpit when he had so many
plans—political and literary (*Norwood* was being drama-
tized) as well as religious—underway. It is very unlikely
that Beecher connived with Duncan to fill the passenger
list—there had been, after all, no *public* announcement of
his intention to join the party; that had been entirely
word-of-mouth publicity, born, in all likelihood, out of
Beecher's casual interest by Duncan's own high hopes—but
Beecher must have known his name was being used. In any
case, when he declared that he would, like a good pastor,
stay put with his parish, almost all his followers decided to
stay put, too. Having demanded no deposit from Beecher's
Plymouth fellows, Duncan now faced a financial crisis, for
he had made large out-of-pocket expenses in securing and
refurbishing the ship.

Beecher's "withdrawal" was only the first calamity.
Scarcely three weeks after Beecher announced his lack of
intention, General Sherman also withdrew. He had said, it
now appeared, only that the itinerary was excellent and
should be followed—not that he would be on board to follow
it. As these constellations fell, lesser stars also dropped

[20] Dr. Abraham Reeves Jackson in *New York Herald*,
November 21, 1867.

away. Maggie Mitchell, who had some fame as an actress, was a last-minute addition—and a last-minute cancellation; even the offer of a free passage for herself and her mother could not hold her. The New York contingent, the "mutual friends and acquaintances" for whom the cruise had originally been planned, now numbered a mere handful, and if they had not already paid their passage money, they too might have withdrawn. The cruise was on the verge of collapse; Clemens was its sole celebrity. "My passage is paid, and if the ship sails I sail on her," he wrote his family, "but I make no calculations, have bought no cigars, no sea-going clothing—have made no preparations whatever —shall not pack by trunk till the morning we sail." [21]

Duncan, however, had no choice but to proceed. If the cruise were canceled entirely, he would have to refund passage money already collected, and this he could not do. He had to make a brave show of it and dragoon as many passengers as he could. Now the "Committee on Applications" began to exercise its functions in a manner that Clemens later satirized. In spite of the show of demanding references and proofs of character, *no* prospective passenger was refused. It became apparent, as Dr. Jackson phrased it, that "the committee was only a myth, and that behind the curtain which veiled the imaginary faces of its members beamed only the bland countenance of the manager himself, and that all the essentials of a good character were covered by the 'twelve hundred and fifty dollars, currency.' " Duncan's efforts were not particularly successful; although he reported to the New York *Tribune* that the cruise was realizing a sum of $180,000, scarcely 70 passengers were finally booked for the *Quaker City,* and although a few more were to join the party in Europe, the minimum quota he had set was barely two-thirds filled.

Duncan's difficulties did not seem to lessen the excitement of the passengers, however. Moses Beach, the editor-publisher of the *New York Sun,* held a gala reception for his fellow travelers two days before sailing, and the style of the party suggests the excursionists' great expectations. "We are to meet at Mr. Beach's next Thursday night," Clemens

[21] *Paine,* vol. 1: 321.

wrote his family, "and I suppose we shall have to be gotten up regardless of expense, in swallow-tails, white kids and everything *en régle*." [22] Uncertain though he was about departure, Clemens was excited by the prospect of meeting the shipmates in whose company he hoped to see half the Western world.

He found the introduction pleasant. He relished being a celebrity, and he always enjoyed making new acquaintances. As the *Sun* was to report the next day, he "enlivened the company with ebullitions of wit." On first encounter he seems to have been delighted with his fellow passengers. "We have got a crowd of tip-top people, and shall have a jolly, sociable, homelike trip of it for the next five or six months," he wrote his good friend Will Bowen the next day.[23] And, indeed, the people who gathered at Beach's home did seem remarkably agreeable, if not very heterogeneous. Almost all were rich—and showed it: "Mrs. Dimon . . . wears the most elegant diamonds I think I ever saw," [24] one passenger remarked of another. Most were from the East Coast, and all were members of upper-class society—all except one, that is; Clemens appears to have been the sole wage earner among them. And initially he was a little awed.

The party itself was a fitting prelude to the elaborate style which the *Quaker City* maintained throughout the voyage. Seventy guests were served an elaborate buffet on the grounds of Beach's home in Richmond Heights, which had a spectacular view of the bay. Such circumstances encouraged fraternization, and when the discussion turned to plans for the excursion, there was remarkable unanimity and gaiety. "Captain Duncan desires me to say that passengers for the *Quaker City* must be on board to-morrow before the tide goes out," Clemens announced. "What the tide has to do with us or we with the tide is more than *I* know, but that is what the *captain* says." [25] How could such a bouyant group be deterred by *any* natural phenomenon?

[22] *Letters,* p. 126.
[23] Clemens to Bowen, June 7, 1867, *Mark Twain's Letters to Will Bowen* (Austin, Texas, 1941), p. 15.
[24] *Journal Letters,* p. 11.
[25] Quoted by Mary Mason Fairbanks, "The Cruise of the 'Quaker City'" *Chatauquan* 14 (January, 1892): 429.

Of course, as readers of *Innocents Abroad* know, Clemens' high regard for his shipmates was to decline rather precipitously after the cruise was actually underway, but the reception at Beach's suggested none of this. Indeed, among the *Quaker City* passengers Clemens met for the first time that evening, there were a few—a very few—persons with whom he remained very friendly, and one, at least, who became a lifelong confidante. The Beach party was a notable experience in Clemens' life, for it was there he met Mary Mason Fairbanks, a woman who was to be not merely a good companion on the voyage but an intimate associate for the rest of her life, one who was to occupy a position in Clemens' esteem shared by only three or four other persons. Their friendship was not an immediate one—the trip was well advanced before they became really close friends—but even at this first meeting they were attracted to one another. The interest was not a romantic one: she was thirty-nine when they met, seven years older than Clemens, and though the difference in their ages was not very apparent, it made it easy for Clemens to call her "Mother" Fairbanks, the name which the younger passengers on the voyage gave her in deference to her affectionate concern for them.

Mrs. Fairbanks was one of seven passengers from Cleveland (the largest contingent from any city outside New York), but she was not, strictly speaking, a Middle Westerner. Although born in Ohio, she had spent most of her life in the East, principally in New York City, and had graduated from Emma Willard's Seminary at Troy. After teaching school for some years, she had married Abel W. Fairbanks, the wealthy editor and publisher of the *Cleveland Herald,* who was eleven years her senior; by him she had two children—a son who was twelve at the time of the *Quaker City* cruise, and a daughter, eleven. Although her husband and children did not accompany her on the voyage, she was not traveling alone; the Cleveland group looked to her as their de facto leader, and the dispatch with which she directed them through Europe suggests that she was no fading Victorian flower but a woman with enormous vitality, a practical turn of mind, and a strong will. "I hardly know how we could have done without her in Marseilles," one of the Cleveland party wrote home.

She became indispensable to the entire ship—a fluent

French interpreter, a gracious hostess when the ship entertained royalty, and a ready conversationalist of wit and
intelligence. In contrast to the acerbity of most of the ladies
on the voyage, her warmth and cheerful demeanor were a
constant source of pleasure. She was also a writer of considerable grace, and her letters to the *Cleveland Herald*,
dispatched more or less regularly throughout the excursion,
reveal her as a person of imagination with taste, perception,
and discrimination. These were qualities Clemens valued
and (as his letters to her suggest) he drew upon them for the
next thirty years.

She was the most refined, intelligent, & cultivated lady in the
ship, & altogether the kindest & best. [he wrote his family
shortly after his return] She sewed my buttons on, kept my
clothes in presentable trim, fed me on Egyptian jam, (when I
behaved,) lectured me awfully on the quarter-deck on moonlit
promenading evenings, & cured me of several bad habits. I am
under lasting obligations to her.[26]

No other person Clemens met at the Beach reception
became as close a friend as Mrs. Fairbanks, but there were
others who at the time seemed compatible. His host, Moses
Sperry Beach, was one of these. Their friendship was encouraged by the fact they were both newspapermen. The
Quaker City roster seemed filled with correspondents
("looks like a reporters' congress," Clemens wrote in his
notebook), but unlike Clemens and Beach most of these
reporters were amateurs, sending letters of incidental observation to hometown newspapers which printed them as free
and mildly interesting fillers. Clemens never scorned such
writing, but throughout the voyage he was pressed by the
necessity of composing regular newspaper letters, and he
could not help being amused by the dilettante authors who
could, if their inspiration flagged, put off writing their letters indefinitely. Beach, however, knew the pressure under
which Clemens worked. He too wrote a regular letter to his
paper ("A Father's Letters to His *Sun*"), and although as
owner he had no deadlines other than those of his own
making, he maintained his correspondence throughout the
voyage.

[26] *BM*, p. 97.

At forty-five Moses Beach was near the climax of a successful but not spectacular career in journalism. He and his brother Alfred inherited the *Sun* from their father when the latter retired, and when his brother withdrew from the proprietorship of the paper in 1852, Moses became, at thirty, one of the youngest owner-editors in New York newspaper history. The paper was consistently profitable, but under his management it seemed editorially ambivalent. Politically, it was nondescript and for a long time it seemed uncertain of its audience.[27] Beach was more interested in the mechanics of publishing than in the newspaper as a medium for information. He was an inventor of some importance and patented several devices, variations of which have become standard in printing: he was the first to feed presses from a roll of newsprint (previously, papers were printed a sheet at a time), and he is credited with being the first to print both sides of a sheet at once. These interests must have made Beach even more attractive to Clemens, who was himself so fascinated by such machines that he was to lose a fortune developing two unsuccessful typesetting devices.

The similarity of their interests serves, however, to highlight the marked difference in their careers in 1867. Beach's concern with publishing was declining when he embarked on the *Quaker City* cruise: after fifteen years as a newspaper owner, he had lost interest in journalism and was preparing to quit publishing and retire. Clemens, on the other hand, was newly committed to newspapers when he embarked on the voyage, and shortly after his return he became part owner of the *Buffalo Express;* it would be several years before he called himself "author" rather than "newspaperman." There was, in addition, a difference in age and in temperament. Beach was fifteen years older than Clemens and, like Captain Duncan, he was a fervent member of Beecher's Plymouth congregation and the superintendent of

[27] For example, for nearly two years Beach turned the paper over to a group of men who published it as a semireligious periodical. By the mid-1860's, however, the paper had become clearly identified as a workingman's sheet, featuring five or six columns of condensed news, a column of editorials, one of jokes and miscellaneous information, and two or more of fiction, of which it made a specialty.

its Sunday school. Clemens was never irreligious, but evangelical piety amused him (it was to be the butt of much light-hearted humor in *Innocents Abroad*), and Beach's religiosity discouraged a close friendship between them. There was, finally, a disparity in reputation which Clemens must have felt. Beach's career was glamorous, but Clemens' pride in his own talent was strong and well-justified; his own jealous self-regard kept him from courting Beach's interest or favor. Although he visited Beach in his home on at least one occasion after the *Quaker City*'s return, and appears to have responded indirectly to the older man's opinions when he revised his letters into *IA*, it is significant that he did not directly seek the aid of the established professional. In the light of these differences it is not surprising that their initial, sympathetic regard for one another did not ripen into fast friendship.

With Beach's seventeen-year-old daughter Emeline, however, Clemens was on different footing. She was to be, at least at the beginning of the voyage, his regular companion: he played chess with her during idle hours on board ship and corresponded with her for a time after the cruise ended. He called her his "old Quaker City favorite" and delighted in her fresh and unaffected manner. "You do say the *naivest* things that ever anybody said in the world, & hit the hardest possible hits, in the most comfortable way," he wrote her when she scolded him for satirizing the ship's prayer meetings, "—but I like it. Your reproofs are so honest, & so pleasant, withal, that I really can't help feeling a strong desire to deserve more of them!" [28] Despite the difference in their ages, Clemens had a great affection for Emeline. The romantic tone of his letters to her suggests that had their friendship been longer and better sustained, and her father more sympathetic to Clemens, their affection for one another might have deepened into love.

The fact that it didn't may have derived, at least in part, from Clemens acquaintance with another passenger at the Beach reception that evening. Charles Jervis Langdon, the "cub" of the group which was to cluster about Mrs. Fairbanks, was not Clemens' close friend on the voyage itself,

[28] Quoted in Bradford A. Booth, "Mark Twain's Friendship With Emeline Beach," *AL* 19 (November, 1947): 222.

but he was to become one of the most important men in Clemens' life. Shortly after the end of the cruise he introduced Clemens to his sister Olivia, whom Clemens soon loved and eventually married. Charlie was the only son of Jervis Langdon, a wealthy lumber and coal merchant of Elmira, New York, who had made his fortune contracting coal with nearby mines and railroads. Jervis Langdon, an ardent abolitionist, was a genial but somewhat severe man (as Clemens was to learn), and it is easy to believe the legend that he sent his son Charles abroad in 1867 to remove him from the scene of an ill-advised love affair.[29] It is easy to believe, too, that Charlie, dark-eyed and diffident, trying to look older than his seventeen years with a sporty if somewhat thin moustache, had been in a romantic scrape of some kind. Charlie is almost certainly the subject of Clemens' notebook description of

the innocent young man—who is good, accommodating, pleasant & well-meaning, but fearfully green & as fearfully slow, [who] began conversation in the smoking room with the remark that well, he believed the papers stated that Max had been captured at last—And got promptly snubbed by somebody who said the news was a week old. Then he exposed the fact that he had gone to sea without a passport.[30]

As might have been expected, it was a one-sided friendship. Charlie sought out Clemens and the humorist was initially annoyed. The boy would lounge in the men's saloon, self-consciously smoking or watching the men play cards and, to their annoyance, kibitzing. On one such occasion he criticized the wrong man. Clemens, who scarcely needed instruction in poker from anybody, looked at Charlie in mild surprise for a moment. "Young man," he drawled, "there's a prayer-meeting forward in the dining saloon and they need you there." [31] Clemens was unlikely to bear any real ill-will to so ardent a fan, however. Although Charlie was never his regular companion, they became

[29] *Journal Letters*, p. 215.

[30] "Unpublished Notebook no. 7" (Typescript, p. 10), *MTP*. An edited version appears in *Notebook*, p. 57.

[31] Jervis Langdon, "Some Reminiscences and Some Excerpts from Letters and Unpublished Manuscripts" (n. d.); copy in *MTP*. Langdon was Clemen's nephew, Charlie's son.

friends and, on occasion, confidants—as when in the Bay of Smyrna Charlie showed Clemens a miniature portrait of his sister Olivia, whom Clemens later claimed to have loved on sight.

Among the excursionists whom Clemens met for the first time at the Beach reception were at least two more with whom he was to be particularly friendly. Emily and Solon Severance were members of the Cleveland party and close friends of Mrs. Fairbanks—a circumstance which no doubt encouraged Clemens' affection for them. Like the rest of the Cleveland passengers, they were staunch members of the First Presbyterian Church, and it is surprising that Clemens should have been so friendly with people who were hardly less pious than other *Quaker City* excursionists whose religiosity he ridiculed. (Even in his teens Solon Severance had a reputation as a virtuous Christian who organized lunch-hour prayer meetings.[32]) The son of one of the earliest merchants of Cleveland, Solon was a very wealthy man, the president of the Euclid Avenue Bank (later to become the First National Bank of Cleveland), a post he had first assumed at twenty-seven. He was thirty-three when he traveled on the *Quaker City* and suffering from a nervous disorder which, although it seems to have hampered his travels very little, nevertheless demanded the constant ministration of his wife. Emily Allen Severance, the daughter of a physician and sister of another, was well able to nurse him. Mrs. Severance, who before her marriage had lived amid the pious radicalism of Oberlin, Ohio, was no less devout than her husband, but she was less severe in her evangelical fervor. Perhaps as a result, Clemens seems to have preferred her to her husband. She was just twenty-seven (the *Quaker City* sailed on her birthday) and, as Clemens noted, a "mild persuasive" woman, short and somewhat stout with a pretty face and luxuriant dark hair. It was for Solon's health alone that they undertook the voyage, for Emily's letters home indicate that, while she enjoyed the trip enormously, she was very homesick for her family and anxious about her three children, the youngest of whom was still a baby. Her devotion to her husband was

[32] William G. Rose, *Cleveland: The Making of a City* (Cleveland, 1950), p. 239.

complete, however, even though he appears to have demanded much from her. Her letters imply that he suffered from periods of depression and ennui, and his actions seem to have been somewhat erratic. Toward the end of the voyage, for example, he seriously considered leaving the excursion and taking up residence in Europe without his wife. He gave up that plan, finally, but not before it had given her much anguish.

There was another passenger who attended the Beach reception whose friendship with Clemens was to last long after the cruise was over. This was Dan Slote, Clemens' "splendid, immoral, tobacco-smoking, wine-drinking, godless room-mate," who was "as good and true and right-minded a man as ever lived." [33] Clemens had met Slote at least two weeks earlier, and he liked him. "He has got many shirts, and a History of the Holy Land, a cribbage-board and three thousand cigars," Clemens wrote. "I will not have to carry any baggage at all." [34] They were not, finally, cabinmates, however; shortly before sailing Clemens was given No. 10, the spacious portside cabin which had originally been assigned to General Sherman. But for the two weeks preceding the voyage they thought they were to be roommates and developed an appropriate camaraderie which continued throughout the voyage. It was a fortuitous combination, for it is unlikely that anyone else on the ship could have been so completely compatible with Clemens. Dan Slote was the thirty-nine-year-old partner in Slote-Woodman Company, a New York banking firm. He was, when Clemens first met him, a round-faced, slightly balding man with a moustache reminiscent of Clemens' own. His humor, too, was like Clemens', droll, dry, and the parlor-car variety which Clemens enjoyed. Dan was Clemens' closest companion on the voyage; except for occasional side trips, they journeyed constantly in one another's company, and this closeness bred unusual loyalty between them. Clemens' attraction to Slote was not derived solely from the latter's amiability; he was charmed, too, by Slote's family, which, he declared, were "the best and most homelike people I have yet found in a brown stone front." There was no "style"

[33] Clemens to his mother, June 1, 1867, *Letters,* p. 126.

[34] *Alta,* May 28, 1867, *TMB,* pp. 247–48.

about them, none of the false politesse which he had learned
to dislike so in the New York "society" he had met.[35] And
yet they lived in the upper-class luxury which Clemens was,
all of his life, fascinated by, and he remarked on the elegance of their house and furniture to his mother. His friendship with Slote continued long after the return of the
Quaker City.

There were two other lively bachelors at Beach's party
who were to serve Clemens well as companions on the
voyage: Julius Moulton ("Moult") and Jack Van Nostrand, both much younger than he. About Moult very little
is known except that he was from St. Louis and therefore
likely to have shared Clemens' own attitudes toward the
eastern company. Jack, a lively youth from Greenville, New
Jersey, appears to have been Clemens' closer friend, and
there are a number of references to him both in Clemens'
notebooks and in *IA* itself. However, Clemens' first impression of Jack was not a happy one. In his notes he described
a "long-legged, simple, green, wide-mouthed horse-laughing
young fellow, who once made a sea-voyage to fortress Mon-
roe in the Oceanica, & now knows it all. He quotes eternally
from his experiences upon that voyage." Jack was, at least
initially, something of a bore. "I am satisfied that we shall
never hear the last of that voyage," Clemens wrote, and he
cared little for the "extravagant, devil-may-care boisterous-
ness & freedom which he imagines to be characteristic of the
man of the world." [36] This first impression was not, fortunately, a lasting one, and Clemens came to like Van Nostrand a good deal and to spend some of his most carefree
hours on the journey with him. He was, Clemens later
recalled, "a good-hearted and well-meaning boy."

Of course, there were other passengers at the Beach reception whom Clemens would get to know and enjoy on occasion; he was far too gregarious a man to limit himself to
any small circle of friends for five months, and he was the
best-known man on board the *Quaker City*. But—excluding
his host—eight alone seemed to find a lasting place in his
affections. Clemens' feelings toward most of the rest of the
"tip-top people" were to change dramatically before the

[35] *Letters,* pp. 127–28.

[36] "Unpublished Notebook no. 7" (Typescript, p. 9), *MTP.*

voyage was ended. The man who started the trip with such expectation ("I am wild with impatience to move—move—*move!*" he wrote his mother before he sailed) and such bonhomie was disillusioned by the end of the voyage and felt real antipathy for most of his fellow passengers. "I don't want their friendship," he wrote Mrs. Fairbanks after their return

I don't want their good opinions, I wouldn't have their good offices. I don't want any commerce with people I don't like. They can hurt me. Let them. I would rather they should hurt me than help me. All the friends I wanted in that ship were: Yourself; Mr. & Mrs. Severance; the cub; Emma Beach; Dan; Moulton; Jack; I don't remember any others—I don't suppose there *were* any others. My opinion of the rest of the gang is so mean, & so vicious, & so outrageous in every way, that I could not collect the terms to express it with out of any less than sixteen or seventeen different languages. Such another drove of cattle *never* went to sea before. Select party! Well, *I* pass.[37]

The comic overstatement he employs here suggests that he was not entirely serious, but the underlying discontent with the other pilgrims was real. A bit overly impressed by good food and good manners, a bit seduced by wealth and culture beyond his experience, he overrated his new acquaintances at the Beach reception. The mutual circumstances of meeting were happy ones, but it was, perhaps, inevitable that he would soon find himself separated from the majority of his companions on the voyage. They were, after all, embarking on a pleasure excursion; he was fulfilling a newspaper commitment. He alone was undertaking the voyage not as tourist but as a full-time newspaper correspondent to whom all his experiences and all his acquaintances were potential subjects to be "used" in his writing. He was, necessarily, a critic as well as a participant—but to the large majority of the *Quaker City* passengers, he was an unacceptable historian and *Innocents Abroad,* an unacceptable chronicle of the voyage.

We didn't amalgamate—that was all [Clemens was to write of the *Quaker City* excursionists]. Nothing more than that. I was

[37] *MF*, p. 5.

exceedingly friendly with a good many of them—eight out of the sixty-five—but I didn't dote on the others, and they didn't dote on me. We were always glad to meet, but then we were just as glad to part again. There was a little difference of opinion between us—nothing more. They thought they could have saved Sodom and Gomorrah, and I thought it would have been unwise to risk money on it. I never failed to make friends on shipboard before—but maybe I was meaner than usual, this trip.[38]

It is a characteristic comment—a humorous overstatement of an essentially serious, trenchant observation. People were, for him, the real source of experience; his imagination was most readily evoked by social situations, and the absence of compatible associates was intolerable to him as a man and debilitating to him as a writer. It was this lack of friendly society which had driven him from New York, that "splendid desert" where, he said, "there is little sociability, and, consequently, there is little cordiality." [39] He was repelled by a social decorum which placed the superficial attitudes of impersonal custom and "good manners" above the simple show of interest and sympathy born of pure fellow feeling. The "little difference of opinion" between him and most of the *Quaker City* Pilgrims was a profound one, for he was probably right in suggesting they assumed a virtue derived not from feeling but from form. His manner offended many of his companions; in the words of one of the passengers, "Clemens was not respectable," [40] and there must have been many ways in which his western vitality seemed crude and vulgar, but to him *their* manners were sham.

On Saturday, June 8, the *Quaker City* was ready to sail. Duncan's dragnet had fished up enough passengers to support the voyage, but for most of them it was their first trip abroad and the confusion of departure was intensified by their excitement. Lost baggage and late arrivals complicated the arrangements. Ships chandlers swarmed over the vessel, delivering turkeys and chickens, geese and ducks,

[38] *Alta*, November 20, 1867; *Traveling*, pp. 310–11.

[39] *Alta*, June 5, 1867, *TMB*, p. 259.

[40] Nina Larrowe in the *Portland Morning Oregonian*, April 22, 1910.

and cattle to be slaughtered en route. The public parlors were decked with flowers from (perhaps) abject friends in the Plymouth Church; huge bouquets stood on all the tables and large hanging baskets of growing plants were hung in the dining saloon. There were guests—every passenger had two or three on board—to be seen off, and letters of farewell to be written and rewritten and sent—as well as salutations to fellow passengers (now old friends!), and amid the furor, the *Quaker Mirror* distributed its first issue, its lead article, "Our Departure," beginning, "Every aspiring knight, in view of an onlooking world, endeavors to create a sensation by some exploit of skill or courage," and running on ". . . humbling to our pride . . . firm foundations . . . we raise, whether foot or pen, in much uncertainty . . . we are sailors now . . . ,"[41] etc. Last-minute telegrams were received and dispatched. "What . . . tearful adieus, waving of handkerchiefs, flinging back of kisses to the weeping, watching ones at the wharf," wrote Mrs. Fairbanks, "my heart is in a whirl."[42]

At exactly 2 P.M. ("so promptly," wrote Moses Beach, "that some watches had not yet fully determined to indicate the hour fixed for sailing,"[43] the *Quaker City* under the command of Captain Duncan, whom the *New York Tribune* called that "well-known sailor and shipping merchant," left its berth at the foot of Wall Street and headed for the sea, leaving behind one indecisive passenger, Bloodgood Cutter, who still pondered whether he should make the trip. Two excursion boats, the *Silas O. Pierce* and the *Fletcher*, carried well-wishers alongside the ship as far as Fort Hamilton, and there—with tears and the ultimate dispatch of more letters—the passengers took their leave of New York.

But not, unfortunately, of New York Harbor. The ship did not sail for two days. Rain had begun to fall as the ship left its pier, and by the time the *Quaker City* entered the lower bay the wind had reached gale strength, and Duncan decided to remain anchored in the calm waters of the harbor until the storm abated. This anticlimax did not lessen the

---

[41] Quoted in *New York Sun*, June 10, 1867.
[42] *Cleveland Herald*, June 11, 1867.
[43] *Sun*, June 10, 1867.

high spirits of the passengers, however. The first days on board were festive, the food good, and almost no one seasick.

Monday morning the weather cleared and the ship began to build up steam for an early departure. At noon, with the ship's boilers almost ready, a long boat was sighted moving out from shore with eight men straining at its oars while a ninth stood wildly waving his arms and shouting something wholly unintelligible. Bloodgood Cutter, his mind finally made up, had decided to join the excursion after all. At

The Start of the Voyage

12:30 the engines were started and the great paddle wheels began to turn. The ship swung about, moving slowly at first and then faster, down the lower harbor, past the Narrows, and into the open sea. As the wake widened behind them the passengers struck up a hymn, "Homeward Bound," from the *Plymouth Collection:*

> Out on an ocean all boundless we ride,
> We're homeward bound.
> Tossed on the waves of a rough, restless tide,
> We're homeward bound,

they sang, while little Harry, the Captain's eleven-year-old
son, accompanied them on the wheezing Mason and Hamlin
organ.

> Far from the safe, quiet harbor we've rode,
> Seeking our Father's celestial abode,
> Promise of which on us each he bestowed,
> We're homeward bound.[44]

In his log, the Captain waxed cheerful too: "Night comes on
with large swell," he wrote. "Pleasant weather and nearly
all the passengers on board sick." [45] The voyage had begun.

[44] (New York, 1864), p. 506.

[45] *Log*, p. 4. The significance of Duncan's log was first noted by
Charles Shain in "The Journal of the *Quaker City* Captain," *New
England Quarterly* 28 (September, 1955): 388–94.

II

"A Crowd of tip-top people . . ."

The voyage thus so auspiciously begun was to be one of the most famous journeys of the nineteenth century. Its fame would derive from the presence of Clemens, who was to rewrite his letters to the *Alta California* and publish them as his first important book, *Innocents Abroad.* Clemens' chief intention in his newspaper letters and in the book itself was to entertain, but he had long since learned, as most of his "phunny phellow" predecessors had not, that to entertain continuously one had to inform and to criticize as well as amuse. Of course *Innocents Abroad* is not a strictly historical account of the voyage; confined by Clemens' intention, it could not be. "Mainly, he told the truth," but he told it like a good storyteller, with his audience clearly in mind, and that audience was American and like himself— iconoclast, intellectually uninhibited, and self-assertive. *Innocents Abroad* projects a distinctively American personality. Other Americans had traveled abroad and written of their journeys with judgment and wit, but Clemens was one of the first to embody in his account a national consciousness no longer restrained by geographical isolation and cultural adolescence, a consciousness intellectually vital and magnificently brash, the evidence of America's coming of age. The book's title was ironic, for Clemens' irrepressibly American persona was intended to be neither inexperienced nor naïve. He was a critic, and his book declared that European civilization was henceforth to be criticized from a peculiarly American point of view. His judgments were frequently outrageous—he was ludicrously unsophisticated at times, and he often illustrated the worst characteristics of American provinciality. But he was more often brilliantly perceptive and exact, and witty enough to give his criticism force.

Significantly, however, *Innocents Abroad* describes not merely Europe and the Holy Land, but the American excursionists who visited those places. Readers of his account may easily see that, if his criticism of Europe is sharp, his implied criticism of American tourists is equally so. Of course, Clemens embarked *expecting* to criticize his fellow passengers for his readers' amusement—caricature had always been one of his chief comic devices, and even before he met his shipmates he had made notebook comments about an imaginary bumpkin, "Blucher," who evinced all the usual provincial attitudes of an American going to sea for the first time. But if his fellow excursionists did not initiate his critical attitude, they certainly encouraged it and gave it substance, for the conventional group of pilgrims who met one another at the Beach reception appeared, once on board the *Quaker City*, to be a *bizarre* group.

Characteristically, the first organized activity of the excursion was a church service. In the light of Clemens' repeated sallies at the religiosity which accompanied the journey one might assume he had an antipathy for ministers. He didn't. If anything, he had an affinity for the clergy, among whom he had several lifelong friends. Never very orthodox himself, he could, nevertheless, live comfortably with the orthodoxy of others so long as it was tempered with a sense of humor. Generally he found preachers pleasant company when they were "off duty," and many preachers found him pleasant too. His interest in ministers may have derived from an unfulfilled desire to be one. "It was the only genuine ambition I ever had," he wrote his nephew Sam Webster about the time of the *Quaker City* trip, "—but somehow I never had any qualification for it *but* the ambition." [1] When he heard there were to be clergymen on the voyage, he welcomed them. "Send on the professional preachers—" he wrote his mother, "there are none I like better to converse with. If they're not narrow-minded and bigoted they make good companions." [2] Unfortunately, he liked none of the clergy aboard the *Quaker City*. Had Beecher come along, things might have been different, for Beecher had attracted several like-minded ministers who wished to accompany him to the Holy Land. But when Beecher left, only three clergymen remained, and they were not a happy lot.

Chief among them was Henry Bullard, a Presbyterian from Wayland, Massachusetts, who, acting as the ship's chaplain, conducted the church service in New York Harbor. He was young, only twenty-seven, and from a family of ministers (his father had been the pastor of the First Presbyterian Church of St. Louis), and his evangelical fervor appears to have been keen—a circumstance which could not have been felicitous to Clemens, who believed his soul his own. Their initial acquaintance was dispiriting. "Rev. Mr. Bullard preached from 11 Cor. 7 & 8th verses about something," Clemens wrote in his notebook following that first service. [3] Bullard appears to have given a somewhat lackluster sermon, the gist of which was that salvation was assured the man who does "as well as he can," a sentiment that most of his listeners, still full of embarkation euphoria, approved.

[1] Samuel C. Webster Collection (Typescript in *MTP*).
[2] *Letters*, p. 126.
[3] "Unpublished Notebook no. 7" (Typescript, p. 10), *MTP*.

(Mrs. Severance, for example, thought the sermon "excellent.") [4] Clemens could have taken the preaching, perhaps, if the "off-duty" personality of the preacher had been other than it was. Although there was only a four years' difference in their ages, they had no interests in common. Clemens was particularly put off by the younger man's salvation manner, which was much too narrow for his taste. A week or so after the ship was underway, Clemens and Bullard were drawn into a religious conversation, at the conclusion of which Bullard remarked to Mrs. Severance, evidently with some chagrin, that he "hoped that from this voyage many souls might be born again." [5] Clemens, however, wanted no part in the clergyman's obstetrical plans.

The other two ministers were much older than Bullard. One, E. Carter Hutchinson, a sixty-one-year-old Episcopal priest from St. Louis, was an acquaintance of Clemens' mother, though this made no difference to Clemens. Hutchinson may have been the passenger described in a letter to the *Alta* as the "solemn, unsmiling, sanctimonious old iceberg that looked like he was waiting for a vacancy in the Trinity" who demanded to know if the excursion would come to a halt on Sundays to observe the Sabbath, and when informed that it could not suggested the passengers should "calculate their chances before doing wrong"; that he had "always got into trouble when he travelled on the Sabbath, and that he should do so no more when he could avoid it." [6] The third minister on the voyage, G. W. Quereau, of Aurora, Illinois, was, at forty, closer to Clemens' own age. One might have expected Clemens to have got to know him well, but he scarcely mentions him.

Clemens' antipathy toward what he considered the excessive piety of the excursion derived, however, not so much from the presence of the ministers on board as from the impression he got from many of the excursionists who, he claimed, gave the trip the tone of a "Grand Holy Land Funeral Procession." The church services he could abide,

---

[4] *Journal Letters*, p. 7.

[5] *Ibid.*, p. 15.

[6] *San Francisco Daily Alta California*, June 6, 1867; *TMB*, pp. 276–77.

but the daily prayer meetings he found obnoxious. Indeed, these public displays of godliness became increasingly odious to him. "There is nothing that gives startling variety to a picnic like prayer meetings," he wrote. The idea of daily prayer services originated not with the ministers on the voyage—although they welcomed them—but with Captain Duncan, who, while not a minister himself, appears to have acquired the demeanor of one. Three days out of New York, the captain announced that henceforth between the hours of eight and nine in the evening interested passengers should attend services in the upper saloon, a room which Clemens soon dubbed the "Synagogue." Every night thereafter the passengers met for devotions, or at least most of them did, and the absence of those who did not was remarked. One of the first meetings, described in Duncan's log, was typical:

At 8 P.M. gong sounded for Prayer Meeting and speedily a goodly company assembled in the Saloon—Meeting was conducted by the Capt. in the Plymouth Church order—viz singing—prayer by Col. Denny of Virginia—another hymn—prayer by Mr. Severance of Ohio—again a hymn—Scripture read—after which addresses and prayers by Messrs. Quereau, Church, Beckwith & Bullard—Closing prayer by the Captain. Doxology—"Praise God from whom all blessings flow" & benediction by Mr. Bullard—meeting lasted just one hour.[7]

Initially, Duncan presided, but other passengers regularly assisted, and eventually a new leader was chosen for each day by the leader of the preceding meeting. Virtually all the male passengers on the ship served at one time or another, and—distasteful though it was to him—Clemens himself led the meeting on occasion. Of course, he was not alone in his distaste; rather soon the meetings became short, less than half an hour, but they remained tedious, and their efficacy seemed doubtful to Clemens: "There were those in the ship's company who attributed the fact that we had a steady siege of storms and head winds for five mortal months solely to the prayer meetings," he wrote on his return. "But I was not of that faction."[8]

[7] *Log*, pp. 14–15.
[8] *New York Herald*, November 20, 1867; *Traveling*, p. 315.

The blame fell inevitably on Captain Duncan, who rather arbitrarily maintained these devotions. Unlike the legitimate men of the cloth, he was to receive harsh treatment at Clemens' hands. The "jolly old Captain" of the first few weeks was to become, before the end of the voyage, an object of distrust and real dislike—a dislike which, abetted by Duncan's own actions, was to lead in ten years to the most bitter quarrel of Clemens' life. Duncan was, according to one advance report of the voyage, a Captain "who never swore an oath—never drank a glass of liquor, and though he has crossed the Atlantic *fifty-eight* times, never suffered a shipwreck, nor lost a man by accident." [9] There was clearly supposed to be some correlation between Duncan's virtue and his good fortune at sea: all his mishaps were apparently deliberate ones.

No doubt the atmosphere of the *Quaker City* which Clemens remarked so often derived from the Captain's somewhat ostentatious piety. The greatest disagreement between them, however, concerned their contrasting attitudes toward drinking. Like many parishioners of Henry Ward Beecher, Charles Duncan was a temperance supporter. Samuel Clemens was not, and his preparations for the voyage showed that he did not intend *his* part of the pleasure excursion to be abstemious. "An importing house sent two cases of exquisite champagne aboard the ship for me today—Veuve Clicquot and Lac d'Or," he wrote his mother before the ship departed. "I and my room-mate have set apart every Saturday as a solemn fast day, wherein we will entertain no light matters or frivolous conversation, but only get drunk. (That is a joke.)" [10] It was, of course; two cases of wine would not support a spree, but the carefree attitude the comment suggests would not have found much sympathy in Duncan or the more severe passengers on the voyage. Clemens was only a casual drinker, and he clearly resented the implication of several passengers that he was an habitual one. The cause of his later feud with Duncan was the latter's public declaration that Clemens had been drunk when he applied for passage on the steamer. This Clemens vehemently de-

[9] *American Agriculturist,* 26 (March, 1867): 86.
[10] *Letters,* p. 127.

nied and suggested in turn that Duncan was a hypocrite who drank in secret, a charge which was certainly untrue.

But Duncan's piety would not have rankled Clemens if it had not been attached, in Clemens' mind at least, with a grasping cupidity. Long before the voyage ended, Clemens became convinced that the cruise had been designed as a strictly commercial venture and that Duncan's description of it as a nonprofit tour was a lie. There is much to support this belief, and many of the passengers shared it, but perhaps the criticism is somewhat picayune. With the exception of General Sherman, the cruise *did* include all that the brochure promised, but as the irritations which accompany such a voyage grew more frequent, Captain Duncan received more and more criticism for what Clemens believed to be, at the very least, disingenuousness. And by the time the ship docked at Marseilles, Clemens had made a list of Duncan's broken promises and hypocritical actions.[11]

His dislike was to grow steadily more emphatic and was never to lessen. Captain Duncan was "the loudest, the longest, the most irrepressible & inextinguishable suppliant among the Quaker City's pilgrims," Clemens wrote several years after the voyage.

These [prayer] meetings could have been made useful to the cause of religion, if the circumstances had been different; but the thought crept into many humble, seeking hearts, that if heaven was to be populated with Duncans it might not be wise to proceed rashly in so serious a matter. There were some lowly, simple souls, who thought the thing over without levity, & decided that barring certain defects, hell had its advantages.[12]

Duncan's middle-class respectability was, perhaps, intensified by the presence on the voyage of his wife and two sons. Mrs. Duncan, whom Mrs. Severance described as a "large, fleshy woman, not particularly prepossessing in appearance," [13] acted, on occasion, as though the ship were her home and the passengers her guests. Harry, the Duncans'

---

[11] "Unpublished Notebook no. 7" (Typescript, pp. 41–42), *MTP*.

[12] Clemens letter to *New York World*, February 18, 1877, manuscript draft in *MTP*.

[13] *Journal Letters*, p. 7.

eleven-year-old son, played the organ during religious services, and George, the older son, was in charge of the ship's
newspaper. The passengers soon tired of Harry's daily encounter with the Plymouth hymns, and since the first (and
last) issue of the *Quaker Mirror* had virtually no news and
cost ten cents for a single 8-by-11-inch sheet, neither were
they endeared to George. Clemens had no stomach for any
of them: "You must always refer offensively to Captain
Duncan," he wrote Mrs. Fairbanks some years later,[14] and
for his part he always did.

Clemens' dislike for Duncan was some time in coming,
however. While it did, there were others on board who began
to make him question his initial judgment of the "crowd of
tiptop people." Some of these were doctors. Unlike most of
his fellow passengers, Clemens took no comfort from the
number of physicians among the excursionists. "I have got
the bly-ak—and there's 8 doctors on board," he commented
sardonically in his notebook after four days at sea. If one
doctor couldn't help his nausea, eight seemed no real advantage. His attitude toward medicine was always ambivalent,
and this ambivalence sometimes showed itself in his feelings
about doctors themselves. Two doctors on the voyage, Albert Crane of New York and Edward Andrews of Albany,
were particularly annoying to him. When Mrs. Fairbanks
dared to say on her return that she missed the *Quaker City*
passengers, Clemens summoned the memory of these saturnine men. "Why mourn for Albert Crane?" he wrote in
mock dismay. "Why sorrow for Dr. Andrews? . . . There
are other Kangaroos that you can scrape acquaintance
with."[15] Andrews he found unusually obnoxious, especially
his manner of spouting guidebook details—usually incorrect
ones—in a sagacious manner. In an early notebook entry
Clemens quotes him by name:

Dr. Andrews at breakfast said: "Which side was the pillars of
Hercules on?"
  "Both"
  "Some think different—Gibbon does." (The old fool had been

14 *MF*, p. 213.
15 *MF*, pp. 6–7.

smelling in a guide-book, and was trying to play it for old
information that had been festering in his brain.) [16]

Clemens did not allow such an ideal subject to remain
undeveloped, and Dr. Andrews appears in *IA* as "The Oracle," a gross and bitter burlesque, who "eats for four and
looks wiser than the whole Academy of France." The innocent notebook entry was made bizarre:

"Do you see that there hill out there on that African coast?" [The
Oracle asks one morning at breakfast]. "It's one of them Pillows
of Herkewls, I should say—and there's the ultimate one alongside
of it. . . . Old Gibbons don't say nothing about it,—just shirks it
complete—Gibbons always done that when he got stuck—but
there is Rolampton, what does *he* say? Why, he says that they was
both on the same side, and Trinculian, and Sobaster, and Syraccus,
and Langomarganbl—" (p. 70)

The narrator quits the Oracle in despair as, indeed, Clemens
did Andrews.

For one of the eight doctors aboard, however, Clemens
developed a real affection. Abraham Reeves Jackson, "The
Doctor" in *IA*, was the ship's surgeon and a man of good
humor and great charm. Clemens probably got to know him
well during the first few days of the voyage when seasickness was almost universal among the passengers; in such
distress Jackson must have seemed a ministering angel.
Although this was his first trip abroad, he was, apparently,
untroubled by the heavy seas the *Quaker City* encountered
out of New York, and he doctored most of the passengers
and many of the crew in a manner which helped to make
him one of the most popular men on board. Although he was
nearly nine years older than Clemens (he celebrated his
fortieth birthday when they had been at sea a week), Jackson became a close friend of the humorist during the voyage.
He was excellent company for Clemens on several trips
ashore, and much of the wit of "The Doctor" was verbatim
from his prototype. In Jackson, Clemens found a companion
with his own mordant sense of humor. It was he who traveled through northern Italy with Clemens, enlivening the

---

[16] *Notebook*, p. 63.

trip by baiting the guides and burlesquing the American tourist abroad. Jackson shared not only Clemens' sense of humor but also his critical view of the voyage; he expressed the hope on his return that the excursion would "be the last of its kind." [17]

It is surprising that Jackson had not been abroad before, for, like Clemens, he had been fascinated since childhood by ships and marine engineering. Unlike Clemens' interest, however, Jackson's remained only a fascination; he stayed on shore, studied medicine, and became an M.D. at twenty-one. He practiced general medicine in his home town of Stroudsburg, Pennsylvania, and during the war had been the Assistant Medical Director of the Army of Virginia for three years. However, despite his joviality, he was not a particularly happy man. Less than two years before the voyage, his wife of fifteen years had died. The end of the war had left him, like many others, with no clear professional direction, and signing on the voyage as ship's surgeon may have been a welcome break with the past. The excursion was, therefore, a significant turning point for him—in fact, he met his second wife among the passengers.

Apart from church services, prayer meetings, and seasickness, the first few days on the Atlantic were uneventful. Monday's weather was clear, though the sea had a heavy swell, and the brilliant sunshine coaxed most of the passengers up on deck. Even those who were becoming seasick stayed topside to bask in the sun. The night brought the rise of a full moon, brilliantly luminescent, and because they were sailing eastward, it seemed to hang motionless, returning each evening at the same spot in the cloudless sky from which it had disappeared the night before. The idleness of the first few days was pleasant. "You may be amused at the ingenuity of persons in inventing amusements," Mrs. Fairbanks wrote home.

. . . A voyage across the ocean must necessarily be monotonous, and we hail with eagerness every incident. Sometimes we rush to the side of the vessel to watch the gambols of a school of porpoises,

[17] See Jackson's letter (signed "A Passenger") in the *New York Herald*, June 20, 1867.

or strain our eyes to catch a clearer view of the whales, whose spoutings look like fountains in the distance.[18]

Some of the ladies crawled upon the paddle boxes to get a better view, and waved ecstatically to the few vessels that passed them—an Irish immigrant ship whose passengers waved back, a German and a French whose passengers did not—and the men learned "horse billiards," as Clemens called the variation of shuffleboard played on the quarter deck. About the deck, groups of passengers read guidebooks and planned European tours. Some played backgammon or dominoes, others wrote home voluminously about the little that was happening. "One is inclined to be too listless even to read or write," [19] said Mrs. Severance. Some merely sat and conversed, or played guessing games. "We spend our days on deck," wrote Mrs. Fairbanks, "—all who are well enough to get up there. 'Mark Twain' sat with us after dinner and amused us. We are each to prepare an original conundrum." [20] (Mrs. Severance, her face badly sunburned, won: "Why is my face like a bird about to fly? Because they are both to soar.")

On Wednesday evening, under the bright, clear sky of the upper deck, Bloodgood Haviland Cutter, Long Island Poet extraordinary, made his debut. It was Clemens' first encounter with the man who was to become the "Poet Larriat" of *IA*, and the introduction was a memorable one. Cutter was the indecisive passenger who joined the ship at the very last minute, and before the voyage was over, most of his fellow passengers were to wish that he had missed it, for he was a self-styled bard who insisted on reading his poetry on all occasions. He was a fifty-year-old Long Island farmer from Little Neck, distinguished by his size (he weighed less than one hundred pounds) and by his penchant for breaking into rhyme with a certain willful persistence. He would compose poems "on all possible subjects," Clemens wrote in his notebook, and give them, unrequested, to any man who came along "whether he has anything against him or not."

[18] *Cleveland Herald,* July 22, 1867.
[19] *Journal Letters,* p. 10.
[20] *Herald,* July 18, 1867.

His verses about the voyage were innumerable, and he published many of them in a flossy limited edition when the *Quaker City* returned to the U.S. "Why, bless your soul," Clemens quotes him as saying, "many and many a time when everybody else is asleep you'll find me writing poetry. And when I feel it coming on, there's no let-up to me." [21] Nor, apparently, for the rest of the passengers, who had to endure his recurring rash of rhyme in silence. He affected penury and piety and initially tried to earn his passage writing and reciting poetry on the voyage (the title "Poet Larriat" was, therefore, a burlesque of Cutter's simpleminded ambition), but when this was refused by the equally penurious Captain Duncan, Cutter decided to pay his way. He could afford to; he was a millionaire. [22]

His doggerel was both obnoxious and hilarious to Clemens, who, as readers of *Huckleberry Finn* well know, had a particular aversion to the homey, nineteenth-century elegy so popular with poets of Cutter's class. Emmeline Grangerford's burlesque lines to the deceased Stephen Dowling Botts ("all covered o'er with spots") echoed the effusions of several would-be poets of Clemens' acquaintance, one of them undoubtedly Cutter, since he made a specialty of writing touching poems to deceased acquaintances. Like many of his compeers, Cutter refused to accept the scorn of his times—he wrote hundreds of occasional poems, printed them as broadsides, and reprinted many of them in his collected works. He was, you might say, indefatigable. The *Quaker City* excursion stimulated his muse; inspiration was everywhere: he wrote several odes to the Atlantic Ocean, and one memorable set of verses to one of its inhabitants ("My friends, to gratify your wish,/ I hang up here a flying fish;/ Last night 'twas said he flew on board,/ And was not to the sea restored" [23]). Furthermore, he was a dangerous man to do a kindness for; almost anything might set him off, as the titles of some of his poems suggest: "Long Island Farmer to Mrs. Dr. Gibson on receiving a slice of tomato

[21] *Notebook*, pp. 59–60.

[22] See John T. Winterich, "The Life and Works of Bloodgood Haviland Cutter," *Colophon*, Part II (May, 1930), no. 5.

[23] *Cutter*, pp. 23–24.

brought by her from the Garden of Gethsemane, and distributed to us in our tent outside the walls of Jerusalem," or "Long Island Farmer to Mrs. Dr. Payne of Boston, one of the Quaker City passengers on receiving from her, her Carte-de-visete, and inquiring about the Baalbec ride." Even his debut that first Wednesday evening encouraged a new flood of sentiment entitled "Recollections of the Pleasant Time on Deck Last Night." Which pleasant time, Clemens was to remark drily, "consisted of his reciting 75 stanzas of poetry to a large, and largely captive audience on the upper deck." It was tedium they would willingly forego in the future.[24] "He is a peculiar man—fancying himself a poet, . . ." Emily Severance wrote. "He may be intelligent in some ways, but is scarcely a poet." [25]

To do nothing, some of the passengers realized, was to leave themselves helpless between Cutter's poems and Duncan's prayers. By Friday (five days out) the sea was calmer and the passengers were eager for more organized entertainment. The first event was suggested by Moses Beach: a gala birthday party for Mrs. Duncan that night. The event which followed was so elaborate and overblown it is surprising Clemens said nothing of it in his *Alta* letters and gave it only a line in *IA*, for it suggests the procedures the excursion had to engage in to entertain itself, and these activities were nothing if not artfully arranged. At eight o'clock the gong sounded and the passengers assembled in the main saloon and elected Dr. Crane chairman of the proceedings. (Every meeting had to have a chairman and every chairman had to be elected.) He, in turn, appointed Beach, Clemens, and Dan Slote to "wait upon Captain Duncan and his lady" and to escort them to the dining room where, with loud applause, Mrs. Duncan took a seat of honor.

The Rev. E. Carter Hutchinson had been elected principal speaker for the occasion and he gave himself up to a rather lengthy series of compliments to Mrs. Duncan (his acquaintance of five days) on her forty-sixth birthday. They were, the Captain noted in his log, "happy, instructive, and impressive" remarks, which ended with a poem

[24] *Notebook*, p. 60.
[25] *Journal Letters*, p. 13.

written by Mrs. Fairbanks ("Ah! pleasant friends, an abler pen/ Than mine should write the praises/ Of her who at this festive board/ Holds Court with all her graces," etc.) at the conclusion of which recitation Mr. Hutchinson placed on Mrs. Duncan's head a wreath several of the ladies had made from ivy growing in the hanging baskets of the dining room. Captain Duncan responded with thanks, "expressing his inability to do justice to the occasion," [26] and then Dr. Crane responded to this response, and Dr. Andrews responded to Dr. Crane's response. Finally, and for the first time on board, Clemens was called for. "This is Mrs. Duncan's birthday," he said. "I make this statement to gain time." When the laughter subsided he continued:

You have spoken of her youthful appearance, but I think she is old. Our life is not counted by years, but by what has been seen and accomplished. Methuselah was but a child when he died, though nine hundred and sixty-nine years old. The world did not improve any while he lived,—he tended his flocks just as his fathers did, and they none of them knew enough to make an iron fence. Mrs. Duncan has lived to see great improvements— [27]

She had lived, he went on, to see the railroads built and "the two continents clasp hands." Methusalah, on the other hand, didn't even "live long enough to see the fashions change." [28]

"Passing to graver subjects," Moses Beach reported of the speech,

Mr. Clemens dwelt upon the wonderful growth of our country within the last six and forty years; upon the progress which had drawn the merely border settlement of St. Louis from its border position to the very centre of a great and still growing country, and from its few rude log houses to be one of the great capital cities of the world. Mr. Clemens concluded by adverting to the really remarkable excursion which the company present had undertaken—the first of its kind in the history of the world—and congratulated Mrs. D. upon being able to associate this also

[26] *Log,* p. 12.
[27] Quoted in *Journal Letters,* pp. 12–13.
[28] Quoted by Mrs. Fairbanks in *Herald,* July 22, 1867.

among those events of her life which, though still in her youth,
give her rank as he had proven beyond the years of
Methusaleh.[29]

Clemens had become an accomplished occasional speaker,
and this is a good example of his style; his audience was not
very discriminating, perhaps, but Clemens was a great success.

Following his speech the *Quaker City* trio (flute, clarinet
and organ) performed, and as an inevitable climax, Bloodgood Haviland Cutter closed the extravaganza with one of
his poems, this one affectionately dedicated to Mrs. Duncan. He concluded it with rending sentiment:

> Once little thought her parents then
> She'd one day see Jerusalem;
> And with her children, on that sod,
> Tread on the soil our Saviour trod.
>
> Or with her husband she would go
> Across the boisterous ocean so;
> As forty years has rolled around,
> On the great ocean she is found.
>
> And on a grand excursion, too,
> The like of this we never knew;
> The same should be embalmed in verse,
> For after ages to rehearse.[30]

When this mortuary function was completed, there was ice
cream, lemonade and a cake especially prepared by the cook
of the ship. The jollification completed, passengers were
called to prayer meeting by Captain Duncan.

By Saturday, the fair weather had turned to foul. Rain
and heavy seas brought the excursionists back indoors after
the pleasant days on deck, and their amusement was of a
different sort. In the afternoon, passengers performed a
hastily convened "mock trial." As Clemens described it in
his notebook, it was a

---

[29] *New York Sun*, July 19, 1867.
[30] *Cutter*, p. 12.

Trial in the Circuit Court of the Commonwealth of Quaker City, of Robert Vail, Purser, charged with stealing an overcoat belonging to Sam Clemens. Judge Crane presiding. Rev. Henry Bullard Clerk, Dan Slote Sheriff, Moses S. Beach, Crier of the Court, Dr. Jackson, Surgeon of the Ship, Counsel for the State, Sam Clemens & Capt. Duncan Counsel for the defendant.—Six Jurymen. Eight witnesses examined. Speeches made. Alibi proven—also insanity of def't. Verdict guilty, with recommendation to mercy. Sentence inflicted on junior counsel [Clemens] in absence of the criminal—solitary confinement of straight whisky in room 10 for one hour & may God have mercy on your soul.[31]

The jury, Moses Beach reported, had "two retirements" to cabin No. 10 before the verdict was announced, occasions which may have helped to lubricate the humor of Clemens' summation. "Many did to that room resort,/ By the evidence before the court./ The witnesses plainly did declare,/ They got a little brandy there,/ And some I think did get some gin," wrote the "Poet Larriat." [32] "The Court was very well conducted, and proved a laughable affair," Emily Severance reported. "Mr. Clemens is the ruling spirit and a capital person for ocean life." [33]

On Sunday the weather began to clear, and the passengers began to get restless. They had been at sea only a week but it seemed much longer, and they were eager to sight the Azores, still four days away. Particularly restless were the younger excursionists. There were not many of these. Clemens reported that three-fourths of the passengers were between forty and seventy years of age, and while this may have been an exaggeration, it was not a great one. Of course, the smallness of number of younger passengers merely intensified their desire to break out of the somewhat sedate life they were forced to live on board, and on Monday evening, the weather clear again, they organized a dance on the upper deck. Immediately after the prayer meeting, ship's lanterns were hung on the stanchions, and the flute, clarinet and organ trio played music for dancing. Clemens

[31] "Unpublished Notebook no. 7" (Typescript pp. 14–15), *MTP*.
[32] *Cutter*, p. 10.
[33] *Journal Letters*, p. 14.

was later to lampoon the proceedings: "The excursionists danced, on three separate evenings, long, long ago (it seems an age), quadrilles, of a single set, made up of three ladies and five gentlemen (the latter with handkerchiefs around their arms to signify their sex)." [34]

Dancing under Difficulties

Actually the dances were rather lively—no quadrilles, but polkas and waltzes and an occasional Virginia reel. The difficulty, as Clemens implies, derived from the pitching deck and the lack of women to dance with. There were only seventeen ladies on board—men outnumbered women four to one and there was an even greater disparity between the number of single women and single men. Indeed, only four women on board were unmarried, although there were several married women traveling without their husbands. It was not a circumstance to encourage romantic notions of

[34] *New York Herald*, November 20, 1867, *Traveling*, p. 314.

shipboard rendezvous; young Emeline Beach appears to
have had rather small competition as Clemens' "favorite,"
but there were attractive women on board with whom he
danced on those moonlit evenings.

One of these was Julia Newell, a vivacious lady from
Janesville, Wisconsin. Her letters to the *Janesville Gazette*
show her to have been a woman of intelligence and great
physical vigor, little deterred by the difficulties of travel in
strange countries. With the exception of Mrs. Fairbanks,
she was the most self-confident and self-assertive lady on
board. Ignoring the difficulties which a single woman traveling alone encountered, she laughed at the possibility that
there was any activity on board or ashore that she was not
quite as able as any man to participate in. For example,
later in the voyage when advised not to travel overland
through Palestine, she was indignant:

Missionaries began to come on board and represent that all except
gentlemen of the most unequivocal strength of constitution had
better give up the route through the country and go direct from
Jaffa to Jerusalem, and to confine their travel to little excursions
from that city to places of interest in its vicinity; that it would be
recklessness for ladies to attempt it, as they would be sure to be
worn out with fatigue—get sun stroke, or take the Syrian fever.
When they went on in this strain . . . one lady at least would have
been glad to lay a hand on the mouth of every missionary who
seemed disposed to open it upon the subject.[35]

Miss Newell went through Palestine—overland—with
aplomb and good humor in spite of the fact that the journey
was fraught with more difficulties than even the missionaries
could envision: thrown from her horse in the ascent of
Mount Carmel, she wiped the blood from her face and re-
mounted; accosted by Bedouin thieves at the Dead Sea, she
scoffed them down. It is easy to see why Clemens liked her;
set among the fussy dowagers on the voyage, she must have
seemed vitality itself. It is also easy to see why he found
her somewhat ludicrous, for he thought self-asserting, dominating femininity comic. But, though his affection was
tempered by amusement, he cared too much for Julia Newell

[35] *Janesville* (Wis.) *Gazette,* November 23, 1867.

to risk offending her even by implication. For example, he spent his final week in Europe traveling through Spain, but there is nothing about this journey in either his *Alta* letters or *IA* because Miss Newell was one of his companions on the trip. He wrote Mrs. Fairbanks that he could not write about Spain, that, indeed, he could barely mention it in *IA*. "If I talked much about the week in Spain I should be sure to caricature Miss Newell. It would surely creep in somewhere," [36] he wrote, and as a result the only account we have of his Spanish sojourn is her own. Clemens danced with Miss Newell on those moonlit evenings, but he was not her usual escort—Dr. Jackson was. The Doctor and Miss Newell were immediately attracted to one another on the voyage, and their friendship developed into the one romantic outcome of the trip; they were married after the *Quaker City* returned to America. Even if Clemens had been less fond of Julia Newell, his friendship with Jackson would have precluded any humorous comment about her in *IA*. It is sometimes asserted that Clemens was willing to turn any relationship to his comic purpose, but this was not so. He could not wound those for whom he felt affection.

Neither did he always turn his comic attack against those he disliked. For Mrs. Nina Larrowe, one of the single ladies with whom he danced, Clemens had real antipathy, but he never mentioned her in *IA* although she was an ideal subject for comedy. Clemens had met her in New York some months before the voyage. He had known her husband, a former state senator of Nevada, during his Virginia City days, and one might have expected this reminder of old times on the frontier to be pleasant to Clemens. It wasn't. He disliked Mrs. Larrowe, who had all the acerbity of Julia Newell and no compensating charm. She seems to have cared even less for him. "He was absolutely no good," she said of Clemens many years after the cruise. "Why, he drank and he swore. The trip was got up by Henry Ward Beecher's church and it was a hard thing to get in. You had to be one of Eastern society and Twain knew nothing of Eastern society." [37] Such unconscionable snobbery would

[36] *MF*, p. 30.
[37] *Portland Morning Oregonian*, April 22, 1910.

have infuriated Clemens, and he was no doubt irritated by Mrs. Larrowe's patronizing air as well. "We made everything as pleasant as we could for him," she said, "He had then no career back of him to make people tolerate his unfortunate habits." [38] Clemens' patience—never too strong—must have been much tried by Mrs. Larrowe and the group of socially self-conscious passengers she represented, but he did not take advantage of their foibles by laughing at them in print.

One of the two remaining single women was little noticed by Clemens. Kate Brown, from Circleville, Ohio, was traveling with her father. She was a willing partner in shipboard dances, but her father's presence may have limited her freedom and made her less interesting to the bachelors on board. However, Carrie Chadeyne, the other spinster, was the subject of speculation and gossip. Like Julia Newell and Mrs. Larrowe, she was traveling alone and had joined the cruise with the understanding that Captain Duncan would take her under special care, a responsibility the captain ignored early in the voyage. This was an unfortunate circumstance, for Carrie Chadeyne was a ready flirt. Clemens hints darkly in his notebook that she made a "questionable" liaison which he does not describe; whatever this unmentionable choice was, Miss Chadeyne was returned to her home in Jersey City safe and, presumably, sound.

As this list suggests, there were always some interested couples when the dancing began; few of these, however, were from among the married passengers, some of whom disapproved of the activity. While it is not true—as Clemens sardonically reported after the voyage—that the dances were "voted to be sinful and dancing was discontinued," [39] they were not popular with the passengers as a whole. The *Quaker City* excursionists were developing another, more popular pastime—gossiping. Miss Chadeyne was one of the better subjects for deck-chair conversation, but not the only one. The *Quaker City* passenger list seems to have had many unusual reputations to be clucked over. For example, for all her flightiness, Miss Chadeyne was

---

[38] Ibid., April 23, 1910.
[39] *New York Herald,* November 20, 1867; *Traveling,* p. 314.

decorum itself contrasted to Mrs. J. O. Green and her dog, both subjects of comment throughout the voyage. She was "Frenchy-looking," Clemens noted, "30, with dark skin, inclined to hairiness, & a general suggestion all about her of coarseness & vulgarity." The dog was a small black and tan terrier mongrel with "long sharp ears that stick up like a donkey's" whom she treated like a child and called "Little Boy." "He jumps into her lap," Clemens wrote, "& repeats it over & over again, & his damned spirit will not down till she takes him to her bosom, wraps her shawl about him & talks affectionate baby talk to him." [40] Mrs. Green was to have been Mrs. Fairbanks' cabinmate, but after several nights of interminable dog conversations, Mrs. Green was encouraged to move elsewhere. She "proves to be very peculiar," Emily Severance wrote home, "and chooses personally to be alone . . . [she] seems not to be exactly sane." [41]

Another passenger who excited gossip went under the title of "Commissioner of the United States of America to Europe, Asia and Africa." He was Dr. William Gibson, from Jamestown, Pennsylvania, one of several "notabilities" whom Clemens regarded with mixed amusement and irritation:

I fell under that titular avalanche a torn and blighted thing. I said that if that potentate *must* go over in our ship, why, I supposed he must—but that to my thinking, when the United States considered it necessary to send a dignitary of that tonnage across the ocean, it would be in better taste, and safer, to take him apart and cart him over in sections, in several ships [pp. 26–27].

Gibson's self-importance and ridiculous manners made him an ideal target for Clemens' thrusts and for the comments of the passengers on deck. A banker and railroad builder as well as M.D., he had accumulated a fortune in Jamestown, and, hearing of the voyage, decided to revel in foreign parts as a United States official. His plan was simple: he wrote the Department of Agriculture offering to collect specimens and data on the trip, and someone for the Department, seeing no harm and some possible good, endorsed him as its

[40] "Unpublished Notebook no. 7" (Typescript, pp. 8–9), *MTP*.
[41] *Journal Letters*, p. 7.

representative—an endorsement Gibson used on every occasion, to the disgust of his fellow passengers in general and Clemens in particular who thought him a "complacent imbecile." Even the patent satire of the reference to him in *IA* would be lost on Gibson, Clemens thought. "Goodness, how I *would* like to see that fellow skip!" he wrote Mrs. Fairbanks, "But he won't—he won't—I shall lose all that. He will think it is a compliment, & go around spelling it over to his asinine neighbors. Now you think I bear that man malice—but upon my sacred word I don't . . . but what he did in the ship is fair prey, & *don't you plead for him.*" [42] Mrs. Fairbanks would not have tried. [43]

There was another Pennsylvania banker on board who was even more bizarre, Judge Jacob S. Haldeman from Harrisburg. He had served a term in the state legislature and built his political prestige into a post in the foreign service: Lincoln appointed him U.S. Minister to Sweden and Norway in 1861, an office he held for over three years. Although only forty at the time of the voyage, he was no longer active in national politics, preferring the relatively quiet activities of the Pennsylvania State Agricultural Society instead. "He is a very peculiar man," Mrs. Severance wrote. "I could imagine him to be a gambler. He wears a red flannel shirt on which are printed hunting figures. Every day he brings out a new necktie, and on his small feet he wears the tightest of patent leather boots." [44] His dress was, however, no more strange than his manner. He was an alcoholic traveling abroad for a cure. Like many misinformed alcoholics in the mid-nineteenth century, he was regularly taking morphine as an alcohol substitute, and as a result he was more or less constantly in a drug stupor. On board the *Quaker City* this does not appear to have made him any the less respectable, but it did furnish an interesting subject for talk.

The excursionists' desire for gossip was not satisfied by private conversation alone, however. These were nine-

[42] *MF*, p. 21.

[43] For details of Gibson's life before and after the voyage, see Henry F. Pommer, "Mark Twain's 'Commissioner of the United States,'" *AL*, 34 (November, 1962): 385–92.

[44] *Journal Letters*, p. 16.

teenth-century Americans traveling not only for amusement but for *edification*. They were determined to assemble facts, to be *informed*. The initial prospectus of the voyage had specifically noted there would be a library on board, and, although Clemens made fun of the books in it, declaring they consisted solely of Robinson's *Holy Land Researches* and copies of the *Plymouth Collection* of hymns, the library did have guidebooks and histories which the passengers read with care. The letters they wrote home were filled with historical detail and statistical information about the places they visited, information that could be had only with effort. Of course, like most travelers they appear to have forgotten nearly all their hard-won information as soon as the inspiration for learning it was out of sight, but— significantly—they had an appetite for knowledge, and it was, therefore, inevitable that one of the activities which they were to organize on shipboard would be a club for what Emily Severance called "the purpose of mental information." On Tuesday, June 18, eight days out of New York and three from the Azores, the passengers gathered in the main saloon after prayer meeting for the purpose of organizing what was eventually to be called the Quaker City Club. The first order of business, of course, was to elect a President, Judge Haldeman, who, although generally tipsy, had nevertheless been abroad before, and an Executive Committee composed of Moses Beach, Dr. Jackson, and Clemens, who, although generally sober, had not. The Club also elected a Secretary, the Rev. G. W. Quereau, whose function was somewhat obscure since the Executive Committee organized the meetings and secured the services of the "authorities" on board who were to lecture the members of the Club.

The *Quaker City* seemed well prepared for such an undertaking. As the excursionists never seemed to tire of telling one another, this was no *ordinary* journey to Europe. There was, in Clemens' words, an "ample crop of 'Professors' of various kinds" on board, most of whom were glad to expound to such an appreciative audience. One of the "Professors" was the famous Samuel B. Parsons, a New York horticulturist and nurseryman who had gained his fame in the late 1830's by introducing the mulberry craze to America (every man to have his own silk farm). Parsons was the American authority on the rose ("its history, poetry, culture, and classification"), but he was most noted for introducing new plants into American gardens. He had already imported the first Japanese maples and Asiatic rhododendrons ever grown in the U.S., and he was going abroad now in 1867 to find new specimens. He was an ideal source of information about the flora of the places to be visited.

Another would-be "Professor" was Anthony Bezenet Allen, a wealthy farm machinery manufacturer who was traveling abroad to study methods to be used in improving American agriculture. He was, Emily Severance noted, "very deaf, but *very* intelligent and interesting," [45] and Mrs. Fairbanks, too, enjoyed his conversation. He had been abroad before and he counseled the other passengers concerning what they should see and where they should buy. A third "Professor" was John Greenwood, Jr., P. T. Barnum's agent who was going abroad to collect specimens for Barnum's Natural History Museum. Greenwood had taken an ad in the New York papers before departure asking the passengers to help him in his search, promising a special room in the museum devoted to the *Quaker City* excursion with each specimen labeled with the name of its donor. Greenwood was an available source of historical and topographical information which he presented to the excursionists (when asked) with pleasure.

Thanks to the advance billing of General Sherman, the ship had several military officers ("chieftains" Clemens called them), men whose experience in the Civil War qualified them, so far as the *Quaker City* passengers were concerned, to discuss some of the sights of the journey— Gibraltar and Sebastopol, for example—with a certain expertise. Two were army men, one a Confederate, the other a Union Colonel. Clemens appears to have liked both. About the Confederate Colonel, W. R. Denny of Winchester, Virginia, he says little, but Denny was congenial enough to be one of Clemens' companions through Palestine. With Colonel J. Herron Foster, the Union officer, Clemens was more

[45] *Ibid.*, p. 29.

intimate. This friendship was encouraged by the fact that Foster was another professional newspaperman, at the time of the excursion editor of the *Pittsburgh Dispatch,* and like Beach, he wrote regular letters to his paper.[46] The journey was a convalescent one for Foster, for he suffered from tuberculosis, and, indeed, died of the disease shortly after his return from the Holy Land. Clemens' affection for him is recorded in his footnote reference to Foster's death at the end of Chapter XX of *IA* and by a two-page manuscript obituary preserved in the Webster Collection, in which he declared his affection for Foster. He was glad, he wrote, "that I who so often speak ill-naturedly of worthy people, wrote nothing unkind of him."[47] Denny and Foster appear to have been good friends, too, a fact which surprised many Europeans who could not imagine enemies socializing so soon after a bitter war.

Clemens' brief experience in the Confederate Army might account for the greater interest he showed the Army vis-à-vis the Navy contingent on board. About the two navy Captains, Lucius Moody from Canton, New York, and W. R. Hoel, of Cincinnati, he said nothing directly.[48] Although he makes fun of the multiplicity of "Captains" on board the *Quaker City* in the first part of *IA,* this comedy was probably directed at other members of the excursion, in particular the owner of the ship, Daniel Leary, of Brooklyn, who was a kind of unofficial overseer of the handling of the steamer, and the several officers of the crew whose self-importance was considerably enhanced when it seemed that Duncan was incapable of maintaining command of the vessel. Indeed, Clemens began to call the first mate "Captain" Bursley, when, before the voyage was half-completed, the mate had to assume operational control of the ship.

Finally, there was another "Professor" on board, a man who practiced a profession which, in 1867, was clothed in

[46] All unfortunately lost. There is no extant file of the *Pittsburgh Dispatch* for the period of the trip.

[47] Quoted in *MF,* p. 22 n., from a MS in the Webster Collection.

[48] Although he seems to have known Lucius Moody well enough to confuse his name with Julius Moulton's in a letter to his family of December 10, 1867. *BM,* p. 97.

scientific mystique. William E. James was a Brooklyn pho-
tographer whose chief concern was to record the voyage on
stereopticon slides and he pursued this objective with a
monumental fervor. Often throughout the voyage the ship
was brought to a standstill to allow James to take a "view."
His cabin was specially fitted up as a darkroom, and there
he would regularly repair to develop his plates. His pictures
were seldom of passengers, usually of sights—both pictorial
and historical—which might be reproduced on his return
and sold commercially.

James's delight in taking pictures was very nearly
equaled by his pride in showing them, and his was therefore
the principal entertainment at the first meeting of the
Quaker City Club. On the same program Clemens gave a
lecture concerning the Azores and Gibraltar, which, considering how little he knew of either of these places, seems a
remarkable choice to begin the series. However, he was
assisted by Captain Duncan and Dr. Andrews (who had
visited the Azores twenty years before) and they at least
may have known a bit about the itinerary. In any case,
James's lantern slides "of places where we expect to go"
(beginning with a view of Greenwood Cemetery, Brooklyn)
proved to be the more memorable entertainment of the
evening. Mrs. Fairbanks and Emily Severance were delighted by Mr. James's slides, but neither mentioned Clemens' speech to their readers back home.

The first meeting of the Quaker City Club was held under
difficult circumstances, the ship's first real storm at sea. Two
days before the ship reached the Azores, torrential rain and
a heavy sea made almost all the passengers very ill, and
most of them took to their berths, packing their life preserv-
ers around them to keep from being pitched headlong to the
deck of their cabins. Even the Executive Officer, "Captain"
Bursley, was indisposed, and for the first time Mrs. Fairbanks missed a meal, not, she explained because she was
seasick, but because she found the movement of the table
back and forth across the dining saloon rather disconcert-
ing. It was very unseasonable, Captain Duncan declared,
very unseasonable indeed for the South Atlantic at that
time of year. Clemens, on his sea legs at last, was not ill but
bored: "Sea so rough to-day we can't play horse-billiards

for'ard," he wrote in his notebook.[49] Amidships, waves were washing over the entire deck, beating against the paddle boxes, burying one wheel and elevating the other almost out of the water and causing the passengers to survey the vessel more apprehensively than before. The *Quaker City* appeared to pass the test: "She rides the waves beautifully," declared Mrs. Severance, "no jarring or creaking." [50] Well, very little, anyway.

At 4:00 A.M. on Thursday, seasick or not, the passengers were summoned to the deck to catch their first sight of a foreign land, the island of Corvo. They had, initially, intended to land at San Miguel, the largest of the Azores islands farther east, but the storm worsened and Captain Duncan decided to dock at Horta, the nearest deep-water harbor, on Fayal. Despite the cold north wind which drove a heavy rain down upon them, the passengers remained on deck watching the passing shoreline. They were eager for firm land under their feet and the sight of it was welcome even in the cold. The land, barely visible, was lush and green, with vineyards seeming to cascade down the mountains to the sea. The terrain was rugged, with deep gorges and ridges which Clemens called "sharp [and] velvety, topped with seeming castles & ramparts—all green in bright spots & handsome." [51] The land was all the more beautiful because not immediately attainable; it was not until the next morning that the ship turned into the bay at Horta, in weather so gray and overcast even Pico Peak towering over the harbor was invisible. No sooner had the port's Health Officer cleared the ship for landing than the passengers began swarming over the sides into the waiting shore boats. The *Quaker City* was to provide for all landing expenses, but in their eagerness the excursionists drove their own bargains with the boatmen—and paid their own (exorbitant) fares. While Captain Duncan was still dickering, as best he could, for their transportation, nearly all of the passengers were landing on shore. The *Quaker City* had reached its first port.

[49] "Unpublished Notebook no. 7" (Typescript, p. 16), *MTP.*
[50] *Journal Letters*, p. 19.
[51] "Unpublished Notebook no. 7" (Typescript, p. 17), *MTP.*

III

HORTA
GIBRALTAR
TANGIER

"A ship is a bad writing desk . . ."

The two days the *Quaker City* lay in Horta harbor were the most exhaustively reported of the voyage. Everybody took notes and almost everybody wrote encyclopedic letters about the "friendly little island in the middle of the great ocean." There were at least seven letters printed in the papers back home which described the activities of those forty-eight hours.[1] The first rush of enthusiasm for a warm

[1] Dr. Jackson in the *Philadelphia Press,* July 22, 1867; T. D. Crocker in the *Cleveland Leader,* July 22, 1867; Mrs. Fairbanks in the *Cleveland Herald,* July 23, 1867; Clemens in the *New York*

and verdant land after nearly two weeks on a cold and pitching ship made every incident seem significant, and the letters recounted the Horta activities in detail: the reception of the passengers in the elegant home of the astonished American Consul, Colonel Dabney, for instance. Dabney was the scion of a line of American consuls who in sixty years had come to own two-thirds of Fayal and to be its wealthiest inhabitant—a significant fact, perhaps, in the context of the great poverty of most of the islanders. The younger Mesdames Dabney (née Webster) excited curiosity and comment among the excursionists, too; fifteen years earlier their father had been executed in Boston for a much publicized murder, and to escape further notoriety they had come to the Azores and eventually married the Dabney sons. ("Well, I suppose you know who *we* are!" one of them said to Mr. Haldeman.)

Some of the letters described the wedding which the Rev. E. Carter Hutchinson performed for a couple who had been waiting, almost in despair, for the arrival of a Protestant minister—surely a happy storm had driven the *Quaker City* to their rescue, for they shunned a civil ceremony and the only clergyman resident on the island was (horrors!) a Roman Catholic priest. All mentioned the trip by donkey into the volcanic mountains surrounding the city and remarked the clarity of the air, the brilliance of the flowers, the size and apparent nearness of Pico Peak across the bay, the insistence of the donkey boys for extra fares, and the interminable begging cries of the ragged urchins who clustered about them wherever they went. The experiences were new enough, and unsettling enough, to encourage elaborate descriptions, and the correspondence from Horta was to be matched in length only by that detailing the pilgrims' entry into Jerusalem several months later.

For most of the *Quaker City* excursionists, correspondence was a self-glamorizing pleasure; for Clemens, it was an everlasting professional chore. When the ship docked at

Tribune, July 30, 1867, and in the *San Francisco Daily Alta California*, August 25, 1867; Duncan (actually written by Mrs. Severance) in the *Independent*, August 15, 1867. And presumably Foster wrote one, now lost, for the *Pittsburgh Dispatch*

Horta, he ceased to be a tourist and became, again, a newspaperman. Heretofore he had taken notes, but written no letters, putting off his correspondence until he had foreign lands to write about. Now, the indolent days on board were behind him; now, began the continuous, sometimes painful, always arduous chore of composition. He was to have no more *completely* carefree leisure moments on the trip. While there would be times when he neither traveled nor wrote of his travels, there would be no time when he did not feel the pressure of correspondence. Free time was, henceforth, time stolen from the rigorous regimen he had set himself for the voyage, for he had guaranteed the *Alta California* 50 letters and had agreed to at least 20 more for the *New York Tribune*.[2] In addition, he had a sub rosa agreement with the *New York Herald* for several more.[3] At the very least, he expected to write 75 letters on the trip, or, in the twenty weeks left to the journey, nearly four a week. The pressure upon him was great, for he had been paid for the *Alta* letters in advance; if he did not complete *that* contract he would have to return money to the newspaper. His commitments to the New York newspapers were important to him also—on their successful completion rested his future reputation in East Coast journalism; while they would not give him great financial return immediately, they offered the promise of future earnings.

These requirements made great demands on his talent. Some critics have implied that for Clemens composition was casual and easy. It wasn't. Only rarely in his life did he have periods when he could write rapidly and painlessly. He was a conscious artist who demanded excellence from himself.[4] Only the most pressing circumstances—illness or loss,

[2] He eventually wrote the *New York Tribune* seven; see Clemens to his family, November 20, 1867: "I am ashamed to go to the Tribune office almost—they have treated me so well & I have not written them a third of the letters I promised." *BM*, p. 95.

[3] See Dewey Ganzel, "Samuel Clemens, Sub Rosa Correspondent," *English Language Notes*, vol. 1: 270–73.

[4] The Mark Twain Papers contain many manuscripts which Clemens refused to publish because he thought them inferior; had he been less fastidious, they would have made him a fortune.

for example—would justify sending in copy which he had
not revised with care. The letters from the *Quaker City*
excursion were extremely onerous in their composition. Like
the correspondence which Clemens had been sending from
New York, they had to be directed to a special audience, the
readers of the *San Francisco Alta California*, and this demanded constant allusion to local personalities and issues.
It sometimes has been argued that Clemens showed his
provinciality by constant reference to San Francisco in his
European letters, but this criticism seems unjust. He was
writing *to order*, and most of the apparently arbitrary local
color was included not because he was unable to free his
imagination from parochialism, but rather because his em-
ployers expected frequent reference to California. Clemens
implies this difference in his comment that his *Alta* letters
as they were originally written were "newspaper matter, not
book matter." [5]

In addition, the letters he wrote had to have in them a
sense of immediacy—a sense that the experiences he described had only just happened. His job was to make the
reader a companion to his experience, and his attempts at
contemporaneity can be traced to this intent. But it was not
easy to maintain such vitality and freshness under the best
of circumstances, and the *Quaker City* was far from being
an ideal writing environment. Contemporaneity can best be
evoked when composition is nearly simultaneous with the
experience itself, and Clemens tried desperately to write his
letters as he went. Unfortunately, even his enormous stamina was depleted in the task of composing while traveling,
and he soon developed a pattern of writing the letters spo-
radically, usually on board ship when there was a lull in his
journey, always attempting to maintain in style and dateline an impression of immediacy.[6] "The worst of it is, that a

[5] *Autobiography*, vol. 1: 245.
[6] A comparison of Clemens' itinerary, Duncan's log, and Mrs.
Severance's letters, makes clear that the dates of many of the
letters, particularly those written in Italy, do not coincide with the
dates he visited some of the places he describes. Occasionally, as in
Naples, he wrote about places he had visited some days before,
listing the month ("July") but no day in the dateline. Prior to the
letters from Palestine, there are ten such vaguely dated letters, all

ship is a bad writing desk, and I can't write on shore because I have too much to see there," he wrote to a friend later in the voyage. "So I neglect my correspondence half the time and botch it in the balance." [7]

His composition was both helped and hindered by another consideration. Even before he left on the voyage, he was making plans to write a book about the excursion.[8] His newspaper letters were therefore written with this end in view: they would be the substance of his first important book—the better their quality, the easier rewriting would be. Indeed, while there were extensive changes in much of his newspaper matter for *The Innocents Abroad*,[9] a far larger amount was carried over into the book with little or no change, a circumstance which suggests not that Clemens was uncritical but rather that, for the most part, he was satisfied with his original composition on the voyage.

The transition to book form was to be facilitated by his notebooks. Like most writers, Clemens kept notes throughout his professional life, but he did so in a rather intermittent fashion, and his use of them was sporadic. In fact, to anyone familiar with the notebooks of his contemporaries, the very term "notebook" might seem a misnomer: although they are voluminous, there is little in them to suggest that Clemens, like Emerson, used notes for private intellectual discourse or, like James, as a repository for ideas to be

<hr />

of which were probably written during periods when his journey was briefly interrupted.

[7] See Clemens to Governor Fuller of Nevada, August 7, 1867, (Typescript in *MTP*); see also Clemens to his family, July 14, 1867, from Genoa, in the Webster Collection: "Since we have touched dry land we have gone to bed after midnight & rose again at 7 to rush all day. I cannot even get a chance to write newspaper letters regularly. . . ." (Typescript in *MTP*).

[8] Doesticks (M. Thomson) to Clemens: "You told me you were to go off in the Quaking [sic] City—you stated that if there was any book-matter in the journey, the ship, the people, or the heathen lands and the inhabitants thereof, you proposed to extract the same and build a book." Reprinted in Fred W. Lorch, "Doesticks and *Innocents Abroad*," *AL*, 20: 447.

[9] See Leon T. Dickinson, "Mark Twain's Revisions in Writing *The Innocents Abroad*," *AL*, 19: 139–157.

developed at a later time. Clemens' notes are not formal: they combine the functions of an intermittent diary, a memoranda scratch sheet, and a schoolboy's copybook. They were written into pocket-sized, leather-bound booklets in rather casual fashion—the books have no pagination and often contain many blank pages; some notes are written in the margins of earlier notes and even, on occasion, upside down. Clemens filled four such books on the *Quaker City* excursion (one notebook was subsequently lost), and they furnish a valuable adjunct to his published accounts of the voyage.[10] Some of the notes are merely private squibs or factual details which he never intended to use in writing; some are introductory comments which he planned later to continue in his newspaper correspondence; some are rather complete descriptions of incidents or detailed data which he might or might not use; and some are merely cryptic notations—single words or short phrases separated by lines— which occasionally correlate with his letters but, as often as not, don't.

For example, he clearly never intended to publish the following note describing the donkey trip in Fayal:

The party started at 10 A.M. Dan was on his ass the time I saw him. At this time Mr. Foster was following, & Mr. Haldeman came next after Foster—Mr. Foster being close to Dan's ass, & his own ass being very near to Mr. Haldeman's ass. After this Capt. Bursley joined the party with *his* ass, & all went well till on turning a corner of the road a most frightful & unexpected noise issued from Capt. Bursley's ass, which for a moment threw the party into confusion, & at the same time a portughee [sic] boy stuck a nail into Mr. Foster's ass & he ran—ran against Dan, who fell—fell on his ass, & then like so many bricks they all came down—each & every one of them—& each & every one of them fell on his ass.[11]

Contrary to popular speculation, Clemens' unpublished works are not filled with obscenities or improprieties, and

[10] Twenty-five years after Clemens' death Albert Bigelow Paine published parts of the notebooks. He implied he printed all, but, in fact, most of Clemens notes remain unpublished.

[11] "Unpublished Notebook no. 7" (Typescript, p. 22), *MTP*.

scatological comments, even innocent ones such as this, are rare in the notebooks.

But many of the notebook comments were intended to be used later in composition. Sometimes they were mere reminders. For example, there is the cryptic comment: "Madame, these attentions are very flattering to me, but—." [12] By itself this means nothing, but it was enough to remind Clemens of an idea for a paragraph in his letter to the *Tribune* about a beggar woman who hounded him for money; a paragraph which began: "Madame, these attentions cannot but be flattering to me, but it must not be— alas, it cannot be—I am another's." Occasionally a notebook entry will suggest an incident which might have been incorporated in his later composition but wasn't. "Couple Custom House officers remained on ship all day to examine all bundles carried ashore by passengers—," he wrote in one entry, "but both stayed on one side, while most of the people went off on the other." [13] Had he chosen to expand this note, it might have been the core of an amusing episode.

Most suggestive of all, perhaps, is his use of figures and historical fact, much of it gleaned from guidebooks. His notes include many statistical references, some useful, some so unimportant that one wonders why he wrote them down at all. However, in his later use of these data Clemens was particularly discriminating. For example, in his notes he wrote: "Population of Horta, 10,000—nearly all Portuguese. Pop. of Fayal 25 to 30,000." In his letters he wrote merely: "The town has 8,000 to 10,000 inhabitants," omitting any reference to the population of the island. This transformation deliberately blurs the statistical effect of the notebook data. While Clemens realized that his audience wanted facts, he knew that it wanted them presented indirectly. One of the faults that he found in the travel books of earlier writers was a certain flatness in presenting statistical information, and he tried to avoid this fault by treating his data more casually, suggesting not so much information read as information recollected. When Clemens used guidebooks—and they were, throughout his career, a useful re-

[12] *Ibid.*
[13] *Ibid.*, p. 20.

source [14]—he did so with care. Rarely, he copied them almost verbatim; more often, he used them only as sources of useful data, being very careful to avoid the reportorial style in which most of the guidebooks were written.

However, just as there is much in Clemens' notebooks which was either never intended for use in composition or intended to be used only with extensive rewriting, there is much in the letters and in *IA* which has no counterpart in the notebooks. Sometimes, it is true, he used his notes systematically, drawing a line through an item when he wrote it into a letter, but one often has a feeling that this was not their only use. As often as not, their text merely parallels Clemens' newspaper correspondence, intersecting it now and again, but never becoming fully integrated with it. One is left with the impression that he kept his notebooks habitually, whether he was writing or not, and that while occasionally he would dip into them for an idea to initiate a letter or for inspiration to carry one to completion, he did not do so regularly.

Clemens was a conscious stylist. His concern with style is clearly revealed in the manner in which he rewrote his newspaper letters into *IA*, but it is also apparent in the newspaper letters themselves, in the shift in manner which occurred in those few instances when he happened to write both the *Alta* and the *Tribune* concerning a single event. Merely writing twice about a subject seemed to bring his material more completely into his control. The two letters he wrote concerning the Azores provide a good example of this effect: the first, to the *Alta California* was begun on June 19, two days before the ship landed at Horta, and is obviously derived, at least initially, from a guidebook of some sort.

The Azores Islands lie on nearly the same parallel of latitude as San Francisco and New York, and are 2,400 miles straight east of the latter city. They are nine or ten in number. The extent of this island of Fayal (pronounced Fy-all) is about 28,000 acres—too large for one farm and not large enough for two. The islands belong to the Crown of Portugal, and were discovered about four hundred and fifty years ago. They are composed of volcanic hills

[14] See Dewey Ganzel, "Twain Travel Books, and *Life on the Mississippi*," *AL*, 34: 40–55.

1. The steamship *Quaker City*, the "right stately-looking vessel"
which transported the Holy Land Excursion for five and a
half months. Although it was thirteen years old, Clemens thought
it "sumptuous." [Courtesy Patten Free Library, Bath, Maine]

2

3

4

5

2. Mrs. Mary Mason Fairbanks, Clemens' long-time friend and confidante whom he met on the voyage. She was, he wrote, "the most refined, intelligent, & cultivated lady in the ship, & altogether the kindest & best. . . . She looks young, because she is so good—but she has a grown son & daughter at home."

3. Solon and Emily Severance, a wealthy Cleveland couple, close friends of Mrs. Fairbanks, who became part of Clemens' inner circle on the voyage.

4. Daniel Slote, Clemens' closest friend during the voyage, in a picture taken while the ship was at Constantinople. He was, Clemens wrote, a "splendid" fellow, an "immoral, tobacco-smoking, wine-drinking, godless" man, "whose blameless conduct and example will always be an eloquent sermon to all who shall come within their influence." In later years they were estranged and became bitter enemies. [Courtesy Mrs. Albert Stuart Angus]

5. Clemens and Charlie Langdon shortly after their return. Charlie, the "cub" as he was called by Clemens' inner circle, was one of the youngest passengers on board. About the time this picture was taken, Charlie introduced Clemens to his sister Olivia Langdon, the beautiful and adored "Livy" whom Clemens later married. [Courtesy The Mark Twain Papers]

6. Charles Duncan, captain of the *Quaker City* and leader of
the excursion to the Holy Land. Clemens first thought Duncan a
"jolly" fellow, but Duncan's piety soon rankled and an
antagonism developed between them. "You must always refer
offensively to Captain Duncan," Clemens warned Mrs. Fairbanks
at the end of the voyage. Their animosity finally erupted some
years later into a protracted public quarrel and lawsuit. [Courtesy
John E. Duncan]

and mountains, and of course the soil is very rich. The hills are
carefully cultivated clear to their summits, and so are the
mountains up to an altitude of eight or nine hundred feet. Every
farm is cut up into innumerable little squares, by walls of lava,
built to protect the growing products from the rude winds that
blow here, and this gives a hill-side the semblance of a vast
checkerboard. All the landscape is green and beautiful; but it is a
quiet, pastoral sort of beauty, for there are no rugged features
about the mountains—all their outlines are soft and gently curved.
Even the Great Pico rises up out of the sea with a smooth
unbroken swell to the height of 7,613 feet—a colossal pyramid of
softest green, without break or breach of any kind to mar its
exquisite symmetry.[15]

This is the second paragraph; before Clemens finished the
letter he had visited the island and his style becomes more
personal, a significant shift which is even more apparent in
excerpts from the letter he wrote the New York *Tribune* on
June 23, after the *Quaker City* had left the island:

We had a pleasant ten-days' run from New York to the Azores
Islands—not a fast run—for the distance is only 2,400 miles
straight east—but an exceedingly pleasant one.
    . . . we steered for the nearest island of the group—Fayal
(the people there pronounced it Fy-all, and put the accent on the
first syllable.) We anchored in the open roadstead of Horta, half a
mile from the shore. The town has 8,000 to 10,000 inhabitants. Its
snow-white houses nestle cosily in a sea of fresh green vegetation,
and no village could look prettier or more attractive. It sits in the
lap of an amphitheater of hills which are from 300 to 700 feet
high, and carefully cultivated clear to their summits—not a foot of
soil left idle. Every farm and every acre is cut up into little square
inclosures by stone walls, whose duty it is to protect the growing
products from the destructive gales that blow there. These
hundreds of green squares, marked by their black lava walls, make
the hills look like vast checkerboards.

The islands belonged to Portugal, and everything in Fayal has
Portug[u]ese characteristics about it. But more of that anon.
    . . . We sailed along the shore of the Island of Pico, under a
stately green pyramid that rose up with one unbroken sweep from

[15] *Alta*, August 25, 1867; *Traveling*, p. 3.

our very feet to an altitude of 7,613 feet, and thrust its summit above the white clouds like an island adrift in a fog! [16]

The second account immediately strikes the reader as a more loosely organized and hence a more casually recounted version than the first; such an effect is the result of art. Although the second omits some details, it gives others, and factually the two are very nearly identical. What is significant is the manner in which these details are given: in the use of parenthetical interjection (note the way the distance from New York is placed between dashes as though it were a sudden recollection) a looser, more vivid sentence structure (for example, "every farm and every acre" for "every farm"; "Portugal" for "Crown of Portugal") and a less stilted and more exact diction ("destructive gales" for "rude winds"; "make the hills look like" for "gives . . . the semblance of"). Significantly, the second version was carried verbatim to *IA*. It is significant, too, that the first version was sent to the California, the second to the New York newspaper. In this instance, at least, the version with the commonplace manner was written for the Eastern audience, the stilted version for the Western, a circumstance which might lead one to question the assumption that Clemens "wrote down" to his Western audience and "up" to his Eastern one.

Clemens characteristic concern is shown not only in his style but also in the subjects he chose to write about. He did not relate every significant happening of the voyage; furthermore, much that he did write about was purely imaginary. This is not to say that he fabricated details and presented them as facts, but, rather, that he wanted to amuse as well as inform his readers. His journey was, in part, an excursion of the imagination, and he knew that the truth of *that* part of the journey could be told not by the reports of a keen observer but by the synthesis of a poetic imagination. Perhaps the most distinctive difference between his account of the voyage and the accounts of the other passengers was his repeated description of imaginary experience. Many of the more amusing situations in *IA* never occurred at all, or occurred in forms far different from

[16] *New York Tribune*, July 30, 1867; *Traveling*, pp. 10–18.

those Clemens described. When he thought his narrative needed a dramatic focus or an amusing anecdote, he had no hesitancy in supplying one from his imagination; a fanciful experience was often included in order to embellish a part of the journey which had little intrinsic interest for his readers. But more often his fabrication was a means of projecting information or attitudes not readily suggested by actual experience. It was not only to amuse his readers that he fabricated, but to tell them the truth of what he saw and thought as well.

It was inevitable that his fabrications should be concerned with imaginary characters—Clemens' imagination was most emphatically evoked in dramatic situations; while he was often brilliant in straightforward narration, he was best when his narration could be shaped around a character, a personality with particular manners of action, dress and speech—particularly speech. This was, indeed, his reason for initially adopting the persona "Mark Twain," a character which was, at least initially, clearly delineated from his creator Samuel Clemens. But the distinction between "Twain" and Clemens was already confused by the time the *Quaker City* cruise was undertaken; the nom de plume had become, at least on occasion, the man himself. The confusion was Clemens' own as well as others: while he usually signed his letters home "Sam," he sometimes signed them "Mark," a name which had no associations for his family. What had originally been a dramatic means for projecting himself to his public had become, in fact, no longer a means but the substance of the projection and therefore less useful as a foil against which Samuel Clemens could fix his imagination. To fill the need for such a foil, Clemens was repeatedly to create new characters, and *IA* was to have its full company of them, characters with whom Clemens could focus his readers' attention, objects of humor which could be developed apart from the experience of the voyage itself, epitomes of attitudes which his critical imagination wished to satirize. With such characters, he was not bound by historical fact, but he could nevertheless be imaginatively stimulated by it. More important, these fictitious characters allowed him to project his imagination in *speech;* such characters could be quoted directly and therefore allow him to indulge in the vernacular humor which he could write so well.

The characters which Clemens "created" in *IA* were at various removes from reality. "The Doctor," for example, seems to have been the exact counterpart to Dr. Jackson, and "Poet Larriat," only a slightly exaggerated picture of the ridiculous Bloodgood Cutter. "The Oracle," more imaginary, was patterned on Dr. Andrews but bore the characteristics of several other overly pious, falsely learned passengers as well. At a still greater remove from actuality was "Interrogation Point," who, in his general naïveté and confounding inquisitiveness, is a lampoon of several of the youngsters on board. These characters allowed Clemens a range of comic comment about the voyage, and all owed their vitality to the manner in which he introduced them into his text. None of them has a continuing function throughout the book, however. Only one of Clemens' creations was to have a regular place in the narrative, and that character, William Blucher, sailed aboard the *Quaker City* only in Clemens' imagination.

Blucher was not a direct result of the excursion itself; even before Clemens embarked on the *Quaker City* he had made notes about him. Moreover, over a quarter of his first letter to the *New York Tribune* concerned the activities of Blucher, a fact which suggests that he was already well developed in Clemens' mind when the trip began. Blucher was a continuation of Mr. Brown, the Clemens' character whose travels with "Mark Twain" filled many of the New York letters to the *Alta*. At first Clemens apparently intended to keep Blucher and Brown distinct—he continued to give regular accounts of Brown to his *Alta* readers, who already knew that gentleman, even while he introduced Blucher to his newly acquired *New York Tribune* readers. But the similarities appear to have been too close for separate development, and after the first letter, "William Blucher" was never again mentioned in his letters to the *Tribune*. Mr. Brown, on the other hand, lived on in the *Alta*. The two characters were one in Clemens' mind, for when he rewrote the *Alta* letters Brown became Blucher, a change which probably derived not from conscious choice but from the fact that the first mention of Blucher-Brown to appear in the book was taken from the *Tribune* letter, and Clemens merely continued the transcription throughout the remaining text. Blucher-Brown has many characteristics in common with his earlier counterpart in the correspondence Clemens had sent the *Alta* from New York: he is from the Far West, a man "of no tact," and possessor of a "ruinous" vocabulary and unabashed naïveté. However, once on the cruise, Blucher-Brown developed other qualities which, though similar to Brown's, result from the circumstances of the journey. His naïveté is qualified; this is his first trip abroad and he suggests all the uninitiated and provincial attitudes which Clemens saw about him on board. Now he is given to touting American ways in preference to all things foreign. Most notably, while not unintelligent, he refuses to believe that "common sense" cannot resolve all complexities. In his first appearance recounted at length in the *Tribune* letter concerning the Azores, for example, he is troubled by his watch which somehow doesn't keep up with ship time:

Thish-yer's a swindle! [he says,] . . . I bought her out in Illinois—give $150 for her—and thought she was good. And, by George, she is good on shore, but somehow she don't keep up her tick here on the water—gets seasick, maybe. She skips, she runs along regular enough till half-past eleven, and then, all of a sudden she lets down.[17]

What Clemens was describing was the difference between "ship-time" and "shore-time"; moving eastward, the *Quaker City* was "gaining" about 20 minutes each day, and the ship's clocks were arbitrarily set forward every night at 11:30. It is significant that this particular fact, unusual enough to anyone who has not traveled across the Atlantic, perhaps, is presented not expositorily but dramatically. The "translation" reveals much about Clemens' art and his awareness of it.

Brown-Blucher derived from no one passenger on board, but he had a special affinity for Jack Van Nostrand. The revision of the letters for *IA* suggests that some of the

[17] *New York Tribune,* July 30, 1867; *Traveling,* p. 11; cf. *IA,* p. 48.

incidents ascribed to Brown-Blucher may have been suggested by Van Nostrand: of 22 references to Brown in the *Alta* letters, 15 were cut entirely from the book text, five changed to Blucher and two changed to "Jack." Jack was much younger than Clemens and younger, too, than Brown-Blucher would appear to be, but he was a source of practical jokes and horseplay. On one occasion, for example, Jack raced to the top of the aftermast and refused to come down until sailors were sent up after him. But Jack was not "Blucher," only a suggestion for him. Brown-Blucher was, in fact, a caricature of Clemens himself, or at least that part of him which was still neophyte, and as such a means— through contrast—for making the other projection of Clemens, the persona "Mark Twain," appear *more* sophisticated. Blucher's concern with his watch was the ludicrous counterpart of Clemens' own fascination with the change in time on the voyage, a change which he comments on several times in his notebooks. His letters were to be essentially experiential, not comic—an important difference from his earliest newspaper writing—and if comedy of naïveté were to appear, as it must, it could not be derived entirely from the character of "Mark Twain," for that persona had to remain capable of serious critical commentary. Clemens wanted a *spectrum* of humor; "Mark Twain" could do well enough for the generalized comic commentary which works throughout the book, but the broad burlesque had to be supplied by another set of characters, among them Blucher.

One of the references to Brown in the *Alta* letters which Clemens cut from *IA* is significant in this regard: Commenting on his sightseeing in Gibraltar, "Mark Twain" noted that he had not acquired many facts about the fortress.

I was so busy looking that I hardly ever asked any questions. Occasionally my conscience smote me, but I quieted it with the reflection that I had taken pains to give Brown the strictest instructions to ask questions and find out everything—to pry into all matters that presented themselves and leave nothing undiscovered that could be of lively interest to the public of the Pacific Coast.[18]

[18] *Alta*, August 27, 1867; *Traveling*, p. 23.

It is only a casual comment,[19] but it suggests something of Clemens' use of Brown-Blucher. He was a kind of comic stand-in which Clemens used for that part of himself which was seeking new experience and new facts which he could present, in due time, to his California readers.

Brown was also a part of the author's own ribald character which could not be acknowledged directly; he figured in some of the relatively immodest parts of *Alta* letters which Clemens later expunged from the book. It is he, for example, who got in trouble in France because he mistook "water closets" in the railway stations [20] and it was he with whom "Mark Twain" watched the women of Odessa bathing nude by the side of the *Quaker City*.[21] Furthermore, he was the focus for a kind of Know-Nothing common-sense disregard for European art. It was he who most severely criticized the art of the old masters in the letters, condemning the paintings in the Vatican and belittling "The Last Supper":

Brown said it looked like an old fire-board. The language was vulgar and irreverent, but it was wonderfully accurate in description. He seems to regard the guide with an evil eye, and doubtless considered him a sort of imposter for bringing us to such a place. At last he said:
"Is this fellow dead?"
"Who?"
"That dobbed this." [22]

The comment was cut from the book, but Clemens was only slightly less condemnatory in his own person; in the *IA* revision, Brown's common-sense manner is superseded by "Mark Twain's" more intelligent disregard.

Clemens use of Brown-Blucher in *IA* is very brief and incidental. Even in the letters it is clear that he had outlived Clemens' use for him long before the trip was finished. Blucher was dropped from the *New York Tribune* corre-

[19] In a notebook comment similar to this, Brown's name is scratched out and Dan's added.
[20] *Alta*, September 5; *Traveling*, p. 41.
[21] *Alta*, November 3, 1867; *Traveling*, p. 140.
[22] *Alta*, September 22, 1867; *Traveling*, pp. 57–58. The comment suggests Dr. Jackson was his source.

spondence after the first letter, and while Brown appeared off and on in the *Alta* correspondence, he did so with increasingly less point as the trip progressed. After the party entered the Holy Land he appeared only once, in a brief reference to Mahomet in Jerusalem which Clemens later cut from the book. Blucher-Brown, the embodiment of the uneducated comic initiate, was no longer useful to Clemens when his own sense of initiation was gone. The disappearance of Blucher suggests a subtle shift in Clemens' view of the voyage and of his task in relating its events. The later letters had less burlesque comedy of the sort Brown-Blucher allowed and more satire of the excursionists' attitudes—the sentimentality of the trip through the Holy Land, for example. As his comedy became less directed at his own initiation, as he became increasingly sure of his place on the voyage, it became less necessary to have a foil for "Mark Twain," and that persona became more subtle, more able to carry the critical function of the book without his shipmate Brown.

Since the stop in Horta had not been scheduled, the *Quaker City* planned to continue to San Miguel when the storm abated, but Friday, the first day at Fayal, was stormy, and the stay in the safe Horta Harbor was extended. The morning of the second day, Saturday, suggested that another gale was on its way, and the ship waited for a safer sea. When it finally weighed anchor on Sunday, June 23, the weather was clear, and the ship, with Sunday bunting flying from the masts and a fine show of farewell gaiety, steamed out of the harbor. But the sky soon became overcast again (so overcast that, though the engines were stopped for the attempt, Mr. James could not photograph Pico Peak through the haze), and the sea increasingly rough. According to the original agreement, the route of the ship could be changed by unanimous vote, and now the excursionists voted not to stop at San Miguel. They had spent two days at Fayal, and after all, they argued, one Azores island was very like another; they were eager for Europe itself.

Clemens had had no time to write letters while at Horta. Although he had begun his first letter to the *Alta* before landing, he did not finish it until after the *Quaker City* was headed for Gibraltar. There was no need for him to complete his Azores correspondence earlier, for Fayal was on no mail route. The only ships which docked there regularly were a small packet from Boston which came every two months and one from Lisbon which stopped no more often, and hence no *Quaker City* mail was left there. From France, on the other hand, there was fast mail service to New York, and this was the route that all of Clemens' correspondence took; even the California letters were sent first from Europe to New York, then south to Nicaragua, overland to the Pacific, and up the coast to San Francisco.

Six days passed before the ship landed at Gibraltar, days consisting largely of bad weather, boredom, and Bible-reading. One day out of Horta the *Quaker City* encountered a head wind of gale force which made the earlier bad weather seem almost pleasant in retrospect. Many passengers tried to write letters, but most took to their bunks and stayed there. Clemens was apparently unaffected by the storm, but—having finished his correspondence—he was bored by the inactivity. Partly at his behest, a debating club was organized and Clemens jotted down several topics for discussion:

Which is the most powerful motive—Duty or Ambition?
Is or is not Capt. Duncan responsible for the head winds?
How can the passengers best see Spain consistently with the ship's
    route as laid down in the original programme?
Is a tail absolutely necessary to the comfort & convenience of a
    dog?—& if so would not a multiplicity of tails augment the dog's
    comfort & convenience by a constantly increasing ratio until
    his ability to carry them was exhausted?
Which is more desirable—the single or the married state? [23]

However, even with Dr. Jackson in the chair, the debating club could not amuse the pilgrims. Seasickness seemed to put a pall over all shipboard activity. "Few incidents have occurred since we left the Azores," Emily Severance wrote home. "With all of the excitement there [at Horta] it seemed rather dull to come back to steamer life." [24]

[23] "Unpublished Notebook no. 7" (Typescript, p. 38), *MTP*.
[24] *Journal Letters*, p. 33.

A second dance was held on the upper deck, encouraged briefly by a moonlit night, but the deck was slick with dew and it pitched and rolled so steeply that there was, as Clemens wrote in his notebook "more fun than comfort about it." [25] The Quaker City Club met again and the Captain and Colonel Foster read aloud to the passengers about Gibraltar. Again Clemens spoke but not, if the other passengers' lack of interest is any indication, very success-

The Rock of Gibraltar

fully. The degree of Clemens' boredom may be calculated from the fact that he actually led one of the evening prayer meetings before the ship arrived at Gibraltar.

There was nothing to do but pray and read guidebooks and look for land—and worry, for the *Quaker City* was running out of coal. Normally it burned 30 tons a day, but the heavy head winds increased its consumption and the bins were almost empty, and without coal the ship would have been in some danger in the storm. By Thursday the sea was worse and the ship, much lightened by the loss of coal,

[25] "Unpublished Notebook no. 7" (Typescript, p. 23), *MTP*.

pitched precipitously. The passengers were not much comforted by the Quaker City Club that evening, either, for the
entertainment was Bloodgood Cutter reciting rhymes about
the Atlantic in a storm.

By Friday all the passengers had given up to seasickness
and retired to their cabins, all except Clemens who, although he didn't feel "very bright," nevertheless stayed up
all night with Mr. Vail, the Purser, playing dominoes and
drinking bourbon until the sun rose. As a result, the two
men were the first to sight land—the coast of Africa barely
visible on the horizon and, to the north of it, Spain, their
first view of Europe. Excited, they woke Dan and the Doctor, and in a short while every passenger was standing at
the rails and squinting into the sunrise to catch a glimpse of
the Rock of Gibraltar. By early morning the gale had
ceased and they were in the Strait, passing within a mile of
Tarifa Point Light House on the southern tip of Spain to
their left, and sighting Tangier, Morocco, thirteen miles to
starboard. Clemens made careful notes of the passing scene:
the water which had been a "lustrous purple-blue" since the
Azores now became green; the great Spanish hills to the left
had, he noted, "rather barren looking sides & grey granite
tops"; here and there he saw a tower, lonely above a sea
wall, or a "town in [the] lap of a valley nestling in shrubbery." There was a splendid breeze; the *Quaker City* was
under full sail and speeding down the Strait; the sky was
clearing.

But while we stood admiring the cloud-capped peaks of Africa &
its lowlands robed in misty gloom [Clemens wrote], . . . a more
magnificent sight burst upon us—a lordly ship with every rag of
canvas set & sweeping down upon us like a bird. All at once a
thrill went through the whole ship & with one impulse every hat &
every handkerchief were swung aloft—she had flung the stars &
stripes to the breeze! She dipped her colors gracefully by way of
salute, & we answered—& so long as the gallant ship was in sight
every eye followed her & every [man] wafted a God speed after
her.[26]

The American ship was described in every letter home.
Clemens expanded his notebook entry into one of the more

[26] *Ibid.*, p. 24.

dramatic descriptions in his letters to the *Alta* in which, by elaborating the initial awe of the passengers for the "beautiful stranger" and delaying the discovery that the ship was American, he intensifies the emotional effect of the scene, concluding that to see an American flag abroad is to see a "vision of home itself and all its idols." [27]

This paean to America was also a prelude to Europe, for it introduces Clemens' description of the first port of debarkation on the Continent:

In a few moments a lonely & enormous mass of rock, standing seemingly in centre of the wide strait & washed on sides by the sea apparently, swung grandly into view, & it required no guidebook to tell us it was famous Gibraltar.[28]

The entrance into Gibraltar Harbor was to have been one of the high points of the trip, for the colony had promised them a grand welcome: a many-gunned salute from the fortress itself, a guard of honor and a parade of the Eighty-third Regiment, and in the evening an illumination of the galleries in the Rock—a momentous show. The welcome never took place, for it had been planned when General Sherman was still listed among the *Quaker City* excursionists. The display was to have been for him, the American general who apparently had as great a following in Europe as he had in the American North. Unfortunately, the authorities in Gibraltar had heard that Sherman was not among the passengers: no Sherman, no show. The excursionists' disillusionment depressed what would otherwise have been an enthusiastic response to their first landing in Europe.

However, even their disappointment could not entirely destroy their awe at the bay and the colossal mountain rising abruptly and magnificently above it. It was, they knew, one of the most spectacular views in the world, and they responded with suitable awe. "I'm sure none of us will ever forget the picture there before us," Emily Severance wrote of the view,[29] and she was right. The *Quaker City*

[27] Cf. *Traveling*, p. 19 and *IA* p. 64.

[28] "Unpublished Notebook no. 7" (Typescript, p. 25), *MTP;* cf. *Alta* letter of August 27; *Traveling*, p. 20; *IA*, pp. 64–65.

[29] *Journal Letters*, p. 51.

entered Gibraltar Harbor at 10 A.M. on Saturday, June **29**. By eleven o'clock the port's Health Officer had cleared the ship and all the passengers were on their way ashore in the ship's boats; by one, most of them had lunched and were scrambling up the Rock of Gibraltar itself, some on the backs of reluctant donkeys, some on foot. The journey up the steep, winding road was as they had expected it: there was the pleasure of exploring the cannoned excavations of the fortress, of watching the Barbary apes that infested the upper reaches of the mountain, and the delight of surveying the Strait, bay, and Mediterranean Sea from the summit. They all agreed that "The Rock" (as they soon called it) was spectacular. As Clemens noted, "There could not be two rocks like that in one kingdom." [30] But for all their initial awe, the Americans could not deny their disappointment. Apart from the exploration of the fortress, an excursion completed the day they landed, there was little to do. To be sure, there was shopping for fruit in the bazaars of the walled English town at the base of the Rock ("The lemons," Mrs. Fairbanks wrote home in some amazement, "were as large as large oranges and were sold at the rate of two for three cents!" [31]), but this was not an activity to hold the passengers of the *Quaker City* for long. For all its foreign air, the rough, wild costumes of the Moors and Jews, and the clamor of the marketplace, Gibraltar was an English colony, and a rather sedate one. English was spoken everywhere—surely that was not what they had crossed the Atlantic for. Without military fanfare, Gibraltar, they found, was not different enough from the civilization they had left behind to be exotic, and their appetites had been whetted for the exotic. At the end of the first day they had, in Captain Duncan's words, " 'done' the place." [32]

However, the ship had to remain at least two days for recoaling—an unscheduled delay—and most of the excursionists sought amusement outside the colony. Mrs. Fairbanks and the Severances went across the Spanish border to San Roque to see a bullfight; they saw the bullring, but no

---

[30] *Alta,* August 27, 1867; *Traveling,* p. 20 and *IA,* p. 65.

[31] *Herald,* July 25, 1867.

[32] *Log,* p. 24.

fight. Others had more elaborate plans: Moses and Emeline
Beach, in company with Rev. Henry Bullard, Charlie Langdon, and two other passengers,[33] decided to leave the excursion entirely for a time. Their plan was to take the ferry to
Cadiz, a day's journey back through the Strait, and from
there to proceed across Spain to Madrid and on to Paris.
They would travel through Switzerland and northern Italy
and rejoin the ship at Leghorn. Beach made his plans on
short notice, for he discovered that *Villa de Malaga,* the
Cadiz steamer, was preparing to leave the afternoon of their
arrival and there was time only for a brief (but sufficient)
view of the fortress before embarking. With effort he per-
suaded Clemens to accompany them, and Clemens nearly
did so. Beach got the French captain of the steamer to agree
to delay until Clemens could join them, and Clemens was, in
fact, climbing into the boat which was to carry him to the
Villa de Malaga when the Cadiz steamer suddenly weighed
anchor and—unaccountably—left without him.

There was, therefore, no trip through Spain to report to
his *Alta* readers, but he was not unhappy at the outcome,
for he had had some doubts about the trip. Three days and
two nights in a railroad car did not strike him as the ideal
way to tour Spain. "Sixty hours? Can we visit the Alhambra, Seville, Valladolid and 50 other places?"[34] he asked in
his notebook. He was not, therefore, disheartened about
missing the *Villa de Malaga.* As a matter of fact, he was
"damned glad" he had, for there was a better alternative.
On Sunday, in company with Dan, Jack, Dr. Jackson,
Major Barry, Julius Moulton, and "five bottles and 75
cigars" he took a steamer across the Strait to Tangier,
Morocco. He had been advised not to go. Tangier had a
reputation for being of little note ("It is a filthy, dirty town,
with narrow streets, and miserable one-story houses," the
Harper's Hand-book warned),[35] and it was assumed to be
dangerous—many travelers had fallen victim to the Riffian
bandits who had their hideouts in the countryside around

[33] Messrs. Sanford and Beckwith of Cleveland.

[34] *Notebook,* p. 63.

[35] W. Pembroke Fetridge, *Harper's Hand-Book for Travelers in
Europe and The East* (New York: Harper and Brothers, 1865), p.
551.

the city. But Clemens and his friends were undeterred. "We will go," he wrote in his notebook. "I shall answer no questions and *not listen* to any damn fears, surmizes or anything else." [36]

The group was absent from the *Quaker City* for only thirty-six hours, but they were the fullest, raciest thirty-six hours Clemens had had on the trip so far. "Tangier is the spot we have been longing for all the time," he wrote the *Alta.* "Everywhere else one finds foreign-looking things and foreign-looking people, but always with things and people intermixed that we were familiar with before, and so the novelty of the situation lost a deal of its force. We wanted something thoroughly and uncompromisingly foreign. . . . And lo! in Tangier we have found it." [37] The forty miles to Tangier took several hours, and Clemens did not waste the time. He took notes. Historical fact, vignette description, incidental conjecture—all were apparently to aid composition back on the *Quaker City.* However, most of these notes were not used in his correspondence, and his comments may be better taken to suggest his state of mind than his journalistic intentions. The trip across the Strait stimulated all of his romantic predilections. He notes, for example, that the Moroccans had busied themselves abducting women from the coast of Spain before the British came and put a stop to it, a story he found believable, for he commented on the beauty of the Spanish girls he had seen in Gibraltar and the thought of their kidnap seemed to stimulate his imagination. Captivated, he was somewhat gullible and indiscriminate: for example, he apparently believed the local tale that Hercules had been an historical personage who lived in Tangier, for he put down fanciful details of the story with no apparent bias.

He fancied the melodramatic, too. The incidental, gossipy nature of his notes indicates that he got his information not from a guidebook, but by word-of-mouth, from an acquaintance who knew the area and its stories well. There are few statistics and fewer historical facts in his notes but there is much local color with dramatic details. Of course,

[36] *Notebook,* p. 63.
[37] *Alta,* August 31, 1867; *Traveling,* p. 26; cf. *IA,* p. 76.

this interest was to be qualified by his intended audience; he could stomach more than his readers, but he had discovered that what shocks in the *particular* can be quite acceptable in the *general*, and his use of some of the details he heard on the way to Tangier suggest how he followed this rule. For example, in his notes he describes the Moroccan punishment for theft in rather grisly detail: "They cut off right hand and left foot—cut round the joint and break it off,"[38] a description particularly evocative to anyone who has carved a chicken. In the *Alta* letter the description is toned down to: "They slice around the bone a little, then break off the limb."[39] It is only slightly less obnoxious, perhaps, but the substitution of "slice" for "cut" and the omission of "joint" abstracts the operation. Even more important, in his letter he omits all reference to the circumstance from which the notes derived, an actual incident in which two men, possibly English, had their hands amputated in this fashion; the hands were then nailed up in the marketplace. One of the men apparently died; "the other," Clemens notes, "got well by re-amputation by English surgeon."[40] Clemens put the general description of the punishment into his *Alta* letter, but omitted reference to a specific case.

The same treatment was given a story of prisoners being pistol-whipped before they were killed and to the execution of a Jew who helped poison a Spanish consul. In Clemens' notes, the poisoner is executed by a squad who "put him at a distance like a target & had marksmen practice on him a good while."[41] In the *Alta* letter this brutality is recounted, but only in general terms; the victim is not described and the experience is less concrete. By being less specific, the information is less distasteful even while it suggests that the Moroccans were consistently more uncivilized than, indeed, they may have been. A note concerning beheading for capital offences Clemens omitted altogether in his correspondence. There were some facts which, however melodramatic, could not be presented to his newspaper audience, and he

---

[38] *Notebook*, p. 64.
[39] *Alta*, September 1, 1867; *Traveling*, p. 32.
[40] "Unpublished Notebook no. 7" (Typescript, p. 27), *MTP*.
[41] *Ibid.*, (Typescript, p. 28).

finally used less than a third of his Tangier notes in his letter.

Landing at Tangier was difficult, for the only way passengers could disembark was on the shoulders of native bearers whose rates were not fixed, and whose threats of catapulting their charges into the sea were real enough. One had to contend not only with the bearer one hired, but with those one refused. The latter, for reasons of revenge as well as competition, tried to trip the successful bearer on the way to the shore. Since there were few passengers and many bearers, it was a harrowing trek. A floating dock would have been safer, of course, but it would have deprived the Moroccans of a means for bilking travelers. Strangely, Clemens says nothing about the trip from boat to shore, an activity which would have been ripe for his satire.[42]

Immediately upon its arrival at Tangier, the American party sought the narrow court called Washington Street which led to the home of American Consul-General McNath.[43] McNath appears to have been a saturnine man. He had been at this post for five years and was eager to leave it; Clemens' description of the boredom of his wife and the drabness of their apartments suggests why. McNath kept his residence at Tangier, he told Clemens, because it was the most civilized port in Barbary ("God help the other ports!" commented Clemens), but he had "no society." He, his wife, and his four-year-old daughter, Katie, were the only Americans in Tangier, and his child was American in name only, for she had been born in Tangier and spoke Spanish and Arabic, but no English. Although there were a number of European consuls at the port, and Gibraltar was only three hours away, the McNaths felt isolated in a

[42] See *Harper's Hand-Book for Travelers in Europe and The East* pp. 550–51 for a contemporary description of travel in Morocco.

[43] The Consul–General's name has been variously reported: Clemens called him "McMeth" in his notebook, "McMath" in his *Alta* letter and, perhaps because of this confusion, omitted the name entirely from *IA*. The *Harper's Guidebook* calls him "McManus," but McKeithan notes (*Traveling*, p. 36) that he has correspondence from the Consul–General's Office in Tangier indicating the man's name was actually "McNath."

hostile, primitive land. Clemens sympathized with them: "Tangier is full of interest for one day," he wrote, "but after that it is a weary prison." [44]

McNath's loneliness probably encouraged the attention he gave the *Quaker City* party. He helped them choose a hotel (there was not much to choose from), and he directed them about Tangier. The need for such a guide was made very clear when Major Barry unwittingly walked into a mosque and was chased down the street by a fanatical mob. Tangier was no place to wander about unescorted, and when Clemens rode alone outside the city walls on the second day he did so only briefly and with trepidation.

Readers of *IA* will recall the variety and detail of Clemens' observations of the city, and his notebook comments were even more various. One of the more frequently remarked subjects in his notes was the veiled women. They were, he concluded, pretty ugly "specimens," whose purdah derived from coquetry rather than modesty—he declared that some of them slyly dropped their veils when he looked at them. The comment was characteristic. Throughout the voyage, his attitude toward non-European women was harshly critical. He had been outrageously denunciatory of the women of Fayal ("Fornication with such cattle would come under the head of the crime without a name," he wrote of them in his notebook),[45] and while he thought the Spanish and English women of Gibraltar beautiful, he thought the Moorish women homely in the extreme. ("If I had a wife as ugly as some of those I have seen," he wrote in a passage later omitted from *IA*, "I would go over her face with a nail-grab and see if I wouldn't improve it.") [46] The coarse way he described the women of Tangier is consistent with this pattern; he seems to have seen them as subhuman objects for ridicule. In describing the Moslem wedding agreement, he notes that "after a reasonable time if she [the bride] don't breed, [the husband can] discharge her—don't take her for better for worse." [47] As these comments suggest,

[44] *Traveling*, p. 35; cf. *IA*, p. 88.
[45] "Unpublished Notebook no. 7" (Typescript, p. 20), *MTP*.
[46] *Alta*, September 1, 1867; *Traveling*, p. 32.
[47] "Unpublished Notebook no. 7" (Typescript, p. 36), *MTP*.

he was strangely crass in his view of foreign society, and unsophisticated about his own cultural shortcomings. One would not expect Samuel Clemens to be shocked by the crude, male-dominated society he found in Tangier; the society he had left in California was also ruggedly masculine and relatively unqualified by women's tastes and attitudes. But one is, perhaps, surprised that he seemed so easily to accept the male prejudice against women which he found in the non-European countries he visited, for he thought women a great civilizing force, and the absence of women in public life must have encouraged his view that Morocco was barbaric. Tangier, he said, was "only remarkable for its fashions—not its civilization," [48] a comment which reveals as much about his ambivalent attitude toward civilization as it does about the society he found in Tangier.

Whether he thought it "civilized" or not, Tangier was a briefly exciting place for Clemens. He saw the usual sights—the Roman bridge, the Alcazar, the public gardens (though the latter two got short shrift in his notes and in his newspaper account). And he evidently saw enough of Barbary night life to convince him that the Barbary Coast of San Francisco, then a notorious red-light district, was well named. He pretended amazement that Moors did not drink hard liquor ("wonderful—wonderful—*will* wonders never cease!") but that did not seem to keep his party from having such refreshments as they chose; a memorandum in his notebook indicates that, though the party of eight spent a mere $4.50 for food during their sojourn in Tangier, they spent $24.50 for ale, whisky, and brandy. It was, by all accounts, a successful trip.

By the time Clemens' party returned to Gibraltar and the *Quaker City*, it was late Monday afternoon and the ship was ready to depart: coaling had been completed that morning and the crew had almost finished sweeping the coal dust from the lower compartments and washing it from the decks; fresh stores had been stowed and the boiler engines had a full head of steam. The African travelers boarded with a boat-load of mementos—enough to suggest a stay of

[48] *Ibid.*, (Typescript, p. 30).

thirty days rather than thirty hours: Moorish clothing, sundry souvenirs, and forty pounds of dates which they meted out to their envious shipmates, most of whom had done nothing more exciting on Sunday than feed the apes and attend the Gibraltar English Church. Clemens and "El Tabeeb," the Arabic title Dr. Jackson had acquired in Tangier, were to have a ready audience for their stories.

Almost as soon as Clemens and his party were aboard, the ship left the harbor. The sun was going down behind Gibraltar, and the Rock, summoning its grandeur for their parting look, exhilarated the passengers, all of whom crowded to the railing for the view. The weather was brilliantly clear and a fresh, fair wind was behind them.

The sunset was soft and rich and beautiful beyond description [Clemens wrote in his notebook]. I shall never forget what a dreamy haze hung about the silver-striped dome of the African pillar—the city and headland of Sudah and the hills beyond the neutral ground, and how the noble precipice of Gibraltar stood out with every point and edge cut sharply against the mellow sky. Nor how like a child's toy the full canvased ship looked that sailed in under the tremendous wall and was lost to sight in the shadows.[49]

The Mediterranean was almost glassy calm, and after dinner all the passengers were on deck, talking and languidly watching the many ships that passed, and, as the night came on, gazing at the brilliant star-lit sky. It was a marvelous change from their earlier days on shipboard; this was the cruise they had anticipated! "After all this racing and bustling and rollicking excitement in Africa it seems good to get back to the old ship once more," Clemens wrote when he went to bed that night.[50]

The scenery the next morning was almost as spectacular as that of the previous evening. To the north, only sixty miles away, the snow-shrouded Sierra Nevada Mountains were clearly visible and made a backdrop for the many ships which passed the steamer; they were now in one of the most busy sea-lanes in the world. The brilliant weather continued, and, delighted by the new experience of many

---

[49] *Notebook*, pp. 66–67.
[50] *Ibid.*, p. 67.

ships around them, the passengers spent most of the day on deck, some, like Mrs. Fairbanks and Emily Severance writing letters home, some reading, some talking.

Clemens, however, had no time for such pleasant pursuits; he was working. During the next two days he locked himself in No. 10 and wrote well over 7500 words to the *Alta* concerning Gibraltar and Tangier. Some of what he wrote derived from his notebook, but much more he set down for the first time in the letters themselves, and the freshness and vigor of his style stemmed at least in part from the fact that he was still engrossed in his activities in those ports. To write three to four thousands words a day as he did in this instance—and was to do again later in the voyage—was remarkable for Clemens. And he thought the quality of these letters good, for he made very few changes (mostly excisions) in them when they were incorporated into *IA*. Of course, his composition had only just begun, he was still fresh from the impetus which new sights gave him, but his productivity suggests something of the experiences which he found most fruitful in composition: the exotic, the wholly unfamiliar, the bizarre—these were subjects he could treat readily in his newspaper correspondence; they lent themselves most directly to the episodic, conversational manner he used in his accounts. He was stimulated, too, by the dramatic and by activities which illustrated manners and social custom. Historical and anecdotal narrative was his forte in these letters, and though he was very sensitive to purely visual experience and could write brilliant description, the descriptive set piece is uncommon in his correspondence. For example, although he had just written into his notebook the fine description of Gibraltar quoted above, he did not use it in his correspondence to the *Alta;* neither did he incorporate it into *IA*. The scene is not described at all in the *Alta* letters, and in *IA* he interpolated a wholly imagined description of the sunset by The Oracle:

"Well, that's gorgis, ain't it. They don't have none of them things in our parts, *do* they? I consider that them effects is on account of the superior refragability, as you may say, of the sun's diramic combination with the lymphatic sorces of the perihelion of Jubiter." (p. 90).

There were times in Clemens' early career when his awareness of his role as a professional funny man caused him to
downgrade or belittle his other rhetorical gifts.

In the letters concerning Gibraltar and Tangier he seems
to be in full control of his style and his subject. Some critics
have suggested that this control was the result of the influence of the refined society of the *Quaker City* excursionists,
that Clemens was beginning to profit from living so closely
with men and women of a higher social and intellectual
class than his own. It is a wrongheaded assumption, but a
popular one, first made by Albert Bigelow Paine in his
edition of Clemens' notebooks. The Tangier letter reveals,
Paine wrote, "a rather sudden development in Mark
Twain's literary style. Cultured association on the ship had
something to do with it. . . ." [51] To one who sees Clemens,
at thirty-one, as the Wild Humorist of the Pacific Slope, a
kind of socially and intellectually uncultivated bumpkin,
the assumption comes easy enough, but the judgment is
unjust to Clemens, who was no neophyte when he embarked
on the *Quaker City* cruise. In 1867 he had been a professional writer for at least five years, and, as the collections of
his early writing indicate, his was no casual career. He had
been doing regular reporting as well as special assignments
in great volume and with notable success; in San Francisco
he had associated with many professional writers, at least
one of whom, Bret Harte, was acquiring a national reputation; furthermore, he had been given the kind of roving
assignment for the *Alta California* which only an accomplished journalist (if lucky) receives. Why, on the face of it,
should he have been professionally influenced by the *Quaker
City* society?

The argument in favor of influence derives most of its
force from his long and close friendship with Mrs. Fairbanks. Indeed, the intimacy of their friendship has encouraged the misconception that the Clemens of 1867 was
a roughhewn Westener and that the cultured lady from
Cleveland refined him, schooled him in the art of social
behavior, improved his taste, and polished his prose style.
Although this view is ludicrously wrong and does a disserv-

[51] *Notebook*, p. 68

ice to both persons, it has been accepted, with varying degrees of emphasis, by virtually every biographer of Clemens since Paine. Mrs. Fairbanks was useful to Clemens when he composed some of the *Quaker City* letters (as we shall see hereafter), but Clemens was by far the more adept artist and critic of the two. There is no evidence that Mrs. Fairbanks was, as some have called her, an "accomplished" writer. She was, rather, an occasional one whose chief claim to publication seems to have been the fact that her husband owned the paper to which her *Quaker City* letters were sent.

Her social influence on Clemens was limited, too. The assumption that she refined his manners is largely founded on his facetious subsequent comments in letters to her; [52] in letters to others, he indicated that he enjoyed teasing her ("because I like her so") with the thought that she was his mentor. Actually, for much of the trip their acquaintance was, at most, a casual one; they were not close friends at the time the Gibraltar-Tangier letters were written, surely. Not until the middle of the voyage were they well acquainted; not until near its end were they intimate associates. The assumption that they were close friends early in the voyage derives from Paine, who suggests that from the beginning of the excursion Clemens read his letters aloud to a select company of fellow passengers:

It requires only a few days on shipboard for acquaintances to form [Paine wrote], and presently a little afternoon group was gathering to hear Mark Twain read his letters. Mrs. Fairbanks was there, of course. . . . The benefit was a mutual one. He furnished a priceless entertainment, and he derived something equally priceless in return—the test of immediate audience and the boon of criticism. Mrs. Fairbanks especially was frankly sincere.[53]

A nice picture—one would like to believe it—but for the first two weeks of the voyage Clemens wrote no letters.

[52] For example, Clemens to Mrs. Fairbanks, January 23, 1868: "I confess, humbly, that I deserve all you said, & promise that I will rigidly eschew slang & vulgarity in future, even in foolish dinner speeches, when on my guard." *MF*, p. 16.

[53] *Paine*, vol. 1: 327–28.

Even if he had, it would have been a sudden departure for
him to be so unsure of himself that he would seek critical
advice from near-strangers, particularly so when these passengers did not represent the audience he was addressing.

There is, in fact, no evidence supporting the assumption
of an early friendship between Clemens and Mrs. Fairbanks. There is, for example, no reference to her in his
personal correspondence, his notebooks, his *Alta* letters, or
his memoirs before Constantinople. Neither do Mrs. Fairbanks' correspondence or memoirs give evidence of close
friendship early in the voyage. Paine supports his claim by
implication, quoting from her letter of June 9 (the day after
sailing from New York) to the *Cleveland Herald:*

We have D.D.'s and M.D.'s—we have men of wisdom and men of
wit. There is one table from which is sure to come a peal of
laughter, and all eyes are turned toward Mark Twain, whose face
is perfectly mirth-provoking. Sitting lazily at the table, scarcely
genteel in his appearance, there is something, I know not what,
that interests and attracts. I saw today at dinner venerable divines
and sage-looking men convulsed with laughter at his drolleries and
quaint, odd manners.[54]

The quotation, unfortunately, is inexact and the impression
of the original is subtly different from Paine's version. Mrs.
Fairbanks refers to "Mark Twain" in quotation marks—an
indication that she distinguished between the persona and
the writer whom, like all of the *Quaker City* passengers, she
called Clemens.[55] It is a distinction she makes very emphatically in her last letter to the *Herald* (December 14, 1867)
when she contrasts "Mark Twain" the professional newspaper writer to "the better man, Samuel L. Clemens." It is
clear that in the paragraph Paine quotes she is speaking of
the persona. Furthermore, as Paine prints the comment
there is the suggestion that it is "Mark Twain's" "scarcely
genteel" appearance which is the "something" which attracts her to him. Mrs. Fairbanks inserted a "nevertheless"
after "something" to make it clear that her interest was in

[54] *Ibid.*, p. 327.

[55] For example, this was Mrs. Severance and Duncan's usual
manner. See *Journal Letters* and *Log.*

spite of these qualities. Finally, she refers not to his "quaint, odd manners," a phrase with pejorative connotations, but his "quaint, original manners," a merely descriptive phrase. The humorist, not the man, is here described, and even he is less outré than Paine's printing of the quotation would have us believe. But even more significant, Paine omits Mrs. Fairbanks' next statement which sharply qualifies her compliment: "To my mind, however," she concludes, "he can never win the laurels that were destined to deck the brow of our poor friend who sleeps at 'Kensal Green.'" It is difficult to determine which of the men buried at the famous London cemetery is referred to here, but it is clear that Mrs. Fairbanks was not giving Clemens the unqualified endorsement of a close friend. In fact, the comment does not even suggest acquaintance—as she describes the scene they were not sitting at the same table. Unfortunately, Paine's misquotation has been requoted often and used to suggest an early friendship of a very special sort.

Although Mrs. Fairbanks refers to Clemens several times before Alexandria, her comments suggest only a casual friendship and, on her part, a deferential one.[56] Her interest

[56] " 'Mark Twain' sat with us after dinner, and amused us," she wrote a few days after sailing from New York. (*Herald*, July 18, 1867) A week later, reporting Clemens' speech in honor of the birthday of Mrs. Duncan, she wrote:

"Mark Twain" paid a handsome tribute to Mrs. Duncan, and then in his own inimitable manner proceeded to prove that Mrs. Duncan was old—years older than Methusaleh [sic]. We were old in proportion to the events with which we were familiar. She had lived to see railroads built, and the two continents clasp hands. Methuselah wore the same kind of clothes his father wore before him. He did not live long enough to see the fashions change. He tended his flocks just as his father and grandfather had done before him, and died without even getting out a patent for a wire fence [July 22].

Here, by quoting him at length, she indicates her interest in the remarks of the famous writer, but later, when she describes the mock trial in which he participated she does not mention him at all. A week later she made an incidental reference to him: "You may wonder what all this has to do with Gibraltar, but as 'Mark Twain' says, 'I'm coming to my subject if you only give me

in "Mark Twain" was at least as keen as her readers', but she had little to report of Clemens' travels because, except for occasional shipboard conversations, she saw little of him at the beginning of the voyage. On none of the numerous sidetrips and excursions away from the ship did Clemens and Mrs. Fairbanks journey together; for example, they were in different parties in Fayal; they did not go through the Rock together; when he went to Tangier, she went to San Roque. Later, although they were in Paris at the same time, they made no effort to see one another there; although they were going to the same places in northern Italy, they took different routes; although they were in Rome and Naples simultaneously, they stayed at different hotels, etc. This does not suggest a close friendship. Furthermore, Emily Severance, who *was* the constant companion of Mrs. Fairbanks, says nothing in her lengthy letters home to suggest even a casual friendship with Clemens during the first four months of the voyage, although she writes of Mrs. Fairbanks and at least a dozen other passengers repeatedly. Only in her last letter of the voyage—from Bermuda— does Mrs. Fairbanks suggest that she and Clemens had become fast friends. It was only after the journey through Palestine that one is aware of Clemens' affection for her, an affection which was to continue unabated until her death in 1898.

There is, then, no real support for the assumption that Clemens was under the tutelage of Mrs. Fairbanks when he wrote his early letters to the *Alta,* and to see him in this light is to distort the real direction of influence on the voyage, an influence which was quite the other way. *Clemens* was the lion of the *Quaker City;* and he was not so easily caged—as the excursionists were to discover. But, while the Tangier letters do not show the result of "cultured association on the ship," they do illustrate another sort of influence. They demonstrate Clemens' intense, new awareness of an historical continuum. For the first time in his life he found himself—in Tangier—in a locale which

time.'" (July 24, 1867). Thereafter she refers to Clemens only twice, once in reference to passports in Russia (October 4, 1867), and again in her last letter from Bermuda (December 14, 1867).

was historically ancient. "It seems like profanation to laugh, and jest, and bandy the frivolous chat of our day amid its hoary relics," he wrote. "Only the stately phraseology and measured speech of the sons of the Prophet are suited to a venerable antiquity like this." [57] Clemens was born on a frontier which was not even a generation old; he was bred in the youngest part of the youngest country of the world, a country so self-conscious of its raw novelty that it was beginning to dot its countryside with towns called Babylon and Bethlehem, Cairo, and Calcutta. It was an age in which the brevity of time present and the antiquity of time past was particularly apparent to sensitive Americans, and to be placed suddenly in a locale older than history charged Clemens' imagination in a new way. "Here is a crumbling wall that was old when Columbus discovered America," he wrote, ". . . was old when Christ and his disciples walked the earth." [58] In such a circumstance it is not surprising that he discovered a breadth in his perception which had not before been apparent. Nor was it a response which came only when Clemens reassessed the voyage in his composition for *IA* [59]—there is evidence of it almost from the beginning in the letters themselves. It can be seen, for example, in his treatment of the Roman bridge of Tangier. His notes say only "Saw remains of old Roman bridge at Mouth of Fishing river (single arch) where Roman dock-yard was—built their ships & took grain in them to Britain 50 yrs before Christ." [60] In the letter this brief comment is brilliantly expanded:

The Phoenicians, the Carthagenians, the English, Moors, Romans, all have battled for Tangier—all have won it and lost it. Here is a ragged, Oriental-looking negro from some desert place in interior Africa, filling his goat-skin with water to sell in these streets from a ruined and battered fountain built by the Romans twelve hundred years ago. Yonder is a ruined arch of a bridge built by Julius Caesar nineteen hundred years ago. Men who have seen the

[57] *Traveling*, p. 27; cf. *IA*, pp. 78–79.

[58] *Traveling*, p. 27; cf. *IA*, p. 79.

[59] His famous invocation to the Sphinx, written on his return, has sometimes been cited as an indication of this development.

[60] "Unpublished Notebook no. 7" (Typescript, p. 35), *MTP*.

infant Savior in the Virgin's arms have stood upon it, may be.

Near it are the ruins of a dock-yard where Caesar repaired his ships and loaded them with grain when he invaded Britain, fifty years before the Christian Era.

Here, under the quiet stars these old streets seem thronged with the phantoms of forgotten ages.[61]

This is a remarkable evocation of disparate places—interior Africa, the Holy Land, Morocco, and ancient Britain; but even more dramatic is its concentration of present and past time—a résumé of a historical sequence followed by the quick recollection of the present moment, moving abruptly into the past, to the eighth century, farther, to the time of Christ, and farther still, to pre-Christian times. One finds in the developing idea of the paragraph, in the repeated evocation of ever-earlier time, a kind of astonishment and wonder at a continuity which pushes back to and even beyond the frontier of recorded history itself and yet remains contained in the immediate present moment. In this excerpt is the infancy of Clemens' historical sense, a sense which was to be most fully developed in his later work. Time was to be a powerful stimulus to Clemens' imagination, and some of the effects of this stimulus are apparent in the account of his first visit to Africa on the Tangier steamer.

Clemens' industry during Tuesday and Wednesday was interrupted briefly by the third dance of the voyage on Tuesday night. A clear night and a placid sea made dancing on board really enjoyable for the first time. The "African Party," as they were now called, dressed for the occasion in the costumes they had purchased in Morocco. Clemens, "El Tabeeb," Dan, Moult, Jack, and the others each wore the white pajama trousers, long white overblouse and head scarf which was the usual dress they had seen in the streets of Tangier. Each wore, too, slippers of bright yellow leather which had been embroidered in the Moorish fashion. The effect was sensational: Bloodgood Cutter wrote a poem to commemorate the event. So successful was the performance that thereafter, throughout the voyage, almost any one of the African Party was likely to enliven an evening by playing the Moor.

[61] *Traveling*, p. 28; cf. *IA*, p. 79.

The dance was only a prelude to more important business: preparing the *Quaker City* for the celebration of the Fourth of July the following Thursday. It was a highly organized affair. Of course, they elected a President of the Proceedings. By unanimous consent, Colonel Kinney was awarded that office; it seemed only proper that the military establishment on board should have the seat of honor. President Kinney appointed a Marshall to attend the flag, and a General Committee for Arrangements which appointed subcommittees for decoration, program, and general festivities. The orator for the day was to be Mr. Crocker, one of the Cleveland company; the music, as usual, would be provided by Messrs. Krauss (organ), James (clarinet) and Church (flute), who played for the dances, and a series of toasts and speeches were planned. July 3 was given over to the preparations, and passengers who might otherwise have been preparing for their arrival in Marseilles (which was to be reached the evening of the Fourth) were hanging bunting and—with great deliberation—preparing toasts. The clear weather continued, and all hoped it would stay pleasant through the Fourth.

It did. At daybreak the ship thundered to the report of the two cannon—so far unused in the ports they entered. The cannon were loaded with charge and fired no fewer than thirteen times, fortunately with no recorded injuries. At 10:00 in the morning the passengers assembled on the quarterdeck. In front of them, seated behind a cable locker with a flag draped over it, were arrayed the President, ten or twelve Vice-Presidents, and the Marshall. After President Kinney brought the meeting to order, there was a prayer—a long, Fourth of July prayer—by Rev. Dr. Hutchinson, followed by "The Star-Spangled Banner" rousingly sung to the accompaniment of flute, organ, and clarinet. Mr. Church, the reader appointed for the day, read the Declaration of Independence in his best elocutionary style, and then the company sang "America," accompanied as before. Mr. Crocker's oration (now mercifully lost) followed, an oration that was, Clemens reported much later in *IA*, "that same old speech about our national greatness which we so religiously believe and so fervently applaud" (p. 92). A chorus of "Home Sweet Home" followed and, finally, after three hours of honorable celebration, the patriots adjourned for the time being.

At 2:00 the celebration continued at a gala lunch which, in the words of Emily Severance, was "exceedingly 'Frenchy,' I suppose to get us used to the cooking and the manner of serving it before we arrive." [62] The meal was followed by a poem written for the occasion by "Larriat" Cutter and read for their edification (and suppressed amusement) by himself. "My friends," he began,

> We have assembled on this sea
> To represent our country free;
> Although now in a foreign land,
> By her true principles we'll stand.
>
> No matter where we are on earth,
> We'll celebrate our nation's birth;
> If we cannot do it on the land
> Then on deck 'neath our flag we'll stand.

Though he evidently had some trouble finding new rhymes, he continued for well over fifteen stanzas, concluding:

> . . . That from north to south, from east to west,
> Our country is supremely blest;
> Our flag now waves o'er every state,
> And we'll the Fourth now celebrate.

A smile for the polite applause and then, almost without pausing for breath, he continued—in prose: "May the celebration of this day unite in hand and heart all the political parties of our country; and may they celebrate it to the memory of the heroes of '76, who gained our independence, and to the heroes of '65, who preserved it." [63]

The poem for the day "done," there followed thirteen regular toasts which, scruples cast aside for patriotism, were made with champagne. There was a toast to Mr. Leary, the owner of the vessel which had carried them so comfortably across the wide Atlantic; one to Mr. Crocker for his oration

---

[62] *Journal Letters*, p. 52.
[63] *Cutter*, p. 30.

of the morning; one to President Kinney who had officiated so admirably; and for Captain Hoel, Dr. Crane, Dr. Payne, and Mr. Nelson for no apparent reasons at all. And to Judge Haldeman, Colonel Foster, and Captain Duncan. And, of course, to Samuel Clemens. Emily Severance thought that "Some of the speeches in response to the toasts were really fine," [64] but Clemens called them "execrable, almost without exception" (pp. 92–93). It is unlikely that anyone judged them too soberly, however, for a good bit of champagne was drunk, and Captain Duncan, for one, soon forgot the names of those toasted. Clemens later wrote that the happiest speech of all was Duncan's calling for more champagne from the locker.

The champagne finished, the meeting adjourned to the deck where, the crew announced, Marseilles had been sighted. At 6:30 the ship passed the islands outside the harbor, picked up a French pilot, and at 7:00 sailed through the narrow passage between the two forts into the largest commercial port in the Mediterranean. At 8:00 the *Quaker City* was cleared and docked and Captain Duncan wrote in his log, "We are safely in our third port."

[64] *Journal Letters*, p. 52.

IV

MARSEILLES
PARIS

"We have done our whole duty by it."

Twenty years before the *Quaker City* docked in Marseilles,
another American journalist for the *New York Tribune*
wrote about the American in Europe. Margaret Fuller described three classes of Americans abroad:

First, the servile American—a being utterly shallow, thoughtless,
worthless. He comes abroad to spend his money and indulge his
tastes. His object in Europe is to have fashionable clothes, good
foreign cookery, to know some titled persons, and to furnish
himself with coffee-house gossip, by retailing which among those

less travelled and as uninformed as himself he can win importance
at home. . . .

Then there is the conceited American, instinctively bristling and
proud of—he knows not what. He does not see, not he, that the
history of Humanity for many centuries is likely to have produced
results it requires some training, some devotion, to appreciate and
profit by. With his great clumsy hands, only fitted to work on a
steam-engine, he seizes the old Cremona violin, makes it shriek
with anguish in his grasp, and then declares he thought it was all
humbug before he came, and now he knows it; that there is not
really any music in these old things; that the frogs in one of our
swamps make much finer, for they are young and alive. To him
the etiquettes of courts and camps, the ritual of the Church, seem
simply silly,—and no wonder, profoundly ignorant as he is of their
origin and meaning. . . . He criticises severely pictures, feeling
quite sure that his natural senses are better means of judgment
than the rules of connoisseurs. . . .

[The third class] is that of the thinking American,—a man who,
recognizing the immense advantage of being born to a new world
and on a virgin soil, yet does not wish one seed from the past to be
lost. He is anxious to gather and carry back with him every plant
that will bear a new climate and new culture. . . . And that he
may know the conditions under which he may best place them in
that new world, he does not neglect to study their history in this.[1]

Miss Fuller's description rests upon the assumption that
there was little that Americans, geographically isolated and
intellectually nondescript, could bring to Europe and that
they were primarily concerned with what they could take
away from it; her types distinguish American manners of
acquisition. The classification is interesting because it suggests the bias which Americans carried abroad in the mid-
nineteenth century. While they were quick to assert the
value of American manners and culture, the assertion
seemed essentially a reaction, a defensive response to the
assumed superiority of all things European which, for all
their chauvinism, most nineteenth-century Americans
conceded. They went abroad to acquire what could not be

---

[1] Arthur B. Fuller, ed., *At Home and Abroad; or, Things and
Thoughts in America and Europe* (Boston: Roberts Brothers,
1875), pp. 250–52.

had at home, and they had no doubt that their life after their return would be immeasurably better than it would have been had they never gone. Miss Fuller's classification was, therefore, well suited to her subject, and likely to be accepted by it. Certainly the *Quaker City* excursionists would have found no fault with her categories; each would, of course, have placed himself in Fuller's "thinking" category; had they not formed the Quaker City Club for "mental information"? Furthermore, although none would admit to being "servile" or "conceited" himself, each would have put at least some of his fellow passengers in those categories; if this had not been the case when they left New York, it was so by the time they reached Marseilles: had not some already indulged their tastes and spent their money buying the tawdry manufactures of Tangier and Gibraltar? Weren't many filling their notebooks and letters with the gossip of travel which was to impress the provincials at home? Had they not, already, discarded the people of the Azores as pleasantly simpleminded and the nation of Morocco as "uncivilized"?

Miss Fuller's classification is interesting, and to a point, exact, but there were and are other kinds of Americans abroad whom she does not describe. Certainly some special category would have to be devoted to those Americans who, somewhat superciliously at times, observe, criticize, and classify their fellow Americans abroad. It was a category in which Margaret Fuller herself would have to be put, and along with her, Samuel Clemens, for his subject was not only the places he traveled, but the Americans he saw there. The name he gave them—*innocents*—suggests the same perspective one senses in Fuller. Of course, other *Quaker City* passengers were quick to judge Americans in this way; their letters are full of criticism of the American traveler abroad, but Clemens was preeminent in this respect; more than any other passenger on board he was sensitive to the typically American foibles of his shipmates and eager to describe them in his letters to the *Alta* and the *Tribune*.

But these were not characteristics of his companions alone—indeed, he himself demonstrated most of them. Although he constantly criticized his fellow passengers for carrying away pieces of the monuments they visited, he himself brought home a large collection of such souvenirs; although he laughed at the precipitous speed with which Americans went through European cities, he could "do" a city as fast as any of them. He did not deny that he shared the foibles he lampooned; indeed, there are several wonderful examples of self-critical humor in *IA*. But his essential stance had to be that of critic; he had to be removed from the subjects he treated for his humor to have its full effect. It was for this purpose that he created "Blucher" and "Interrogation Point" and the rest—even as he had created "Mark Twain"—to objectify his experience and make it viable.

Certainly Clemens illustrated all of Fuller's categories the first few days he spent in France. He was "servile" enough, "spending his money and indulging his tastes" and "retailing his experience to those less traveled at home." He was eager to sample all of Marseilles' specialities—and he was impressed by them. Some he thought the epitome of civilization: French waiters, for example, he noted with astonishment were noiseless, intelligent and, unlike their American counterparts, always polite regardless of tip. And he was "conceited," too. How scornfully he noted the lack of soap in French hotels, a circumstance which suggested to him that the people of Marseilles, unlike Americans, did not want to be clean! But he was "thinking," as well, in his regard for French streets and roads, whose construction and maintenance he thought America should copy. Typically, too, his most severe criticism during his first days ashore in Europe was of another American who, he noted "talked very loudly and coarsely, and laughed boisterously where all others were so quiet and well-behaved" (p. 99). Clemens, who frequently talked loudly and coarsely and laughed boisterously did not, apparently, sense the irony of his remark. He was typical indeed.

Because of his typicality, it is unfortunate that the day-by-day details of his first week in Europe are lost. The first letter he sent the *Alta* concerning Paris described his arrival and two-day sojourn in Marseilles, his trip by railroad to Paris and his first two days there sight-seeing and visiting the Exhibition. But that letter was lost somewhere in transit across 7500 miles. The loss was to be debilitating, for in writing *IA* Clemens needed his correspondence to sharpen his memory and quicken his imagination; it was difficult for him to recapture the contemporaneity of his letters without his original account to guide him, and the new material he composed for this lost section of his correspondence (and for other lost sections) lacks the freshness which he transferred from his newspaper letters to other parts of the book. The chapters of *IA* treating Marseilles and Paris (X through XV) were written several months after the *Quaker City* returned to New York, and, while both amusing and informative, they suffer in comparison with other sections which first appeared as letters.

For example, the immediacy which one senses in the Tangier and Gibraltar chapters is lacking in most of his description of Marseilles. Although Clemens spent two days and nights in the port before continuing to Paris, there is little that is concrete or specific in the account of his sojourn there. The chapters are largely composed of his animadversions about his hotel, his fanciful comparison of one of the birds in the Zoological Gardens to sanctimonious passengers on the *Quaker City,* and an overly elaborated account of his visit to the Chateau d'If, an account that owed as much to Dumas as it did to Clemens.

His description of Paris in *IA* is also strangely incomplete and flat, suggesting what was indeed the case, a reliance on the facts of a guidebook to inspire his recollection. The guidebook interpolation is skillfully done, and it demonstrates Clemens' sophistication in his use of sources, but the new chapters are different in kind from the earlier ones. Those have the impetus of connected experience—the continuum of action derives directly from the experience itself. The Paris chapters have no such organic unity. They contain funny anecdotal scenes—an experience with a French barber, for example, or his Parisian guide's attempt to force him into a silk shop, but either of these incidents could have happened to anyone; they do not suggest unique experience—indeed, they may be entirely hypothetical, although there is no reason to assume they are. They suggest "stories" brought back from one's travels, rather than the experience of traveling itself. That Clemens was trying to maintain an appearance of the latter is clear from his use of present tense verbs: he tries to suggest that the chapters were written while he was in Paris. "I think we have lost but little time in Paris," he wrote at one point, "We have gone to bed every night tired out" (p. 125). But the reader senses that this is exhaustion recollected in a later tranquility. That Clemens fails to achieve an immediacy is apparent in the distance one feels from the narrator in the telling. At another point and in a more candid mood he wrote: "That first night on French soil was a stirring one. I can not think of half the places we went to, or what we particularly saw" (p. 97). The careful reader becomes aware of the absence of particularity.

When memory failed, imagination served—or tried to. The new section contains a lot of padding. For example, incidents unrelated to the excursion are described, sometimes at length; one such is the long description of a trip by stagecoach across the American Great Plains. There is a certain coarseness, too, in the way purely imaginary experience is substituted for actuality, or historical detail elaborated into grotesque comic effect, as in the lengthy, burlesque retelling of the story of Abelard and Heloise, which is arbitrarily incorporated into a description of Père-Lachaise Cemetery. Here one senses for the first time in *IA* the difficulty which Clemens had in synthesizing two essentially different kinds of narrative. He was trying to combine the historical facts of the voyage with his humorous awareness of them, and, since the facts were not always amenable to comic treatment, he sometimes had either to drop his comic manner or pass over the facts. But he was even more frustrated in his attempt when the facts were incomplete—when the historical circumstances of the cruise became vague, inexact, or nonexistent in his narrative. At those times the book tends to become purely imaginary and, inevitably, given his initial context, false, for Clemens' humor requires a continuing correlation with objective reality to be most effective. At its best it is satirical and demands a foil. It is this lack of objective reality which is missing from his account of Marseilles and Paris.

Most of the *Quaker City* passengers left Marseilles for Paris by express train at 10:00 P.M. on July 5, the day after landing. Some, like Julius Moulton and Messrs. Allen and

Parsons, would not stop at Paris but would continue to
England and rejoin the *Quaker City* several weeks later at
Naples. Others, like Jack Van Nostrand, Mrs. Fairbanks,
and the Severances, would stay in Paris for a week and then
proceed through Switzerland and northern Italy, joining the
ship at Leghorn. A few would return to Marseilles from
Paris and continue to Genoa on the *Quaker City* herself,
and among these were Clemens, Dan Slote, and Dr. Jackson. Unlike the rest of the *Quaker City* pilgrims, Clemens'

A Railroad Official in France

group did not depart immediately for Paris. The reasons for
their delay are unknown: perhaps they wanted to travel
apart from familiar faces, perhaps they found Marseilles
unusually attractive (although Clemens does not suggest
this is the case), or perhaps they simply missed the train. In
any case, they remained two nights in Marseilles, and,
contrary to Clemens' report in *IA*, probably on board the
Quaker City, for the ship was to serve as their hotel in
port—this, indeed, had been one of the attractions of the
voyage—and there is no good reason why Clemens and the
others would not avail themselves of this economy. (When
they returned to Marseilles from Paris, however, they

stayed in a hotel, the Grand Hôtel du Louvre et de la Paix, for the ship was recoaling and to remain on board then would have been unpleasant.)

Those two days in Marseilles were spent in rather frantic sight-seeing; through the museum at Château Borely in jig time, with guide and carriage down the handsome boulevard Prado, into the Zoological Gardens and—more than once—to the Grand Casino for entertainment. Clemens' description of Marseilles is a composite of his two sojourns there (for example, he did not visit the Château d'If until his return from Paris), and much of the activity of those first days was overlooked or omitted when he wrote *IA*, but his introduction to France was frenzied. When Clemens stumbled aboard the Paris express on Saturday night, July 6, he was exhausted.

The journey to Paris was uncomfortable. Most of the excursionists found the European railway cars vastly inferior to their American counterpart. In particular, Clemens was troubled by the absence of sleeping cars (then an innovation on American railroads); the European coaches were compartmented, without connecting aisles which later models adopted, and he felt claustrophobic when the conductor locked the passengers in without water or heat. The seats were comfortable for sitting but not for sleeping. "The backs of the seats were upholstered above where our heads reached, and would have seemed easy for a few hours," Mrs. Severance wrote, "but not for all night." [2] It was an uncomfortable ride for a tired tourist, and Clemens slept little. Neither was there passing scenery to alleviate his boredom: although the train stopped at Arles and Avignon, it did so in the middle of the night. The engine exhaust was even more irritating. The train went through tunnel after tunnel—nearly forty of them—and each time smoke filled the cars choking the passengers and depositing soot on their clothing.

At daybreak they discovered they were following the Rhone River and heading due north; the rocky terrain gave way at last to lush, rolling hills, a patchwork of well-cultivated farms. They stopped for breakfast in Lyons, a city made famous in America and England by Bulwer-

---

[2] *Journal Letters*, p. 57.

Lytton's play ("We saw the lady of Lyons," Clemens wrote, "and thought little of her comeliness" [p. 111]), and then continued up the Saône Valley to Dijon where they detrained for lunch. From Dijon they went west to Tonnerre, and on to Sens, then up the valley of the Yonne to Montereau where the Yonne flowed into the Seine. They were close enough to their destination now to become excited. Fontainebleau passed by their windows, then Melun, and then, finally, at precisely six o'clock, after twenty hours en route, the train came to a halt in Gare de Lyon.

Although in later years he came to dislike the city intensely, Clemens' first impression of Paris was one of admiration and delight. He liked the decorum and efficiency he saw ("What excellent order they kept about that vast depot!" [p. 112] he wrote). The control, he knew, derived from an authoritarian, autocratic political regime, but he apparently did not condemn it on that account. He was impressed as well by the ease with which they secured a hackney coach outside the station, and delighted by the dispatch with which it proceeded at a trot through Paris—past the Place de la Bastille, up the rue Antoine into the rue de Rivoli and finally past the Louvre to their hotel.

The Grand Hôtel du Louvre was one of the largest and most sumptuous in the world. It occupied an entire block, nearly two acres, bounded by the rue de Rivoli on the front and rue Saint-Honoré on the rear, and as a result it commanded a magnificent view of the Louvre, the Place du Carrousel and the Tuileries. It and its sister hotel, the Grand Hôtel de la Paix (both were run by the huge credit combine, the Compagnie Immobilière de Paris), were the most expensive in Paris, and the appointments were as elegant as any American could well have imagined; in fact, its design was the archetype of most of the American grand hotels built during the next fifty years. Its main entrance was through one of two identical courts, each enclosing a large private parking area in which *voitures de remise* ("the better sort of hackney," Clemens was informed) awaited guests of the hotel. In each court, a porte cochere led to an elaborate passageway flanked by a telegraph office—in itself a symbol of importance—a public restaurant, and various concessionaire shops, and this passage in turn opened to a spacious central court several stories high and covered with a glass roof. Here the entering guest would register, change money and be assigned a waiter from one of the "service" offices of the upper floors, and with the waiter he would ascend an ornate double staircase, walk through the elaborate Corinthian-columned "Conversation Room" and up the stairs to his floor. There he would be presented to a concierge who would lead him to his accommodation, which, on the lower, most expensive floors might consist of several rooms—drawing room, bedroom, bath—and on the upper, least expensive ones, perhaps only a bedroom. For camaraderie—not economy—Clemens, Dan and Dr. Jackson roomed together, and the suite they shared was, in Clemens' word, "sumptuous." The other public rooms were equally so: the periodical room was an elegant saloon, in which one could find current newspapers and magazines from all over the world. The billiard room—one of Clemens' first resorts—was also elaborate. Off the "Conversation Room" were various lounges for guests, a breakfast room, a tea room, and the main dining room. The latter Clemens was to know well. It was decorated with gigantic frescoes representing the four seasons and was elegantly furnished with crystal chandeliers, damask hangings and handsome furniture. It was the model for Clemens' "palatial barber-shop" which he later gave an account of in *IA*, that "imaginary" room in which he described himself "with pictures about me, and sumptuous furniture; with frescoed walls and gilded arches above me, and vistas of Corinthian columns stretching far before me" (p. 113). All in all, the hotel was as impressive as the gentleman from San Francisco could have wished.

The hotel's location was excellent for Clemens' purpose: it was directly across the street from the Louvre—a fact which indicates that Clemens' description of the Doctor's difficulty in getting their guide ("Ferguson") to drive them to the Museum was a comic invention. They were in the middle of the shopping center of Paris—next door to Wall, the famous Paris tailors (from whom Clemens was to purchase his "Paris linen"), and down the block from Galignani's Book Shop, the most important publishers of English books in Europe, in whose reading room English and American travelers congregated to browse and read. Galignani's also published the best continental English newspaper, the *Messenger*, a periodical which would have been of interest to Clemens. At its rear, the hotel abutted the Palais Royale, one of Paris' most popular public buildings, around whose beautiful gardens a famous colonnade enclosed the most elegant jewelry shops in Paris. It was probably here that the three Americans went after they had settled in their hotel rooms, for at the north end of the garden were three of the best cafes in the city—Véry's, Trois Frères Provençaux and Véfour's—at one of which they probably ate the "lingering dinner" Clemens described in *IA*. After dinner they sauntered through the colonnade looking at "the dainty trifles in variety stores and jewelry shops." It is clear that Paris was what Clemens had expected it to be with "music in the air, life and action all about us, and a conflagration of gaslight every where!" (p. 113).

Unfortunately, the gaslight was everywhere but in his room, for when he returned that night and climbed into his "sumptuous" bed the gas was unaccountably off, and he had to read his guidebook by candlelight. He was in no mood to read anyway—exhausted and excited, trying "to make head or tail of the wild chaos of the day's sights and experiences," he was ready to sleep.

We can be sure that Clemens saw all the sights in Paris that a robust American man could crowd into three days. "We have done our whole duty by it," he wrote in *IA*. "We have seen the Tuileries, the Napoleon Column, the Madeleine, that wonder of wonders the tomb of Napoleon, all the great churches and museums, libraries, imperial palaces, and sculpture and picture galleries, the Pantheon, *Jardin des Plantes*, the opera, the circus, the Legislative Body, the billiard-rooms, the barbers, the *grisettes*—" i.e., *everything* (p. 150). We know, too, that during his stay in Paris he wrote the lost letter to the *Alta* covering these first days. Unfortunately, the notebook he kept while there was also lost, although apparently only after Clemens used it for writing *IA*, but if the Paris sections he composed anew for the book are any indication, he had little help from his notes, for his description of Paris is vague and generalized and devoted almost entirely to imaginary incidents like the barbershop story, the escapades with "Ferguson," and activities of a generalized, historical nature (such as the military review of Napoleon III and Abdul Aziz) which might have been derived from the recollections of other passengers. His notebook comments may, therefore, have been few, for on those occasions when Clemens wrote letters while traveling, his notes tended to be brief. His chief source in rewriting the Paris section of *IA* was not his notebook but a guide, *Galignani's New Paris Guide for 1867,* which he probably purchased soon after his arrival in Paris. That he used a guidebook as a direct source was itself an indication of his frustration at the loss of his Paris letter, for several times in his letters and notes he scorned writers who take such works as primary authorities. One remembers, for example, how roundly he berated The Oracle who "reads a chapter in the guide-books, mixes the facts all up, with his miserable memory, and then goes off to inflict the whole thing on somebody as stuff which has been festering in his brain for years, and which he gathered at college from erudite authors who are dead, now, and out of print." [3] And elsewhere, too, he speaks condescendingly of passengers who copy information from a guide (pp. 511–12). He scorned the use of outside printed sources because he thought it a kind of plagiarism, and he had been stolen from enough to appreciate how bitter such theft was. Then, too, he thought that a writer should know what he pretends to know and his account should be what it pretends to be. Travels derived from other men's writings could never be honest in this respect. But, though he condemned taking information directly from guidebooks, he succumbed to the practice several times in his composition of *IA*. At times he did so very directly and without indicating his debt, but on most occasions he used his sources in a manner which most writers would think legitimate; after all, he had to get his facts from somewhere, and would it not be more honest to take his information from the best source available? This, at least, was the probable rationale that Clemens used when, in

[3] *Traveling,* p. 23; cf. *IA,* p. 70.

extremis, he borrowed from the works of others to fill out his own books.[4]

Galignani's Guide was a logical choice; it was in English and up-to-date enough to have a section on the Exhibition which he would have thought useful. The synoptic nature of his account of Paris suggests that, writing the sequence concerning Paris several months after his return from the voyage, he first recollected particular places of interest to him and then turned to the guidebook for the details which his memory could not immediately supply. This is, perhaps, most apparent in his description of Notre Dame, the Bois de Boulogne and the Père-Lachaise Cemetery. At no point does he copy the *Guide* directly; rather, he selects factual details and compresses them into his narrative, rounding off dates, deliberately blurring sharp distinctions, and enlivening the narration to avoid the guidebook's flat style. For example, concerning Notre Dame Cathedral *Galignani's Guide* noted:

It appears certain that a temple existed on this spot in the time of the Romans, the foundations being discovered in 1711, when nine large stones were found: [here follows a detailed description of the stones]. . . . On the site of this temple a church dedicated to St. Stephen was erected about 365, in the time of Valentinian I. This was rebuilt by Childebert, about 522, and is spoken of by Fortunatus, ... The high altar was consecrated in 1182 by Henry, legate of the Holy See. . . .[5]

Clemens reshaped this information:

They say that a pagan temple stood where Notre Dame now stands, in the old Roman days, eighteen or twenty centuries ago—remains of it are still preserved in Paris; and that a Christian church took its place about A.D. 300; another took the place of that in A.D. 500; and that the foundations of the present

---

[4] Later in his career, when similarly pressed writing *Life on the Mississippi*, he turned to guidebooks once again. See Dewey Ganzel, "Twain, Travel Books and *Life on the Mississippi*," *AL*, 34: 40–55.

[5] *Galignani's New Paris Guide for 1867* (Paris: A. W. Galignani, 1867), p. 310.

Cathedral were laid about A.D. 1100. The ground ought to be measurably sacred by this time, one would think [pp. 130–31].

Once or twice, however, his information is more directly derived from the guidebook. For example, in describing the structure itself, the *Guide* says:

The portals are bisected by square pillars. That of the central one was removed on Jan. 1st, 1852, on the occasion of the thanksgivings [sic] for the renewal of the President's powers, but has since been replaced.[6]

Clemens' description is very close to his original:

The portals of the great western front are bisected by square pillars. They took the central one away, in 1852, on the occasion of thanksgivings [sic] for the reinstitution of the Presidential power—but precious soon they had occasion to reconsider that motion [sic] and put it back again! [p. 131].

In like manner, specific details about Croix Catelan in the Bois and the tombs at Père Lachaise were taken from *Galignani's Guide* and put in *IA*.

In view of the difficulty he had rewriting the account of his stay in Paris, it is surprising not that he took information from a guidebook but that he took so little. Given the passage of time and the number of sights which he saw but had no record of, one might have expected him to take much more, for there are many experiences in Paris which he must have had about which he says nothing. For example, he devotes scarcely a page to the Exhibition which was supposed to have been one of the chief attractions of the cruise and was certainly one of his favorite subjects when he first contemplated the journey. The fair apparently left him unmoved. "We went there on our third day in Paris—and we stayed there *nearly two hours*," he noted sardonically. He continues that that "was our first and last visit" (p. 124). It was not lack of interest in the Exhibition which kept him from returning but the knowledge that to see anything of it at all would demand more time than he would

[6] *Ibid.*, p. 311.

be willing to give it on such a short stay. Viewing inanimate exhibits was never so interesting to him as looking at people, and there is, therefore, very little about the Exhibition in *IA.*

As a matter of fact, the Exhibition was all but ignored by most of the *Quaker City* passengers, a surprising circumstance considering how large it loomed in the weeks before departure from New York. Moses Beach, arriving in Paris from Madrid, apparently never saw the fair at all—at least he said nothing of it in his letters, and Mrs. Severance was much too fatigued to spend much time about the exhibits. Only Mrs. Fairbanks appears to have explored the fair with any perseverance. Of course, she had an advantage: L. F. Mellon, the American in charge of the United States concession, was an old Cleveland friend who personally escorted her through the University Exhibition grounds on the Champ de Mars, and she was impressed:

It was as if we had suddenly passed from Paris into another city, [she wrote to the *Cleveland Herald*]. Having paid our franc at the gate, we entered the enclosure, where we were at once bewildered with the strange and constantly changing panorama before us. Every country was represented, in the costume of the people, their style of houses, their mode of living, and the fabrics which they manufacture. Flags of all countries floated from different cafés and cottages; languages of every nation came to our ears with the most meaningless jargon. . . . There were galleries of machinery so bright in all their finish, and so complete in all their parts, that I would not wonder at the pride of possessors. There were flowers from every clime—indeed it was like a bazaar of the whole world; the embodiment of an idea, that it appears to me could only have been conceived in Paris.[7]

The plan was a unique one: in a single Grand Palace, seven concentric elliptical circles housed seven doughnut-shaped galleries devoted to various subjects of manufacture (for example, the first—innermost—gallery was devoted to fine arts; the second to the liberal arts, etc.). While it was generally agreed that the structure had no architectural distinction, it was nevertheless functional. The participating

[7] *Cleveland Herald*, August 3, 1867.

countries were each given a section which cut through all seven galleries (like a wedge of pie), and hence each had space in all of the various categories. The exhibitors were all individual manufacturers, but governments leased space for their country's exhibits. Nothing was for sale, and, indeed, the Governors of the Exhibition forbade any obvious commercialism, for the purpose of the fair was solely to display the manufactures of the world and to award 800,000 francs in prizes for what were to be judged the best of its products. The United States section was seventh in size but thirteenth in number of exhibitors. It was not, therefore, a stand-out at the Exhibition, but, considering the distance the exhibits had to come, it was an impressive showing, and its exhibit of a mobile military hospital won the Medal for Humanity. Two of the largest exhibits in the American section were sent by the State of Illinois: a full-scale Western Farm House and a Western Primary District School Building complete with all school furniture and supplies. They were, said Mrs. Fairbanks, to "interpret to the emigrant the democracy of American life—that he may make for himself such a home in the New World, and his children enjoy the advantages of good schools." The entire Exhibition was an elaborate if somewhat utilitarian display. Mrs. Fairbanks was delighted with everything she saw. "Imagine it the most wonderful, the most bewildering, the most ingenious, the most beautiful, and the most *French,* and you will be in the way of a popular verdict," she concluded.[8]

Clemens might have agreed had he had the time to see more of the fair, but on the day of his visit there was a parade elsewhere which he would not have missed: Napoleon III entertained Abdul Aziz, the Sultan of Turkey, in a Grand Military Review on the Champs Elysées. Clemens says in *IA* that he heard of the review by chance at the Exhibition, but this is unlikely. The parade had been planned for weeks and the *Quaker City* excursionists had looked forward to it ever since they had seen the Sultan's warship in Marseilles and heard of the activities of state which had been scheduled for his visit. On their arrival in Paris they had learned that the court was in mourning for the Archduke Maximil-

[8] *Ibid.*

ian and that, except for the military review, all public
appearances of Napoleon III had been canceled. It is unlikely that Clemens would have had to be reminded of his
only chance to see Louis Napoleon in full regalia.

The prospect was a particularly exciting one, for Clemens
had an unbounded admiration for the emperor. He was, said
Clemens, "the greatest man in the world to-day," greater
even than Bismarck. "There is no element of true greatness
which Napoleon does not possess,"[9] he wrote. This was
rather fulsome praise for an American to pay the "Democratic Despot" of France, perhaps, but it illustrates Clemens' ambivalent attitude toward governmental authority.
Although he was emotionally committed to representative
democracy, he was, nevertheless, intellectually autocratic,
and this tension between authoritarianism and democracy
remained unresolved in his mind. While he was convinced,
for most of his life at least, that the individual man was
essentially good and inherently rational, he nevertheless
had a distrust of man in the mass, whose judgment he
thought suspect and whose goodness he thought corruptible.
It was a duality which was to appear in many of his works,
most emphatically, perhaps, in *Huckleberry Finn,* in which
Huck's moral affirmation and Colonel Sherburn's moral
cynicism are never really synthesized or resolved. In the
Louis Napoleon of 1867 Clemens found a beau ideal ruler,
the benevolent despot, a shrewd, wily, ruthless dictator who
manipulated his subjects for their own good. "He has taken
the sole control of the Empire of France into his hands,"
Clemens wrote, "and made it the freest country in the
world—perhaps—for people who will not attempt to go too
far in meddling with government affairs. No country offers
greater security to life and property than France does, and
one has all the freedom he wants, but no license—no license
to interfere with anybody, or make any one uncomfortable"
(p. 128). The use of "perhaps" suggests that Clemens may
have been aware of the contradiction inherent in his statement, for he certainly would have believed "meddling in
government affairs" part of the "freedom one wants"—his
activities in Washington on his return to the United States

[9] *Alta,* September 5, 1867; *Traveling,* p. 40.

make this clear. Yet he liked order in community affairs, and order was what Clemens thought Napoleon III had brought to France. How impressed he had been with the efficiency of the railroad station on his arrival, with the police control of hackney prices, and with the government control of the sale of gold jewelry! This order, this efficiency enforced by law, was, he thought, derived from one man, that "genius of Energy, Persistence, Enterprise," whom he saw for the first time that day on the Champs Elysées.

It was a dazzling sight. In spite of the official mourning, Louis Napoleon was brilliantly attired in a flashing gilt helmet with white ostrich plumes, a military coat, and red velvet trousers with a black stripe running down to his polished boots. Across his chest he wore a broad green sash from which was suspended a gilt scabbard. His saddle was gilt too, and his horse was a spirited bay which seemed unaffected by the cannon bursts that punctuated the progression down the boulevard. Behind him, and, after he dismounted at the Palace of Industry, passing in review before him, were twenty thousand soldiers marching twenty-eight abreast in close order in a parade which continued uninterrupted for well over two hours. It was a spectacle to turn any democrat's head!

Clemens' respect for Louis Napoleon was probably enhanced by the comparison with Abdul Aziz. "Was ever such a contrast set up before a multitude till then?" he asked. The Emperor was all hauteur and intelligence; the Sultan, all vulgarity and stupidity. The contrast reveals something of Clemens view of civilization: Abdul Aziz could hardly have been anything but crude, for the people he "represented" were, Clemens wrote, "by nature and training filthy, brutish, ignorant, unprogressive, superstitious" (p. 126). It is significant that this section of *IA* was written after Clemens returned to the United States—after, that is, he had visited Turkey and become disgusted by it. His recollections of that day in Paris were filtered through his dislike of the "civilization" of Constantinople and the prejudices he acquired there, and the attack he made on Aziz in writing of Paris derived largely from gossip he heard later in the trip. Clemens, like most nineteenth-century Americans, assumed that civilization was determined by the superficial characteristics of society; that order, whatever its cause, was an earmark of social and governmental excellence, and that a lack of order was a sign of a backward civilization.

Seeing Napoleon was the high point of his Paris visit, but Clemens crowded much more into his three-and-a-half days there. His days were filled with sight-seeing and writing the lost *Alta* letter; his nights, with the gay life of Paris after dark. Monday night he went to Jardin Mabille, perhaps the most famous of the French *bals,* country dance pavilions which were open for two or three nights a week during the summer months. The Mabille was an elegant garden with a large dance floor and comfortable places to take refreshment. Here and there throughout the gardens were other amusements—games of chance such as *jeu de bagues* and quoits and swings and Chinese billiard tables. Clemens, of course, was immediately attracted to the billiards, but it was not the game he knew and the tables were very bad. The *bals* were respectable places of amusement, certainly, but they were not all propriety; women, for instance, could attend unescorted and were always admitted free. "The company at this elegant garden," *Galignani's Guide* says of the Mabille, ". . . generally comes under the description of 'the gayest of the gay,' and the licence of the dance is frequently carried beyond the limits of propriety." [10] It was probably here that Clemens first saw performed the cancan which he describes with mock modesty in *IA*.

Clemens' taste for Parisienne dancing was evidently whetted by the Jardin Mabille, for the next night he went to another *bal*, the Jardin Asnières, the most elaborate of them all. Asnières, a chateau built by Louis XV, had recently been acquired by an American. It was noted for its park, a large garden laid out with gravel walks through spacious grass plots and shady groves, which, *Galignani's Guide* noted, afforded "that wicked demon, Opportunity, ample space for laying his wily snares." [11] Clemens was delighted with it. "Heavens!" he said of the dancing there, "Nothing like it has been seen on earth since trembling Tam

[10] *Galignani,* p. 479.
[11] *Ibid.,* p. 481.

O'Shanter saw the devil and the witches at their orgies that stormy night in 'Alloway's auld haunted kirk' " (p. 137), and he was probably not referring to the cancan alone. Asnières was the likely scene of Clemens' encounter with the French barman whose sign "All Manner of American Drinks Artistically Prepared Here" attracted him. American tourists were among the most numerous at the Exhibition, and special attempts were made to lure them into business establishments—usually with the unhappy results Clemens describes.

It was probably to Asnières that Clemens took Lily Hitchcock, a beautiful twenty-five-year-old San Francisco bluestocking whom he had known in California when she wrote for the *Alta California* and the *Overland Monthly*. He had made a special point of calling on her while he was in Paris, for she was a gay, outdoor-loving girl whom he enjoyed. Her knowledge of Paris [12] and her ability to speak French were useful to Clemens, who had little of either. As it happened, Lily was living at Clemens' own hotel, a circumstance which made their visiting easy, and he probably spent much of his sight-seeing in her company. The note he wrote her when he left Paris suggests that they were very good friends indeed. She promised him a picture of herself and he promised to return to Paris. Neither promise was kept, however, and Clemens' cavalier manner with her suggests that there was no romance between them: he promised to meet her for breakfast on Thursday although, as he later wrote his family, he "knew perfectly well I would be on my way to Marseilles by that time. How the world is given to lying." [13]

On his last day in Paris Clemens traveled to Versailles, and his experience there was described to his *Alta* readers in a letter which did not miscarry. He thought Versailles more beautiful than it was possible for any place in the world to be; it was, he said, "worth a pilgrimage to see." Significantly, his view was an historical one. For all the magnifi-

[12] She had lived there for the first part of the Civil War when she was expatriated by her mother who had Confederate sympathies. It was on her return to San Francisco, the war nearly over, that she met Clemens.

[13] *BM,* p. 94.

cence of the scene, he could not ignore in it the suggestions of extravagance and decadence which, in true American fashion, he deplored. And not past history alone. He juxtaposes his description of Versailles with that of Faubourg Saint-Antoine, an area he would have known from Dickens' *Tale of Two Cities,* and implies the political consequences of extremes of wealth and poverty. As was usual with him, places and things led his imagination to people and events.

The days in Paris ended much too soon. In order to be sure not to miss the *Quaker City* he had to leave July 11. He had planned to spend ten days in Paris; [14] he had spent four. Clemens boarded the express train for Marseilles early Thursday morning and spent the next day in a long, sleepless, uneasy journey back to the ship. The excitement of Paris as much as the discomfort of the carriage kept him awake. He had had, he wrote home, a "gorgeous time in Paris. It isn't any use to try to say anything about it—I am only writing to let you know I am well. Oh, confound it, I can't write—I am full of excitement." [15] He couldn't write, but he had to, and when he arrived at Marseilles he shut himself up in a room at the Grand Hôtel du Louvre et de la Paix to complete his *Alta* letter. It was a good one which contained his description of Versailles, and Clemens was later pleased enough with the letter to incorporate it virtually without change into *IA.* Writing that letter took much of Friday, but by afternoon it was finished and Clemens went for a sail in Marseilles harbor, and out to the Château d'If.

Clemens' journey to Paris must have been of great interest to the excursionists who had remained in Marseilles. By all accounts their stay had been a dull one. "There is little of interest in Marseilles," Captain Duncan complained. It had, he noted, "large and increasing docks, a few old churches—some fine streets, tricky shopmen, clean and contented looking lower classes [and]one fine drive." Not enough, perhaps, to hold inquisitive travelers for nine days. Bloodgood Cutter was one of those who had remained behind, and he had, by Duncan's account, "probably walked

[14] See Clemens to Bret Harte, May 1, 1867, *Letters,* p. 124.
[15] *BM,* p. 94.

through every street, lane and alley, into every church and public building and learned more of Marseilles than any one else on board," [16] but even he was not much inspired by the locale: "This is indeed a solemn place,/It seems a city of the dead," he wrote. There had been a bit of excitement when the crew of the *Quaker City* engaged some British sailors in a fight for several nights running, but this was quickly dissipated by Bursley, and, indeed, was not important enough to be recorded in Duncan's log. When the *Quaker City* steamed out of Marseilles harbor at noon, July 13, none of the twenty-two passengers she carried was sorry to be leaving.

Clemens himself was glad to be at sea again. "It was like home to us to step on board the comfortable ship again, and smoke and lounge about her breezy decks" (p. 159). The weather was delightful with a fresh southwest wind behind them, and the sights along the rugged coast were interesting: they passed near Toulouse harbor and were signaled, to the passengers' delight. The night was clear and farther along they could make out a large fleet of men-of-war anchored close in shore. It was a quiet, peaceful night, and after the excitement of France Clemens slept well.

[16] *Log,* p. 27.

V

GENOA MILAN COMO VENICE FLORENCE

"We grow wise apace."

He woke the next morning in Genoa. No city in Europe was
to excite him more. "I want to camp here," he wrote. "I had
rather not go any further." [1] Genoa harbor was one of the
most beautiful the *Quaker City* visited and Clemens' view
from the ship's deck was a remarkable one. Off to the left,
outside the harbor, was the lighthouse whose beacon, just
now extinguished, had guided them the last two hours of the
voyage. Directly in front was the Palazzo Doria, the mag-

---

[1] *Alta,* September 8, 1867; *Traveling,* p. 41; cf. *IA,* p. 160.

nificent sixteenth-century structure whose towers commanded the entire harbor and whose formal gardens cas-
caded to the water's edge. To the right was the crescent
of docks, busy even at this hour, and above them, tiers of
palaces and public gardens mounted the hillsides, giving
way finally to villas and vineyards at the hills' summits.
And all about him the magnificent bay lay bright in the
first rays of the sun just beginning to appear above the hills
which cradled the harbor. It was indeed "Genoa the Superb."

In spite of the early hour, the excursionists were eager to
disembark. As soon as the ship was cleared, they took boats
to shore, some to entrain for Milan and Venice, some, like
Clemens, to find a hotel for a short stay in Genoa itself.
Clemens' hotel was the Crois de Malte, one of the most
famous in Italy. Like most of the grand hotels of Genoa, it
had once been a private palace, and its marble floors,
frescoes, and gilded ceilings showed the splendor of an earlier time which delighted Clemens' romantic spirit. He could
imagine, he wrote some time later, that in the time of the
Crusades "mailed sentinels once kept watch and ward in its
massive turrets and woke the echoes of these halls and
corridors with their iron heels" (p. 168). Of course the
palace was nowhere near that old, and the only connection
the hotel had with the Knights Templars was its name. It
had, however, one of the best locations in Genoa, for it
overlooked the Aquasola, a beautiful park laid out on the
inner town ramparts, the fortifications of which once ringed
the harbor and protected Genoa from attack when it was
the most powerful city-state in Italy. Because of the Aquasola's height, it had a sweeping view of the harbor, and this,
along with its carefully tended plots of flowers and shaded
walks, made it the most fashionable promenade in the city.
It contained, as well, the Cafe Gran Corso, the city's most
elegant restaurant, which boasted an entirely gas-lit courtyard where the society of Genoa took wine and ices in the
evening. It was here that Clemens spent his first evening in
Genoa and discovered the beauty of Genoese women, that
"freshlet of loveliness" which awed and delighted him. "I
fell in love with a hundred and eighty women myself, on
Sunday evening," he wrote the *Alta* in a passage later

omitted from *IA*. "One can see more real fashion, among gentlemen and ladies both, in one day in Genoa, than he can in three in Paris." [2]

Clemens' hotel was one of the magnificent buildings which had given Genoa the title "City of Palaces." Although many of these were still private residences, most were open to the public at specified times during the week, and before Clemens left Genoa he visited several. Only a few doors from his hotel was the renowned Pallavicini Palace, probably the original of the "immense, thick-walled pile" he described in his letter to the *Alta*. Although he deliberately suggests a composite description, he mentions the feature for which the Pallavicini Palace was famous—the "grand *salons* hung with pictures by Rubens, Guido, Titian, Paul Veronese," a collection unmatched in Genoa.

Clemens was an indefatigable tourist. "Since we touched dry land we have gone to bed after midnight & rose again at 7 to rush all day," he wrote his family on the second day in Genoa. "We tired ourselves out here in this curious old city of palaces yesterday & shall again today." [3] His original plan was to stay in Genoa only two days and two nights but he found so much to amuse him that he stayed an extra day. But, though he seems to have been the typical tourist, he was not the typical European correspondent. His letters to the *Alta* do not suggest the encyclopedic narration which other correspondents sent home in their dispatches; what he was describing was his *experience*, the special perspective which his point of view brought to his travels. Clemens was always aware that his purpose was not merely to describe but to present; the consciousness of the narrator rather than the substance of the narration was his first concern.

As a result, much of his sightseeing in Genoa did not appear in his newspaper letter. He wrote nothing about many of the conventional tourist attractions; nothing of the Castellaccio, or the Palazzo Doria, the Palazzo Rosso or the Palazzo Municipale—all places he visited. He wrote, in-

[2] *Traveling*, pp. 42–43.

[3] Clemens to his family, July 15, 1867, Webster Collection, Typescript in *MTP*.

stead, of the beautiful Genoese women, the beggars who salvaged his half-smoked cigars from the gutter, and the obnoxious guide who misdirected him about Genoa. His selection was not arbitrary; Clemens knew his audience, and his choice was a calculated one. *IA* gives the appearance of being so casual a narrative that it is sometimes assumed that its composition was almost accidental, but this misconception is an unintended compliment to his skill, for he knew that the greatest art was that which hides its artistry. His account of his visit to the Pallavicini Gardens,

Women of Genoa

the famous villa at Pegli twelve miles from Genoa, illustrates his awareness of this dictum. The gardens, he wrote, were an unforgettable "mimic land of enchantment."

You go wandering for hours among hills and wooded glens,
artfully contrived to leave the impression that Nature shaped

them and not man; following winding paths and coming suddenly upon leaping cascades and rustic bridges; finding sylvan lakes where you expect them not; loitering through battered mediæval castles in miniature that seem hoary with age and yet were built a dozen years ago; meditating over ancient crumbling tombs, whose marble columns were marred and broken by the modern artist that made them.[4]

What is striking about this description is his awareness of the essential artificiality of the gardens; the picturesque was, in this instance a calculated creation, and Clemens delighted in it. And yet the artificiality was so contrived as to suggest its opposite, to suggest that "Nature . . . and not man" had shaped it. The culminating experience of the garden was the most artificial and the most successful of all:

The chiefest wonder *is* reserved until the last, but you do not see it until you step ashore, and passing through a wilderness of rare flowers, collected from every corner of the earth, you stand at the door of one more mimic temple. Right in this place the artist taxed his genius to the utmost, and fairly opened the gates of fairy land. You look through an unpretending pane of glass, stained yellow; the first thing you see is a mass of quivering foliage, ten short steps before you, in the midst of which is a ragged opening like a gateway—a thing that is common enough in nature, and not apt to excite suspicions of a deep human design—and above the bottom of the gateway project, in the most careless way, a few broad tropic leaves and brillant flowers. All of a sudden, though this bright, bold gateway, you catch a glimpse of the faintest, softest, richest picture that ever graced the dream of a dying Saint, since John saw the New Jerusalem glimmering among the clouds of Heaven. A broad sweep of sea, flecked with careening sails; a sharp, jutting cape, and a lofty light house on it; a sloping lawn behind it; beyond, a portion of the old "city of palaces," with its parks and hills and stately mansions; beyond these, a prodigious mountain, with its strong outlines sharply cut against ocean and sky; and over all, vagrant shreds and flakes of cloud, floating in a sea of gold. The ocean is gold, the city is gold, the meadow, the mountain, the sky—everything is golden—rich, and mellow, and dreamy as a vision of Paradise. No artist could put upon canvas its entrancing beauty, and yet, without the yellow

[4] *Alta*, February 9, 1867; *Traveling*, p. 243; cf. *IA*, p. 521.

glass, and the carefully contrived accident of a framework that
cast it into enchanted distance and shut out from it all
unattractive features, it was not a picture to fall into ecstasies
over.[5]

It is clear from this description that Clemens was convinced that art was dependent on artificiality, that, indeed,
nature unadorned, unselected, unframed, was not necessarily beautiful. It was from the selection of detail and an
artful combination of impressions that beauty derived, and
this same conscious artistry can be seen in his own selection
of relevant items for his letters, in the manner in which he
filters details through his own "golden" consciousness and
artfully combines them. If he omitted details of his journey,
rearranged experiences, was seemingly inexact about dates
and days, it was not because of an inability to keep details
straight or a lack of interest in exactitude but because the
journey he was narrating was one of the imagination. The
wholeness of the book he would fashion would derive not
from fidelity to historical fact but from aesthetic coherence.
Such an intention allowed great latitude in his use of his
materials: he could freely interpolate apparently extraneous
information and, indeed, occasionally could fabricate experience; he could ignore events which another, more orthodox narrator would have described in detail; he could be
relatively unconcerned with time and narrative order (the
description of the Pallavincini Gardens, for example, was
given three months after he left Italy in a letter ostensibly
concerned with Mount Tabor in Palestine). The completeness of his work was to be found not in its affinities with a
guidebook tour through Europe and Palestine but with the
continuing development of an attitude toward what he saw
there.

Clemens' selection of incident therefore reveals much of
his consciousness during the voyage. For example, although
he visited several churches in Genoa, he describes only two.
Certainly he saw San Ambrozio, which had the reputation
for being the most beautiful in the city, and San Siro, which
was the oldest and most historically significant of all the
Genoese churches; either of these would have encouraged

[5] *Traveling*, pp. 244–45; cf. *IA*, pp. 522–23.

another narrator (or, perhaps, Clemens himself at another time) to write at length of art or architecture or historical events. But Clemens does not even mention San Ambrozio or San Siro. Instead he wrote of the far less significant Church of the Annunciation (Santissima Annunziata del Vastato), which seems to have caught his fancy because "one family built the whole affair, and have got money left," a relatively insignificant fact which he may have gleaned from *Harper's Handbook*. What the comment reveals is Clemens' growing awareness of an aristocratic culture, a civilization founded on a moneyed intellectual class. One family had built the church hundreds of years before, and that same family still lived and ruled in Genoa. It was a profoundly disturbing idea because it challenged the democratic convictions which Clemens had grown up with and encouraged his own dissatisfaction with the somewhat easy assumptions of American republican society.

Likewise, Clemens' comments about the Cathedral of San Lorenzo, the most important church in Genoa, tell less about Genoa than they do about Clemens' own ambivalent attitude toward Catholicism. San Lorenzo was the first of many Italian cathedrals, those monuments to piety and art, which were to arouse this curious ambivalence in him: although he admired their magnificence, he distrusted their purpose. San Lorenzo was, he admitted, "about as notable a building as we have found to-day," but its religious relics evoked a typically sardonic disclaimer. "Isn't this relic business a little absurd?" he asked. He doubted that the Chapel of John the Baptist really contained John's ashes, "because I had seen St. John's ashes before, in another Church. I don't think St. John had two sets of ashes." [6] He scorned such faith as mere superstition. Awed by the magnificence of the church, he could not appreciate the faith which created it or recognize San Lorenzo's function as a shrine. On the one hand, he was moved by the elaborate aesthetic ramifications of Roman Catholic art; on the other, his own vague and simplistic Protestant faith was intellectually antithetical to the origins of what he saw. The Chapel of John the Baptist was notable to Clemens not

[6] *Traveling*, p. 45; cf. *IA*, p. 165.

because St. John's ashes were or were not enshrined there but because women, the inheritors of Salome's lust, were allowed to enter it only on St. John's feast day. Clemens thought the custom as significant as the faith.

His sojourn in Genoa revealed another of his predilections: for all his reverence for the past, he had an affinity for the new. On his last day in Genoa he visited Campo Santo, the famous burying ground one and one-half miles north of Genoa which had been laid out only twenty years before but was, nevertheless, one of the city's most popular tourist excursions. The design was a dramatic one: the entrance was a large rectangular area surrounded by arcades with sumptuous single monuments in recesses; extending from this area, flights of steps and broad inclined planes led to the upper galleries, the focal point of which was a rotunda surmounted by a dome supported by monolithic columns of black marble. The effect was evidently awesome to Clemens who was charmed by its size and elegance. "Our last sight was the cemetery," he wrote, ". . . and we shall continue to remember it after we shall have forgotten the palaces." He was most impressed by its newness.

On either side, as one walks down the middle of the passage, are monuments, tombs, and sculptured figures that are exquisitely wrought and are full of grace and beauty. They are new, and snowy; every outline is perfect, every feature guiltless of mutilation, flaw or blemish; and therefore, to us these far-reaching ranks of bewitching forms are a hundred fold more lovely than the damaged and dingy statuary they have saved from the wreck of ancient art and set up in the galleries of Paris for the worship of the world [p. 170].

The new was attractive because it was complete and pristine. When the old suggested the complete, he revered it too, but he was scornful of the monuments of the past which, mutilated and fragmentary, could only suggest what they had originally been; the pyramids would impress him because they were so close to what they had been millenia before; "The Last Supper" he would ridicule because, though comparatively new, it was hopelessly decayed. Clemens' letter to the *Alta* contains no mention of the Campo Santo because it was written early Tuesday, July 16, and

Clemens made his trip to the cemetery that afternoon. It was not until several months later when he rewrote his Genoese letter into *IA* that he recollected his pleasure at the famous monument. His strictures on dilapidated ancient monuments were probably derived, therefore, at least in part from his experiences in the Holy Land, where, he was to discover, there was virtually no means for separating the genuinely ancient from the consummately "restored."

Wednesday morning he replenished his supply of cigars and boarded the train for Milan. It was a journey of only five hours and part of that time was spent changing trains at Alessandria, but he later complained he spent "all day" on the train. The first two hours must have seemed that long. The railroad cut a tortuous path through the Apennines; there were many tunnels on the route, some of them long, and the passengers were occasionally plunged into darkness for twenty minutes at a time while the soot from the engine settled on the carriages, soiling clothing and making breathing difficult. At Alessandria, Clemens had a short stopover and he spent his time visiting the battlefield of Marengo, two miles outside the city, the scene of Napoleon's great victory over the Austrians in 1800. The battlefield had a special attraction for tourists (*Harper's Handbook*, for example, devoted a page and a half to it), and Clemens was so impressed he wrote an entire *Alta* letter describing it, a letter unfortunately lost.[7] We can only imagine what he saw, for his impressions were evidently set down directly in his letter. When he later wrote about northern Italy in *IA* he said nothing of Marengo, for his notebook apparently had no details of his visit there.

The journey through the Po Valley from Alessandria to Milan was more pleasant than the earlier part of the trip. Now the terrain was relatively flat, and the travelers could see for many miles in all directions. Long before they arrived at Milan, its cathedral was clearly visible ahead of them, dominating the plain for miles about the city. It was a momentous sight, fading yellow pinnacles against the faintly blue outline of the Alps beyond, and Clemens was

[7] *Letters*, vol. 1: 135.

enthralled by it. "What a wonder it is!" he wrote. "So grand, so solemn, so vast! And yet so delicate, so airy, so graceful!" [8] In fact, the cathedral seemed to push all other experiences in Milan into the background. "We were in a fever of impatience; we were dying to see the renowned cathedral!" (p. 171) he wrote.

It was to be a while before he could satisfy his desire, for as soon as he arrived at Milan station he was ushered to a room and "cleansed," a process he was later to call "undergoing purification, suffocation and fumigation through the medium of a combination of miraculous stinks and stenches such as only Italian ingenuity could contrive." [9] He was to be "cleansed" repeatedly during his travels in Italy. All of Italy was experiencing a cholera epidemic which had reached plague proportions; nearly every city had minor outbreaks of the disease and feared major ones. Travelers arriving at a city from a supposed source of infection were therefore forced to undergo "fumigation"—an ill-advised and virtually useless method for controlling cholera. It consisted of putting the traveler in a closed room in which chloride of lime and sulphur were being burned and leaving him there for up to thirty minutes while the infection was, presumably, driven from his person and his belongings. Occasionally trunks and suitcases would be opened and their contents drenched in the fumes and then hung out to air for a few hours. It was a tedious, noxious operation which every traveler denounced. "If [tourists] have picked up any cholera," Clemens was to write later, ". . . they might survive it easily enough with a little care; but whether they can undergo Italian purification and live is another matter." [10]

However, he said nothing of his purification in Milan in his letters; perhaps his expectation of the cathedral made him overlook it. Or perhaps the surroundings in which it took place eased his discomfort, for the railroad station at Milan was an impressive one, well befitting the aspirations

[8] *Traveling,* p. 48; cf. *IA,* p. 171.

[9] *New York Herald,* August 22, 1867.

[10] *Ibid.*

of the fastest growing city in Italy. As Mrs. Severance, (who arrived there from Switzerland a day or two after Clemens) described it, it was palatial.

A wealth of art is exhibited in sculptures and frescoes, which, not having seen, one can scarcely imagine. Above the arches in the depot are pictures emblematic of the city, embracing the finest buildings. In the first and second class waiting rooms are frescoes of fancy scenes beautifully colored, and statues everywhere.[11]

Clemens recounts in *IA* that he rushed off to spend "half of that night" looking at the cathedral. He may have, but it is unlikely, for after dark little could be seen either inside or outside the structure. It is more probable that he settled down at the Cavour, a spacious, comfortable hotel directly opposite the railroad station where most of the *Quaker City* excursionists stayed and that he saw the cathedral for the first time early in the morning. He had to be early to have the view from the tower, for by mid-morning the sultriness which had bothered him on the train the day before would have begun to cloud the atmosphere and reduce visibility which, on good days, was over thirty miles. The top of the cathedral was therefore Clemens' first resort. He went up the 158 steps to the first roof from which the facade could be viewed at close range ("long files of spires, looking very tall close at hand, but diminishing in the distance like the pipes of an organ"). From this roof he ascended yet another winding staircase (177 steps) to the platform of the dome, and finally yet another (193 steps) to reach a gallery just beneath the feet of the statue of the Virgin that crowned the cathedral. From there the most spectacular view of all was to be had—and had *best* through a telescope which the guard on duty lent for a price. According to the letter Clemens was to write the *Alta*, the guard also sold beer to willing pilgrims, and Clemens declared he was "full of sublimity" when he went back down the stairs—a confession he later omitted from *IA*.

Clemens' awe of Milan's cathedral encouraged an elaborate description (only the church of the Holy Sepulcher in

---

[11] *Journal Letters*, p. 70.

Jerusalem was to be described in greater detail) and much of it was guidebook data which he probably received from his sacristan guide. He was aware of the undue amount of historical detail in the *Alta* letter, and he attempted to disguise his data by putting it into the mouth of his character Brown. Brown's vernacular description ("and then this old sport lit some more candles and began to grind a crank in the end of the coffin like a hand-organ") spiced what would otherwise have been a rather dull recounting. Clemens further softened the guidebook effect by continuing the humorous skepticism which he had earlier suggested in the cathedral at Genoa. He called the various parts of the church "side-shows" and commented sardonically on the constant request for money ("I never felt so out of funds in my life before"). The holy relics moved him not at all (a bone of Judas Iscariot, he noted, was "very black"), but he was genuinely amazed by the sheer size and complexity of the building itself, so much so that in uncharacteristic fashion he gave his readers its minute specifications—the number of its spires, statues and bas reliefs, for example, along with the number still to be added. He was impressed by the fact that although the church was almost five centuries old, it was still under construction and would not be finished for still another century. "The third generation hence will not see it completed," he wrote with apparent awe. Such group effort over so long a period was a new experience for a man of the American frontier.

The Duomo was the first stop on any itinerary through Milan, and the second was the church of Santa Maria delle Grazie, for on the wall of its convent refectory Da Vinci painted "The Last Supper." Clemens' famous criticism of the picture was harsh. It was, he said, "the mournful wreck of the most celebrated painting in the world," and he argued with some vehemence that the picture was far too obliterated to have any aesthetic value. The comment may seem ludicrous to twentieth-century readers, but to Clemens' contemporaries it was not an uncommon view; it was, rather, the consensus. Almost every guidebook remarked the painting's shabby state: "How much of Da Vinci's handiwork can remain?" asked one contemporary account. "We can be sure of nothing more than the outline of the figures, if of so much." [12] Said another, "But few years can pass before it will be entirely obliterated from the view of those who would wish to behold this lovely composition, all efforts of modern artists to restore its former beauty having proved ineffectual." [13] And most visitors to the refectory echoed their guides. "It is so nearly obliterated," wrote Mrs. Severance, "that one can scarcely imagine what it must have been." [14] Mrs. Fairbanks also belittled it, saying that "the antiquity of this picture is now its principal recommendation." [15] Although Clemens couched his comments in a tone which suggested iconoclasm, he was really echoing the opinion of the majority who saw "The Last Supper."

But his comments nevertheless reveal a great deal about himself: a certain lack of sensitivity toward graphic art, an inability to imaginatively reconstruct a fragmentary picture. "It is battered and scarred in every direction, and stained and discolored by time, and Napoleon's horses kicked the legs off most of the disciples when they were stabled there more than half a century ago. So, what is left of the once miraculous picture?" he asked, and then used his perspective for comic effect: "Simon looks seedy; John looks sick, and half of the other blurred and damaged apostles have a general expression of discouragement about them. To us, the great uncultivated, it is the last thing in the world to call a picture." [16] The antipathy inherent in the words "the great uncultivated," the pugnacious affirmation of untutored experience it makes, was an attitude Clemens maintained most of his life, and it accounts for much that is intellectually vulgar in his work. He belittled those who claimed to find value in experience he could not share. His most sardonic comments concerning Da Vinci's masterpiece were aimed not at the picture itself but at those who were

[12] C. B. Black, *Guide to the South of France and to the North of Italy* . . . *etc.* (London, 1873), p. 473.

[13] W. Pembroke Fetridge, *Harper's Hand-Book for Travelers in Europe and the East* (New York: Harper & Bros., 1865) p. 277.

[14] *Journal Letters*, p. 72.

[15] *Herald*, September 9, 1867.

[16] *Alta*, September 22, 1867; *Traveling*, p. 57; Clemens omitted the last part of this comment ("Simon looks seedy . . .") when he wrote *IA*.

moved by it. "I only envy these people; I envy them their honest admiration, if it be honest—their delight, if they feel delight," he was later to write in *IA*. The impression is clear that to Clemens such feeling was fabricated. "I am willing to believe that the eye of the practiced artist can rest upon The Last Supper and renew a lustre where only a hint of it is left. . . . But *I* can not work this miracle. Can those other uninspired visitors do it, or do they only happily imagine they do?" (pp. 192; 93). It was a typical nineteenth-century attitude: the coterie pretended to understand art, but only the mass could give it value. Such "no-nonsense" description delighted his readers who were, unfortunately, all too ready to evaluate what they could not understand. "Now forevermore I am down on the old masters," [17] he told his *Alta* readers in a comment later omitted from *IA*. He was indeed.

Clemens described only the Duomo and "The Last Supper" to his *Alta* readers, but he saw much more, some of which he was to describe when he rewrote the letters into *IA*. From Santa Maria della Grazie it was an easy walk past the Castello Sforzesco, the fifteenth century castle of Milan (then closed to the public), to the Piazza d'Armi, the great public garden which was bounded on three sides by the city walls, the Castle, and the Arco della Pace, a triumphal arch marking the principal entrance to the city from the Simplon Road. The arch impressed Clemens, but he refused to climb to its top—his exercise in the Duomo had made such exertions difficult—preferring to view it from its base and compare it to the Arc de Triomphe in Paris which, the proud Milanese proclaimed, had been copied from it. The fourth side of the Piazza d'Armi was bounded by the Arena, an open-air equestrian circus capable of accommodating 30,000 spectators. In *IA*, Clemens calls it "a huge Roman amphitheatre, with its stone seats still in good preservation. Modernized, it is now the scene of more peaceful recreations than the exhibition of a party of wild beasts with Christians for dinner" (p. 185). Perhaps Clemens was "stretching" the truth for the sake of his comic comment, or perhaps he was simply misinformed by the guide, whom he complains of in *IA*. In any case, the Arena was not an

---

[17] *Alta*, September 22, 1867; *Traveling*, p. 57.

ancient amphitheatre—it had been built scarcely sixty years before with the materials reclaimed from the demolition of the old castle fortifications; certainly it was never the scene of Roman spectacles, a subject which was to capture Clemens' fancy several times during his tour of Italy.

From the Arena, a short walk past the north side of the castle would have brought Clemens to the Palazzo di Brera, the Palace of the Sciences and Fine Arts, a building which contained the Pinacoteca, the finest collection of old masters in Milan, as well as the newly established Archaeological Museum and the Ambrosian Library. His prejudice against old master painting notwithstanding, Clemens saw the collection of the Pinacoteca, and although he was beginning to scorn Roman antiquities, that "damaged and dingy statuary" which he seemed to find everywhere, he probably went through the two rooms of the Archaeological Museum as well. His real interest, however, was in the Ambrosian Library, the oldest public library in Europe, a famous collection of books and manuscripts established in the early seventeenth century by Cardinal Frederic Borromeo, a nephew of the Archbishop Borromeo whose blackened body Clemens had viewed in the crypt of the Duomo. Significantly, what impressed Clemens was not the size of the collection (140,000 volumes, 15,000 manuscripts) but the romantic associations of some of the items. For example, the letters to Cardinal Bembo from Lucrezia Borgia caught his imagination, for Lucrezia was, he said, "a lady for whom I have always entertained the highest respect, on account of her rare histrionic capabilities, her opulence in solid gold goblets made of gilded wood, her high distinction as an operatic screamer, and the facility with which she could order a sextuple funeral and get the corpses ready for it" (p. 185). This penchant for the melodramatic turned to comic effect directed much of Clemens' attention in his travels and shaped the letters he wrote about them. To such an interest, the incidental was more valuable than the monumental. For Clemens' purpose, Petrarch's copy of Virgil, certainly one of the more important literary treasures of the Ambrosian Library, was not valuable in itself but useful only as a starting point for satirical comments about Petrarch's love affair with Laura. The drawings of Da Vinci he saw there were merely an opportunity to comment on Italian pronunciation. And some of the greatest treasures—such as the third-century illuminated manuscript of Homer or the fifth-century palimpsest of the Pauline epistles—he mentioned not at all.

After the Piazza Duomo and Piazza d'Armi, the largest square in Milan was the Piazza della Scala, named for the great theater which faced it. Clemens had a desire to see La Scala, perhaps because he thought (incorrectly) that it was the largest theater in the world. He took a guided tour through the building and was, apparently, impressed by its grandeur and by the class distinctions which he saw in its seating arrangements. He did not see a performance at the theater, for during the hot summer months there were none. Most of the city's night life was diminished during Clemens' visit, for the highborn society which made it were at their country villas. There was, nevertheless, much for Clemens to do in the evening—he took a ride into the surrounding countryside in an open barouche; he sipped wine in the New Public Garden opposite his hotel and strolled along the Corso Vittorio Emmanuele; he listened to the bands which played in the Royal Gardens and enjoyed the leisure and the calm which he was beginning to think typically European. "Just in this one matter lies the main charm of life in Europe—comfort," he wrote in *IA*. "In America, we hurry —which is well; but when the day's work is done, we go on thinking of losses and gains, we plan for the morrow, we even carry our business cares to bed with us. . . ." (p. 186). He was prepared to acquiesce to this comfort—at least for a time. "The change that has come over our little party is surprising," he wrote. "Day by day we lose some of our restlessness and absorb some of the spirit of quietude and ease that is in the tranquil atmosphere about us and in the demeanor of the people. We grow wise apace. We begin to comprehend what life is for." (p. 187). For two days he tried to adopt this custom, and in part he succeeded—at least he wrote no newspaper letters while he was in Milan.

But it was unlikely that a spirit as vigorously restless as Clemens' could have been quiet for long, and by Saturday, July 20, he was ready to leave Milan and proceed to Lake

Como. It was an easy journey by rail, only 28 miles, slightly over two hours' traveling time. His destination was not the city of Como but rather Bellagio, a town situated on the promontory between Lake Como and Lake Lecco and reputed to be the most beautiful in the Italian lake district. It could be reached either by carriage along a winding road which edged the lake or by steamers which left Como several times a day. Clemens and his friends had decided to go by steamer, and since this meant a delay of several hours in Como and the few sights of that city did not attract them—another duomo, more city ramparts—they decided to continue on the train to Chiasso, Switzerland, only three miles beyond Como. It was all Clemens was to see of Switzerland during the voyage—but it impressed him enough to be the subject of a letter to the *Alta*. The letter, unfortunately, was one of those which never reached the newspaper, and we therefore have no idea of what he saw in his glance at Switzerland. Certainly there wasn't much to see at Chiasso, a rustic small town notable only as the chief entry of Italians into Switzerland. The scenery, however, was spectacular, and, although Clemens was later to forget the name of the town, he did not forget its locale. The excursion to Chiasso was brief, and they returned to Como in plenty of time for lunch before the steamer sailed.

Viewed from Como, the lake was somewhat disappointing to Clemens. He had expected a vast expanse of water similar to Lake Tahoe, which he had come to love in California. Once on the steamer, however, his disappointment changed to enchantment. What he found was a twisting, elongated body of water which impressed not with its size but with its constantly changing aspect as the steamer wended its way around points and between bluffs, now passing close to the silent, densely wooded shore which rose abruptly at the water's edge, now suddenly revealing a vista of several miles which, after a brief view, would as suddenly disappear behind a promontory. For three and a half hours the steamer took its way up the lake to Bellagio, stopping intermittently on both the east and west banks at villages which were little more than entries into the forest countryside, a green expanse which did not quite hide white palatial houses with elaborate formal gardens at the water's edge.

The lake had scarcely a ripple, and the silence of the shore intensified his feeling of pleasurable isolation. Lake Como captivated him. "At eventide when everything seems to slumber, and the music of the vesper bells comes stealing over the water," he wrote, "one half believes that nowhere else than on the Lake of Como can there be found such a paradise of peacefulness and repose." [18]

At Bellagio they were "fumigated" again, but even this did not lessen Clemens' delight. His room at the Grande Hotel Bellagio had a superb view of the lake from its adjoining veranda: to the left, across the lake, the mountainside rose abruptly to a height of 1800 feet; directly in front, the lake stretched out—as he had imagined it might—to a horizon line, for here Lake Como became wider and its vista much longer. The view evoked Clemens' lyrical mood: In the evening he watched the sun set over the water, watched a single boat cut a path through its placid surface, watched the hazy mountain backdrop turn from purple to blue. It was, he said, "beyond all question . . . the richest, softest, dreamiest picture I have ever looked upon." [19]

Bellagio was a place to *be*—as well as a place to see. The hotel had a beautiful garden skirting the lake from which steps extended to the water's edge for swimming and sunning one's self. Guests at the hotel had free access to the Villa Serbelloni, a "ducal estate" whose elaborate gardens with their old, palm-shaded walks extended to the tip of the promontory (Punta di Bellagio) and afforded the best view of the juncture of Lake Como and Lake Lecco.

But Clemens did not spend much time in sight-seeing. He planned to be in Bellagio only two nights and a day and he had several *Alta* letters to write. He wanted to describe his experiences in Milan before his memory cooled and his reminiscences of that city became hopelessly confused with his other travel memories. It was a real problem for him. Traveling as rapidly as he was through a great variety of terrain and experience, the particular quickly became the general in his tired, overstimulated mind. His constant enemy was "drowsy brains harassed with a mad panorama

[18] *Alta*, September 22, 1867; *Traveling*, p. 53; cf. *IA*, p. 202.
[19] *Alta*, September 22, 1867; *Traveling*, p. 54; cf. *IA*, p. 203.

that mixes up pictures of France, of Italy, of the ship, of the ocean, of home, in grotesque and bewildering disorder" (p. 201). If he waited too long, even his notebooks could not help him revive the freshness of his first experience. He was, therefore, busy in Bellagio, but not too busy to spend some time with another *Quaker City* pilgrim, Colonel Foster, whom he unexpectedly met there. Foster had come through Switzerland and planned to rejoin the ship at Genoa before it sailed. They had, therefore, stories to exchange.

It is likely that Foster was Clemens' courier as well, for the two letters he wrote in Bellagio were the last to reach the *Alta California* from northern Italy; the fact that letters Clemens had written up to the time he met Foster were safely received suggests that the latter carried them to the ship. Although Clemens was to write at least nine more letters during his travels to Venice, Florence, Pisa, and elsewhere, all of them would miscarry. It was not a surprising circumstance. Italy was in a state of intermittent civil war, and mail service was badly disrupted. In addition, the none-too-efficient service was further curtailed by the fear of cholera which many thought could be transmitted by letter; mail was often deliberately destroyed. The loss of these nine letters was to create an enormous difficulty for Clemens when he came to write that part of *IA* which concerns northern Italy, for it was impossible for him to recreate the experience many months after the event, and as a result the new Italian material he composed for *IA* is somewhat farfetched, overly dependent on the artificial narration of fanciful stories and improbable experience.

The loss is a real one to readers of *IA*, but so far as the actual narrative of Clemens' journey is concerned it is not so great a loss as might be imagined, for at least half of the lost letters were concerned with the single day's trip from Bellagio to Venice. Early in the morning, Clemens' party took the steamer from Bellagio up Lake Lecco, generally considered inferior to Como in picturesqueness and luxuriousness of vegetation. The trip was less romantic than the one Clemens had taken two days before, and it was also much shorter (Lecco was only twelve and a half miles long). But in its own way the scenery was more dramatic; the mountainsides descended to the water more precipi-

tously, and the sight would have been closer to Clemens'
memory of Lake Tahoe. At Lecco they hired a carriage for
Bergamo, a distance of about twenty miles and left at once,
for there was little in Lecco to hold their interest—only a
fourteenth-century stone bridge which they crossed leaving
the town and, high above it, on the city side, the ruins of a
fortified tower which may have been the inspiration for
Clemens' story of Count Luigi, the burlesque tale he incorporated into *IA* partly to fill the space left by his lost
letters. The journey to Bergamo was very pleasant. For the
first half hour they followed the road around Lake Garlate
and continued along the Adda River to Brivio, where they
crossed the river and continued through the foothills of the
Bergamasque Alps, across the Brembo River at Ponte and
on into Bergamo, a ride of almost two hours. It was a
delightful trip: a magnificent view of the Alps continued on
their left, now mirrored in glassy lakes, now obscured by the
trees when the road passed through dense woods. The
weather was brilliant and the company good. They arrived
in Bergamo only 45 minutes before their train, the express
from Milan to Verona, arrived, and they had little time,
therefore, for sight-seeing. Bergamo was divided into two
cities about half a mile apart—the upper town, the oldest
section, an old Roman fortified city and the lower, the modern metropolis. Clemens was able to see nothing of the
upper city in his short stay, but he saw a good bit of the
lower on his arrival, entering through the Broseta Gate,
passing through the two principal squares, the Piazza Pon-
tida and the Piazza Cavour, turning in front of the Teatro
Donizetti to arrive, finally, at the railroad station.

He boarded the train at two, and six hours later he was in
Venice. It was, he said, "a long, long ride." But it took him
through more beautiful countryside, past the Lago di
Garda, the largest of the Italian lakes, which Clemens
called "handsome," and through the fertile irrigated vineyards and farms of the central Po Valley. The journey took
him through fabled cities, too, cities which, had he had the
time, he would have explored with interest—Brescia,
crowned by its ancient and forbidding castle; Peschiera, an
ancient frontier-fortress guarding the Lago di Garda; Verona, with its reminders of "Montagues and Capulets, their

famous balconies and tombs of Juliet and Romeo *et al.*" (p.
216); Vicenza; and Padua—he would have found much in
each of them to see, but he hurried on to Venice. His speed
did not keep him from writing of these places, however, and
he sent four letters to the *Alta* about these and other cities
of northern Italy. It is a pity they are lost, for it would have
been interesting to see what Samuel Clemens found to say of
cities he never visited.

At 8:00 P.M. he arrived in Venice, and, after the ritual of
fumigation had been performed, he, Dan, and Dr. Jackson
entered a gondola to be transported to their hotel. It was
dusk, and Venice was dramatic.

In a few minutes we swept gracefully out into the Grand Canal,
[Clemens wrote] and under the mellow moonlight the Venice of
poetry and romance stood revealed. Right from the water's edge
rose long lines of stately palaces of marble; gondolas were gliding
swiftly hither and thither and disappearing suddenly through
unsuspected gates and alleys; ponderous stone bridges threw their
shadows athwart the glittering waves. There was life and motion
everywhere, and yet everywhere there was a hush, a stealthy sort
of stillness, that was suggestive of secret enterprises of bravoes
[sic] and of lovers. . . . Music came floating over the
waters—Venice was complete [pp. 218–19].

His hotel, the Grand Hotel d'Europe, had one of the best
prospects in Venice. It fronted the Grand Canal at the point
where it joined the Canale della Giudecca opposite Isola de
Giorgio, and Clemens' room commanded a view of the
church of San Giorgio Maggiore made famous by Caneletto
and Turner. Around the corner, scarcely two minutes' walk
from his hotel, was St. Mark's Cathedral fronting the superb square which, for Clemens, as for most tourists, was
the epitome of Venice.

But, for all the expected glamor which Venice had promised, the city was not very memorable to Clemens. Although
he was to remain there for three days and four nights (he
left on Friday, July 26), he spent little time in sight-seeing,
for he was behind in his letters. He must have written five
while in Venice: four were the lost letters concerning Lecco,
Bergamo, Padua, Verona, and some other cities in northern
Italy; a fifth described Venice—the only one of the group to

reach San Francisco. It is not, therefore, surprising that this Venice letter [20] suggests a very brief tour of the city: "What would one naturally want to see first in Venice?" he asked. "The Bridge of Sighs, of course—and next the Church and the Great Square of St. Mark, the Bronze Horses, and the famous Lion of St. Mark." [21] This would be a start, surely, and the second lost letter might have made the tour more comprehensive, but the new section in *IA* which Clemens wrote to replace the lost correspondence does not suggest his tour of Venice was much more than a brief, one-day affair. He saw the Doges' Palace (and described it in detail), the dungeon and the Bridge of Sighs, and the Basilica of St. Mark—but that was all. Despite his initial comment, nothing of the Bronze Horses, nothing of the Square, no description of the campanile, no clock tower, nothing of the pigeons—all subjects treated in detail by other travelers.[22] Neither was there anything added to suggest Clemens made a Grand Canal tour. He never mentioned the Rialto (although he summoned up the ghost of Shylock), and he said virtually nothing of the palaces or the museums. Although he implies he saw many pictures in Venice, he describes only hypothetical works. Neither did he visit Murano or the Lido. Of course, he may have visited all of these places and deliberately chosen to ignore them in his letters, but if this is the case, his selection is even more bizarre, for he excluded in his account virtually everything which made Venice attractive to the American. His lack of interest seems strange in one who later wrote so eloquently of "the widowed bride of the Adriatic" and her glorious past (p. 217). But this veneration was a later attitude, perhaps, one evoked when he was filling out the letters to make them into a book. At the time, his view may have been less romantic.

[20] *Alta*, misdated "July 29" (*Traveling*, p. 59). Clemens was in Leghorn on this date; it was not his usual practice to deliberately make itinerary and date conflict. The letter was printed out of order, indicating that it arrived late in San Francisco; the *Alta* editor might, therefore have misread the date, or changed it.

[21] *Traveling*, pp. 60–61; cf. *IA*, p. 222.

[22] See, for example, Mrs. Fairbanks' letter concerning Venice *Herald*, September 9, 1867.

Writing nearly 5,000 words a day, he didn't have time for a Venetian romance.

Of course, he may have cared as little for Venice as his friend Mrs. Fairbanks did. She arrived on Wednesday (July 24), and for two days she tirelessly toured the city—or at least her letters sound as though she did—but Venice seems to have been too much even for her usually methodical mind. Unlike her earlier letters, her Venice column seems disjointed, almost chaotic. ("There is no order in Venice," she confided to her readers.) The strain of extended travel in a foreign country was beginning to tell on them all. She was tired. The Bridge of Sighs? "In my humble judgment every bridge in Venice may justly claim that name." Clemens may have been experiencing a similar exhaustion—with 10,000 words to dispatch before he went on. The initial glamour—that moonlit journey among the romantic gondolas—gave way, finally, to broad daylight reality which enabled one to see objectionable things floating in the canals. It turned out to be a dirty, hot city. "Venice," Mrs. Fairbanks concluded, "has been to me one grand disappointment." [23]

Clemens, however, showed his disaffection only indirectly. There is nothing in his surviving letter or in his later additions to indicate he intended to unsettle his readers' romantic attitudes about the city. "It seems a sort of sacrilege" he was to write later, "to disturb the glamour of old romance that pictures her to us softly from afar off as through a tinted mist, and curtains her ruin and her desolation from our view" (p. 217). But neither is there much to suggest that he sincerely shared these attitudes. When filling in the gap left by the missing letter he was clearly hard put to remember any significant details of his stay: only his description of Santa Maria Gloriosa dei Frari has anything like concrete particulars—and these (despite the fact that he misnamed the church) were almost certainly cribbed from a guidebook.

It is significant that, unlike his practice in other parts of *IA,* he did not take more from his guidebook concerning

---

[23] *Herald,* September 9, 1867.

Venice. It would have been relatively easy for him to have lifted details about the Rialto, for example, from several sources—among them Mrs. Fairbanks' correspondence to the *Herald* which he saw before he rewrote—but instead of guidebook details simulating experience, he took the occasion of the Venice interlude to treat three themes which were to be recurring motifs in *IA*. The first of these, the provinciality of Americans abroad, was apparent from the very beginning of the voyage. In his correspondence Clemens seldom missed an opportunity to suggest the inexperience of the American in Europe for the first time; as often as not he himself was the butt of the joke—as when, seduced by the flattery of a salesgirl in Gibraltar, he buys gloves too small for him and tears them to shreds putting them on (pp. 73–74). In such a situation, the American is an "innocent"—gullible, perhaps, but ultimately aware of his pretense and able to laugh at it. The American as novice, Clemens could treat with good humor. But another side of this provinciality—the American as pretender—he treated sardonically, increasingly so as the trip progressed. At the outset of the letters Clemens attacked this pretense in individuals (The Oracle's supposed knowledge "got from a guidebook," for example), but the criticism soon became more generalized and directed at Americans who pretended to the sophistication and attitudes of the European, those, for example, who found "The Last Supper" a masterpiece because they thought they ought to do so. He was particularly scornful of those Americans who pretended a knowledge of a foreign language when they knew only English, and that barely. In the newly written sections on Venice he was emphatic in attacking the pretense of knowing French. Among his friends on board the *Quaker City*, only Mrs. Fairbanks, apparently, actually knew the language well enough to speak it, but after the Paris sojourn many were dropping French phrases with abandon. It was a mannerism Clemens scorned increasingly, and he used the subject for at least one lecture ("Back From Yurrup") on his return. "It is not pleasant," he wrote in the new Venice section, "to see an American thrusting his nationality forward *obtrusively* in a foreign land, but Oh, it is pitiable to see him making of himself a thing that is neither male nor female, neither fish, flesh, nor fowl—a poor, miserable, hermaphrodite Frenchman!" (pp. 234–35). American affectation as Clemens exploited it in *IA* had two extremes: the American who asserts his grossly provincial Americanism at every opportunity and who is, because of it, a victim, and the American who is too easily assimilated into foreign cultures, who too readily pretends foreign manners. Clemens is amused by the vanity of the first; he is, more often than not, scornful of the hypocrisy of the second.

Clemens' ambiguous attitude toward conventional, "old world" romance is also suggested by his new Venice material. Throughout his life he had a penchant for the mystery and drama associated with exotic locales and a mythic past, but this appetite seldom existed without the qualifying interest in the realistic present—the everyday world of necessity. He could play the dichotomy either way: he might show the pragmatic Connecticut Yankee Hank, trying to bring the practical nineteenth century into King Arthur's Court or, on the other hand, he might depict Tom Sawyer, fed on exotic romance, trying to force Huck and Jim into a medieval pageant of escape. It is the juxtaposition which appealed to Clemens' comic sense: the commonplace thrust into the outre world or the outre into the commonplace. Perhaps the most exotic characteristic of Venice to the *Quaker City* Pilgrims—indeed, to any foreign traveler—was its canals and, in particular, the gondolas which worked them. Clemens never described the Grand Canal, but he devoted a large part of the Venice section to the gondola. Although he already had nearly 700 words of description of his initial gondola ride in the letter that survived, he added another 1300 words concerning the gondola in the new material he wrote for *IA*. What caught his imagination was the combination of the exotic gondola performing everyday, mundane tasks. "It seems queer," he wrote seven or eight months after he had left Venice, "—ever so queer—to see a boat doing duty as a private carriage" (pp. 229–30). And he extends this juxtaposition to its comic conclusion: A "young lady" making a call by gondola and making a return invitation:

We've moved into the new house, O such a love of a place!—so
convenient to the post-office and the church, and the Young Men's
Christian Association; and we do have such fishing, and such
carrying on, and *such* swimming-matches in the back yard—Oh,
you *must* come—no distance at all, and if you go down through by
St. Mark's and the Bridge of Sighs, and cut through the alley and
come up by the church of Santa Maria dei Frari, and into the
Grand Canal, there isn't a *bit* of current . . . [pp. 230–31].

It is Missouri in Venice, the commonplace in the surroundings of the exotic, a pattern he was to use again and again in
IA.

A third motif, Clemens' attack on the paintings of the
"old masters," also appears in the new Venice material he
was later to compose for the book, and it is, in a sense, an
amalgam of the two just described: the glamour of viewing
famous works of art was real to Clemens—he frequently
evinces a certain awe in being face to face with a certified
masterpiece: "I shall remember the Transfiguration [by
Raphael]" he was to write later, "partly because it was
placed in a room almost by itself; partly because it is
acknowledged by all to be the first oil painting in the world;
and partly because it was wonderfully beautiful" (pp.
302–3). And yet, as this quotation suggests, the glamour,
while initiated and supported by the judgment of "all," is
nevertheless qualified by his own sensibility. He was self-
conscious of his lack of training, remarking in the new
Venice section that "one has no opportunity in America to
acquire a critical judgment in art" and that he "could not
hope to become educated in it in Europe in a few short
weeks" (p. 237). But, although he is an admitted "innocent," he was determined not to be a victim, and he asserts
his own critical preference for the historically commonplace
rather than the romantic conjecture: "To me there is nothing tangible about these imaginary portraits [of martyrs],
nothing that I can grasp and take a living interest in. . . . I
think posterity could have spared one more martyr for the
sake of a great historical picture of Titian's time and
painted by his brush" (p. 237). This attitude suggests the
tension in Clemens' mind between the conjectures of a romantic imagination on the one hand and verified historical
fact on the other, and this tension was to be one of the chief

characteristics of his writing not only in *IA* but in most of his later work as well. Clemens needed facts to ground his imagination (later in life he would visit his boyhood haunts to stimulate the composition of *Life on the Mississippi;* he would read Lecky to help him compose *The Prince and the Pauper*), and yet there was nothing more stultifying to him as an artist than unadulterated fact. It was, apparently, impossible for him to recount historical detail without embellishment or imaginative extrapolation. The dichotomy between imagination and fact was the equivalent of that between romance and the commonplace, and he was no more able completely to resolve the tension between the one pair of extremes than the other. Ultimately Clemens would find a working equivalent for this resolution in *IA*—an arbitrary and changing preference for one or the other attitude made without apology. This was possible only in retrospect, when the physical exhaustion of continuing foreign travel was past.

Clemens, Dan, and Dr. Jackson left Venice on Friday, July 26, traveling by way of Bologna and Pistoia to Florence. They may have been accompanied by Mrs. Fairbanks, who made the trip on the same day, but Clemens does not mention her. "We were a little fatigued with sightseeing," he wrote later of the trip, "and so we rattled through a good deal of country by rail without caring to stop" (p. 244). Leaving Venice, they left the Austrian Empire and entered the Kingdom of Italy. They crossed the Po Valley, much of it cultivated in orchards and vineyards heavy with ripening white grapes ("they have not the delicious flavor of our own [Ohio] catawbas" Mrs. Fairbanks remarked),[24] through fields marked by graceful Lombardy poplars and round-trimmed locusts beneath which white cattle shaded themselves, through Ferrara, through Bologna, into the Apennines and, finally, to Florence, the ancient city which had only two years before been made the capital of the Kingdom of Italy. It was a long day's journey and they stopped only for meals—a circumstance which did not, however, prevent Clemens from later writing a letter to the *Alta California* (now lost) about Bologna, a letter which must have been

[24] *Herald,* September 11, 1867.

derived wholly from a guidebook, for he took few notes on this journey and he had virtually no experience of his own to remember and relate. The journey to Florence was not an uncomfortable one—all the Americans spoke well of the Italian trains, of the comfort of their appointments and the courtesy of the handsomely uniformed employees. "There is no rushing through a crowd," wrote Mrs. Fairbanks, "Everything is done upon time. . . ." [25] It was only during the latter part of the trip that Clemens grew restive, when, passing through the Apennines he complained of being "robbed of all the fine mountain scenery on our little journey by a system of railroading that had three miles of tunnel to a hundred yards of daylight" (p. 244). It was after dark when they arrived in Florence and Clemens stopped at yet another "Hotel de l'Europe," this one in the center of the city on the Piazza Santa Trinità, a convenient location within easy walking distance of the major sightseeing attractions.

"Florence pleased us for a while," Clemens wrote later, encouraging his readers to assume he had a long sojourn in that city. Actually he was in Florence for only forty hours and his memories of them were not happy. He was tired; he was eager to rejoin the *Quaker City* now anchored at Leghorn scarcely fifty miles away by train, and he had no heart for sight-seeing. Still, he did it. He apparently visited Santa Croce (although he could not have gone there "from time to time" as he says) and Piazza della Signoria, whose "great figure of David" he described. He claimed to have traveled through both the Pitti Palace and the "Ufizzi" Gallery, and he remembered the Medici Chapel in detail. He also got lost on one of his two nights there. It was a busy forty hours, the exact details of which we will never know, for the letter which he wrote shortly after leaving Florence was one of those lost, and the notebook which covered this part of his journey is also missing. When he came to describing Florence in *IA* he was nonplussed. Florence was to have been one of the major points of interest on the journey (it would later be one of his favorite cities, one where he would live as an expatriate), yet he devotes scarcely four pages to his stay

[25] *Ibid.*

there, and most of that is a description of Florentine mosaics, details of which he probably got from reading Mrs. Fairbanks' letters after the trip was long completed.[26]

But he was near exhaustion. In the ten days since he had left Genoa he had been under an intensive regimen of travel (over 600 miles) sight-seeing (four major cities) and writing (nine letters). It is not surprising that he was in a hurry to reboard the *Quaker City*. Passengers going overland through northern Italy were not expected back on board before Monday, July 29, but Clemens wanted to return before that. On Sunday morning he set out for Leghorn by way of Pisa, stopping there for several hours between trains to see the "strangest structure the world has any knowledge of—the Leaning Tower" (p. 249). The sight was worth a letter, and he wrote it shortly after he got back on board the *Quaker City*. (It too was lost, and Clemens once again resorted to a guidebook when it came to describing Pisa in *IA*.) He arrived in Leghorn late Sunday afternoon.

We never entirely appreciated, before, what a very pleasant den our state-room is; nor how jolly it is to sit at dinner in one's own seat in one's own cabin, and hold familiar conversation with friends in one's own language [he wrote on his arrival]. Oh, the rare happiness of comprehending every single word that is said, and knowing that every word one says in return will be understood as well. . . . We shall not go ashore in Leghorn. We are surfeited with Italian cities for the present, and much prefer to walk the familiar quarterdeck and view this one from a distance [p. 253].

[26] Cf. *Herald*, September 11, 1867 and *IA*, pp. 245–47.

VI

LEGHORN
ROME
NAPLES

"Wonderful monuments of human folly . . ."

Only two weeks had passed since the *Quaker City* docked in
Genoa harbor. It seemed much longer. For Clemens the
fortnight had been packed with the experience of a month;
for the passengers who remained with the ship, the time had
been stretched by boredom. There had been some excitement
at first: shortly after Clemens' departure, a gunboat seized
the ship and the dozen passengers who remained on board
and held them in durance until a superior officer arrived and
ordered their release; on another occasion, Captain Duncan
was taken ashore under guard and questioned; and during

the nine days the *Quaker City* remained in Genoa, guard boats were stationed about the ship at night and the movements of the Americans watched in port. Rumor had it that two steamships were being sent from an unidentified country to aid Garibaldi's cause, and the *Quaker City* was thought to be one of these. Americans were notoriously pro-Garibaldi—had he not lived in the United States for a number of years before returning home to agitate for a United States of Italy? It was not without reason, Captain Duncan wrote home, that "the 'Quaker City,' an ex-war steamer, loafing about the Mediterranean, professing to be on an excursion, but showing scarcely a dozen passengers, is suspected of being connected with the movement." What *was* surprising, perhaps, was how lightheartedly the passengers took the experience in Genoa harbor. "The shadows are after us," Captain Duncan remarked. "Well, let them watch; it pleases them and does us no harm." [1]

Under the circumstances it was foolhardy to contemplate visiting Garibaldi himself, but Duncan apparently was keen to try. The original prospectus for the voyage had suggested a call at Caprera, one of the small Tuscan islands near Elba where Garibaldi had a villa, but this was to be done only "if practicable," and certainly no one had much hope of meeting the great man himself. In Genoa harbor it seemed even more hopeless: even if Garibaldi were willing to meet a group of itinerant Americans, there would have been official difficulties, for both the Kingdom of Italy and the Papal States feared insurrection and would not willingly have allowed foreigners—particularly Americans—to visit the chief insurrectionist himself. Nevertheless, despite the difficulties and official threats, Duncan was determined—and ultimately successful. If Clemens had arrived back on board a scant five hours earlier—had he, for example, foregone Pisa and arrived Sunday morning rather than Sunday afternoon—he might have joined one of the more interesting excursions of the journey. The mischance denied him an experience he would have relished.

It also denied us the pleasure of his account, and we must settle for that of Captain Duncan who led the party of nine

[1] *Independent*, August 29, 1867 (Dated July 21, 1867.)

who visited the "Grand Revolutionary." It is not entirely clear how the meeting was finally arranged, for Garibaldi was not in Caprera but in a villa at Vinci near Empoli. It is possible that Dr. Gibson, that plenipotentiary extraordinary, arranged it, perhaps by using General Sherman's name, but—from whatever fortuitous circumstance—on Sunday morning the party received a last-minute invitation for an audience with Garibaldi. Gibson and his wife, the Duncans and their two boys, Colonel Kinney, Dr. Birch, and Jack Van Nostrand set out at noon for Vinci, their train undoubtedly passing Clemens' going in the opposite direction. "There were some scruples, of course, against making such a journey on the Sabbath," the dutiful Duncan was to write home later,

even to see such a personage as Garibaldi; but then might not good grow out of it? Might not our pious example and conversation have a good effect upon the great revolutionist, and be the means of inducing him, while fiercely denouncing the Romish priesthood, to exhort his people to become Congregationalists, Presbyterians, Baptists and Methodists? Possibly. Surely the effort should be made, and no day so suitable as the Sabbath to carry out such pious purposes. We resolve to go." [2]

Resplendent in this evangelical fervor the group entrained for Empoli where they took a carriage to Vinci about an hour and a half away. Garibaldi, surrounded by an armed retinue, met them in his bedroom, one rheumatic leg propped up on a chair before him. He did not disappoint them—he wore his red shirt and greeted them warmly in broken English ("We were surprised that he spoke English so imperfectly," Duncan reported later), commenting that it was too late for him to learn a foreign tongue. He was particularly eager to talk of the American Civil War, and when he learned that Kinney had been a Colonel in the Union Army under Sherman he became enthusiastic. It was, he declared, "a glorious war, a war for mankind. If you had failed," he confided, "I and my friends might have gone to Australia, to China, or to the devil!" Sherman was, he said,

[2] *Ibid.*, (Dated August 3, 1867.)

"a *great* general" and the march to the sea "A grand campaign." "He spoke warmly of America" Duncan was later to write in his log, "He had . . . visited many parts of it, and alluded with a merry laugh to the time when he had made candles on Staten Island." [3] He offered the party wine which they, like true Christian warriors, refused, but they did accept his offer of autographs: one for each of them, an extra one for Henry Ward Beecher, and two more for General Sherman and General Grant to be sent in the care of Colonel Kinney. Duncan invited Garibaldi to join the excursion—at least as far as Naples, but he declined, blaming his rheumatism, and bade them a friendly farewell. They were back on board the *Quaker City* by 9:00 P.M. "We hope our missionary efforts may not prove fruitless," Duncan averred on his return.[4]

The day and a half Clemens spent on the *Quaker City* in Leghorn Harbor was a productive time for him. There were scarcely ten passengers on board when he, Dan and the Doctor returned, and the ship, anchored a mile from shore, presumably to keep the sailors in check, was cool and quiet—a good place to write. Although he was tired, he did not lose the opportunity offered by this respite and wrote four more letters—those he later referred to concerning Bologna, Florence, Pisa and Leghorn—describing experiences real and imagined in places still fresh in his mind. Like many of those which went before—and were to follow—all of these were lost en route to San Francisco.[5] His labor was lost because, despite the notorious uncertainty of the mails,[6] Clemens had neither the time nor the patience to make copies of his letters.

Clemens was probably hard at work in No. 10 when the

---

[3] *Log*, p. 33.

[4] *Independent*, August 29, 1867.

[5] If, as is likely, these were mailed at Leghorn, their miscarriage might have been occasioned by the fact that that port was shortly to be quarantined—all ships leaving it would have had to prove their good health in subsequent ports and all mail carried from it by sea would have been subjected to various disinfecting procedures, some of which might have ruined Clemens' manuscripts.

[6] See *Journal Letters*, p. 83.

passengers began to return to the *Quaker City* on Monday. The Beaches, fresh from Spain, France, and Switzerland, had returned to the ship in Genoa, and had gone, like the Severances, to see what they could in two days in Florence.[7] Mrs. Fairbanks had stopped in Pisa before returning on Monday afternoon. The pilgrims arrived with plunder from all over Europe ("the convenience of having a ship became evident," Duncan noted in his log). Small boats clustered about the ship offering alabaster statuary, mosaics, and jewelry, and although heavy-laden, the pilgrims continued to buy. They were delighted to be on board again, "quite satisfied," as Beach was to write, "after their little experiences to accept thankfully the lesser evils of shiplife of which, once, they had been disposed to complain."[8] Reunions were intermittent throughout the day—punctuated with expressions of pleasure after long separation and the exaggerated descriptions of experience real or imagined. Captain Duncan, who had been forced to stay with the ship, viewed the return with a jaundiced eye.

Everybody has seen more than anybody else, [he wrote to *The Independent*] and everybody is satisfied."
Paris has been done in a day, the Exposition in an hour and a half! Churches, galleries, palaces, and cities have been visited . . . in one side and out at the other—the idea being to get through. This rushing of things, this guzzling, is altogether unnecessary and unwise. Swallowing everything and digesting nothing. There is an abundance of all that is rare and rich which can be seen and enjoyed leisurely with the time at our disposal; but this would not be American. *We* must rise early, sit up late, bolt our food, race, rush, work, and sweat, if we would have real enjoyment.[9]

A valid criticism of the excursion, certainly, but it comes with a certain lack of grace from Duncan who had planned it that way—and who himself did not maintain a hectic pace only because he could not leave his ship.

[7] Beach was later to write an "eyewitness" report of the visit to Garibaldi although he did not himself go to Vinci. See *New York Sun*, November 25, 1867.

[8] *Sun*, November 23, 1867.

[9] *Independent*, August 29, 1867.

According to schedule, the *Quaker City* was to leave Leghorn on Monday night and arrive in Civita Vecchia the next morning. From Civita Vecchia, passengers who wished could continue by rail to Rome and return to the ship at Naples. It was a logical plan, but it reckoned without the cholera epidemic. Early Monday morning a dispatch from Florence informed Captain Duncan that Civita Vecchia had been declared an infected port and that any ship which sailed from there to Naples would certainly be held in quarantine for seven days. Civita Vecchia was immediately dropped from the itinerary, and many of those who planned to disembark there hurriedly made other arrangements to catch a train from Leghorn to Rome leaving the next morning.

Clemens and Dan Slote, however, didn't choose to wait for the train. They'd had enough of that kind of travel for a while, and, because of the cholera, rail travel was thought more dangerous than going by sea. As Clemens reasoned, once they got to Civita Vecchia they could go ashore and take the short train trip to Rome, for Leghorn was not quarantined and "they do not quarantine the cars, no matter where they got their passengers from" (p. 254). They therefore quickly booked passage to Civita Vecchia on a French steamer leaving Leghorn that evening. It was just as well they did so, for the next two days on the *Quaker City* were frustrating ones. Monday night Duncan telegraphed Naples to confirm the report of the Civita Vecchia quarantine and on Tuesday morning he received word that it was not true; the rail passages were canceled, and the *Quaker City* prepared to continue to Civita Vecchia. However, departure was delayed by the absence of Mr. Leary, the ship's owner, who was unaccountably missing, and the *Quaker City*, steam up, lay waiting for over eight hours. It was an unhappy circumstance, for with Mr. Leary came the information that in the eight-hour interim *Leghorn* had been declared an infected port, that the *Quaker City* would now be quarantined in any Italian port where she subsequently dropped anchor, that for seven of the eight days to be spent in Naples those who stayed with the ship would be able to view the city only from the harbor. Mr. Leary was not very popular that evening. Now all but fifteen passengers sought rail transportation to Rome, and, since none was available until 9:00 the next morning (Wednesday), the passengers voted to lay over one more night in Leghorn.

When the rest of the *Quaker City* passengers finally boarded the train in Leghorn Clemens was already in Rome—indeed, he had been there for 12 hours. His voyage on the French steamer was not a comfortable one—the ship was small and crowded, and nobody spoke English. If one is to believe Clemens' account of the 12-hour voyage written some months later, it was a rather sleepless night, for he describes a monk and a French sailor ("the leader of a marine band of a French man-of-war") who played the piano and "sang opera turn about; they sang duets together; they rigged impromptu theatrical costumes and gave us extravagant farces and pantomimes" (p. 261). The customs procedure at Civita Vecchia made him no happier. The Papal States were one of the few countries in Europe which demanded a passport and visa for entry. Clemens, like the rest of the *Quaker City* passengers, had a passport, and he had had the forethought to get a visa in Florence. But apparently all Americans looked like Garibaldian conspirators to the Roman authorities, and he and Dan were delayed in the port for some hours while his luggage was ransacked; his passport was not returned to him until he arrived in Rome. "This is the vilest nest of dirt, vermin, and ignorance we have got into yet," he said of Civita Vecchia.[10]

Of Clemens' sojourn in Rome we know very little, for the one letter he wrote to the *Alta California* concerning his stay there was lost and the notebook he carried with him is also missing. We have only a few reminiscent notes concerning Rome in the notebook he began in Naples. Rome was too important to be ignored in writing *IA*, but it was, apparently, difficult for Clemens to reconstruct his experience there. The Rome portion of *IA* amounts to forty printed pages, yet they say less about Clemens' journey than any comparable section of the book. The text suggests that he himself was dissatisfied with what he wrote: "I

---

[10] *New York Tribune,* September 6, 1867; *Traveling,* p. 72. He later toned down the language of this letter when he printed it in *IA,* pp. 262–65.

wished to write a real 'guide-book' chapter on this fascinating city, but I could not do it, because I have felt all the time like a boy in a candy-shop—there was everything to choose from, and yet no choice. I have drifted along hopelessly for a hundred pages of manuscript without knowing where to commence" (p. 307). It is an accurate judgment of the section: over half the additions are pure fabrications, and some of them have virtually nothing to do with Rome—for example, the Judge Oliver story that evoked Nevada in the middle of a description of the Coliseum.

Of course, as we have seen, Clemens' intention was never merely to recount his journey abroad: he wished, in the broadest sense, to entertain—to cast a fresh eye on the things he saw on the trip and to comment on them in a vital, amusing way. But he was not a mere funnyman. At its best, his humor was satirical and dependent on a comic correspondence to the real world of fact and reason. In most of his writing prior to the *Quaker City* excursion, he had addressed an audience that knew the subjects of his satire, but in his *Quaker City* letters he was exploring a world new to his readers, and it is this circumstance which determined the structure of the book, a point of view which oscillates between the self-conscious traveller and the objective satirist. Conveying the reality of Europe and the Middle East to his audience was the more difficult because it was not wholly real to Clemens himself. This may have been the source of his difficulty in writing about Rome: it was all new and yet in a sense all recollected; he was seeing the Eternal City as concrete reality for the first time and yet he had heard about it almost all his life and had blended it—perhaps beyond separation—with the extravaganza of schoolboy fantasies. He was a boy in a candy-shop—his appetite driving out all discrimination.

But his method demanded something concrete to work his style against and, several months after his return, in the absence of on-the-spot correspondence, his memory serving not at all, he turned once again to the kind of source which had helped him earlier—a guidebook, in this instance one written by William H. Neligan.[11] Unlike his earlier use of

[11] William H. Neligan, *Rome: Its Churches, Its Charities, and Its Schools* (New York: James B. Kirker 1858).

Galignani's Guide in the Paris sections, however, Clemens used Neligan intending to satirize him, and he was, therefore, much more direct in his reference: he named his authority and quoted it verbatim on occasion. But he did so only to laugh at what he believed to be Neligan's "undoubting, unquestioning simplicity" in accepting Christian tradition concerning the scenes he describes. Clemens' manner was characteristic; he had adopted it earlier in his letters and was to do so again, particularly in his treatment of William Prime's *Tent Life in the Holy Land* in the Palestine section.

What he indulged in here was a good-natured, but nevertheless pointed, debunking of attitudes he encountered throughout the voyage but found particularly evident in Rome and in Neligan's guidebook. Clemens had a typical middle-class Protestant prejudice against Roman Catholic political power; it was a prejudice he shared (as we have seen) with virtually all of the *Quaker City* passengers, and Rome brought it to full flower. Even so gentle and generous a lady as Mrs. Severance was repulsed by what she saw there: "I feel more than ever the degradation of Popery," she wrote home from Rome, "and wish that its days might soon be ended. Such mummery, such superstition, such innocence, such ignorance! I try to thank God that we have cut this yoke of bondage in our land." [12] And Mrs. Fairbanks, while she was clearly in awe of the splendor of St. Peter's, could not forget that it was, after all, the "temple of the Pope and priesthood," [13] a phrase which suggests more accurately than any other what these travelers (who were not blatant bigots) found most nefarious—not Catholicism but "Popery." The Papal States were an independent kingdom—one of the most restrictive to travelers on the entire continent; they seemed to carry all the trappings of political totalitarianism as well as religious repression, and this in a context of great extremes of poverty and wealth. As Mrs. Fairbanks wrote:

Surely "the beggar is the just antipodes of the Pope rather than the King." Our way to the Vatican was through streets whose filth and offensive odors would be a disgrace to my beautiful Cleveland,

[12] *Journal Letters*, p. 95.
[13] *Herald*, September 26, 1867.

while our carriage was beset by beggars who pursued us to the steps of the palace. The Pope, however, has put between himself and the outer world such a barrier of architecture that he need never look upon the Lazarus who sits at his gate.[14]

It was, ironically, the very splendor of the Vatican which made the *Quaker City* travelers suspicious of it. Their own Protestant ethic defined Christian virtue in the context of good works, something akin to selling all that one has and giving to the poor. A church wealthy amid the dire poverty of its people seemed to them a sacrilege. This was, perhaps the dominant impression that Clemens himself carried away from his Italian sojourn, and he refers to it both in the letters he wrote at the time and in the subsequent additions he made to *IA* afterward. "As far as I can see," he wrote to the *Alta California* upon his departure from the country,

Italy, for fifteen hundred years, has turned all her energies, all her finances, and all her industry to the building up of a vast array of wonderful monuments of human folly, and starving half her citizens to accomplish it. She is to-day one vast museum of magnificence and misery. All the churches in San Francisco put together could not buy the jewelled trumpery in one of her hundred cathedrals. And for every beggar in San Francisco, Italy can show you ten thousand—and rags and vermin to match. It is the lousiest, princeliest land on the face of the earth.[15]

This attitude explains his choice of Neligan and his use of Neligan's book, for Neligan's announced purpose was to provide devout American Catholic tourists with a guide to the city. Actually, Neligan is factual and restrained, but he assumes a kind of faith and an acceptance of Papal power which Clemens could never abide. Clemens attraction to the guide probably lay in this very antipathy. Neligan served a dual function for him: he provided the essential factual

---

[14] *Ibid.*

[15] *San Francisco Daily Alta California*, September 26, 1867; *Traveling*, p. 69. I conjecture this letter was written after his visit to Rome; it is clearly recollective of his visit there, although it incidentally concerns Florence, and it must have arrived at San Francisco in the company of the other Naples letters discussed below.

details that grounded Clemens' narrative in concrete reality
and at the same time he served as a butt for Clemens'
sardonic humor. Clemens laughs, for example, at the string
of academic degrees and professional associations which
Neligan printed after his name and implies that, for all his
education, Neligan was naïve—Clemens laughs at academic
authority even while he uses it. Furthermore, he doesn't
hesitate to misread Neligan; in two of the three direct
quotations in which he cites the guidebook he belittles it
unfairly by misquoting in one instance and misunderstand-
ing the author in another.[16] This treatment seems particularly unfair when one realizes that, although Clemens sati-
rizes Neligan by name for bad information, he felt no apparent hesitancy in using his book—without naming it—as
his prime authority in other parts of the Roman chapters,
particularly in his description of St. Peter's [17] and in that of
the Catacombs. In the latter, he pieces several references in
Neligan into a concerted whole.[18] The quotations are widely

[16] He laughs at Neligan's comment that "the heart of St. Philip
Neri was so inflamed with divine love as to burst his ribs" (*IA*, p.
296), but Neligan had not written "burst his ribs" but, rather,
"cause his ribs to be broken" (p. 432). The fact is the same,
perhaps, but the effect is somewhat different. Clemens also
mistakes Neligan's use of the term "to confirm," meaning "to
celebrate," with that meaning "to prove" and from this misreading
implies an overweening faith. Cf. *IA*, p. 297, and Neligan, p. 77.

[17] Cf. *IA*, pp. 271–73, and Neligan, p. 161.

[18] Neligan wrote:

In these same Catacombs St. Pontian, St. Antherus, St. Fabian,
and St. Cornelius took refuge, from the year 235 to 252, during
the time of their pontificate. St. Stephen, who began to reign on
the 13th of May, 253 . . . [was killed by] the ministers of the
Emperor's vengeance when they thrust him back into his
episcopal chair and murdered him . . . Thirty years later than
this, St. Caius lay hidden there during eight years of his pontificate, and only left them to join the noble army of martyrs
[p. 411].

There appears to have been about 160 different Catacombs,
bordering on the different public ways. . . . [A calculation]
would give about 900 miles as the length of the streets in all the
Catacombs taken together [p. 406].

spaced in Neligan, and Clemens' carpentry here suggests how carefully he read his source—and how useful Neligan actually was to him. For Neligan was not a bad contemporary guide to the city, and the things for which Clemens particularly chastizes him, Christian miracles and Popish politics, are a very minor part of his book. Had Clemens looked a bit farther he might have found other guides which would have served his satirical purpose better—but none which would also have been a good stimulus to recollection.

Clemens' general disaffection with Rome probably de-

Under the church of St. Sebastian is a Catacomb. . . . It is, however, interesting from its associations, as there St. Bridget was wont to kneel, wrapt in contemplation. Here St. Charles Borroméo was wont to spend whole nights in prayer . . . [pp. 431–32].

From these disparate references Clemens pieced together a connected paragraph implying that his information came from a priest who guided Clemens' party through the catacombs:

Five or six of the early Popes—those who reigned about sixteen hundred years ago—held their papal courts and advised with their clergy in the bowels of the earth. During seventeen years—from A.D. 235 to A.D. 252—the Popes did not appear above ground. Four were raised to the great office during that period. Four years a piece, or thereabouts. It is very suggestive of the unhealthiness of underground graveyards as places of residence. One Pope afterwards spent his entire pontificate in the catacombs —eight years. Another was discovered in them and murdered in the episcopal chair. There was no satisfaction in being Pope in those days. There were too many annoyances. There are one hundred and sixty catacombs under Rome, each with its maze of narrow passages crossing and recrossing each other and each passage walled to the top with scooped graves its entire length. A careful estimate makes the length of the passages of all the catacombs combined foot up nine hundred miles. . . .

In the catacombs were buried St. Cecilia, St. Agnes, and several other of the most celebrated of the saints. In the catacomb of St. Callixtus, St. Bridget used to remain long hours in holy contemplation, and St. Charles Borroméo was wont to spend whole nights in prayer there [*IA*, p. 295–6].

rived primarily from his own ambivalence toward Catholicism and the formal trappings it wore in Italy—its "monstrous" churches, as he called them, its "ubiquituous" priests ("one man for every ten" declared Mrs. Severance),[19] and its totalitarian government which seemed to hem the traveler in on all sides. But there were other qualities which Rome shared with the rest of Italy which probably prejudiced Clemens against it: the beggar population, the filthy streets, the uneducated, unkempt citizenry, and the general lack of mechanized progress. Rome was surely one of the most unhealthful cities in Europe (the Pontine marshes were not yet drained and malaria was a constant danger) and, of course, it was crowded with Americans (they were "monopolizing the hotels and the guides," declared Mrs. Fairbanks [20]), a circumstance which was abhorrent to Clemens who liked Americans, but preferred them at *home*.

How long Clemens remained in Rome is uncertain, but he and Dan probably made the eight-hour train trip to Naples on Sunday, August 4. Unlike his earlier journeys by train, it would not have been a difficult journey. The weather was clear and cool. "We were most agreeably disappointed finding it not dusty," wrote Mrs. Severance after she had made the trip. The views were splendid; for a long distance Rome was visible, the dome of St. Peter's shining against a bright blue sky, and on either side of the route, ancient monuments appeared—mysterious, unidentifiable ruins and an ancient aqueduct 15 miles long. The route twisted among the rocky hills, now passing vineyards whose vines were festooned between the trees and heavy with the large, sweet grapes the tourists had enjoyed in Rome; now through fields where women harvesting hemp paused and waved as the train went by; now past clumps of cork trees where men were cutting away the thick black bark. And never far away, often in sight, lay the Mediterranean splendid under the summer sun. At the border there was, of course, the usual difficulty with luggage, but, that finished, the train continued past carefully tended gardens, burrowing occasionally

[19] *Journal Letters*, p. 91.
[20] *Herald*, September 26, 1867.

through rocky hills until finally it arrived at the Stazione Centrale, Naples. Like most of the *Quaker City* passengers who arrived from Rome, Clemens settled in a hotel overlooking the magnificent bay and found, among the hundreds of ships at anchor there, the *Quaker City* herself small in the distance, bravely flying from her mast a flag of quarantine.

The ship had been there for nearly four days, and three more would pass before she would be given a clean bill of health and her fifteen passengers allowed to come ashore. Before the ship had sailed from Leghorn there had been a hope that quarantine would not be imposed on the vessel, and a small letter-writing foray had been planned to secure release if such quarantine were imposed. Before he left the ship at Leghorn, Clemens had written a letter to the editor of *The Observer,* an English-language newspaper in Naples, and sent it with the ship with permission to print it in the event of quarantine. Clemens' intent was clearly to cajole freedom with humor, but the letter, published on August 3 before Clemens himself arrived, had no effect.[21] Bloodgood Cutter, for his part, petitioned the health authorities of Naples in a dozen stanzas which ended with these enduring lines:

> I'll tell you now you may depend
> You will not gain with us a friend.
>
> Why don't your doctor come on board
> And see what in our ship is stored;
> Although our ship is nice and clean
> On her at all he is not seen.
>
> But no, he came near us in his boat,
> Under his umbrella there doth float;
> Says a few words then goes away,
> Leaving us confined in Naples Bay.[22]

---

[21] The letter was later published in the *Alta* (probably from a clipping sent by Clemens), September 16, 1867. The *Alta* incorrectly noted that Clemens was on board the *Quaker City.*

[22] *Cutter,* p. 48.

But even Cutter's lines were unavailing. "We had expected that, on hearing part of it read, rather than be afflicted with the remainder, they would immediately issue an order for our release," W. E. James wrote home, "but, as in many other things concerned with this excursion, we were doomed to disappointment." [23]

The quarantine had small—very small—pleasures. The passengers were allowed to row about the harbor—so long as they touched no other ship (and took a guard along to make sure they didn't). And they could make purchases from the many boats that clustered about the *Quaker City*. The port's Health Officer was quite willing to act as interpreter during the transactions, and the salesmen were equally willing to take the excursionists' contaminated

The Bay of Naples

money. As the overland passengers began to assemble at Naples, some, Clemens among them, rowed out to the ship to express their sad-faced condolences and to voice their vexation at the unfairness of Italians in general and port authorities in particular—before they rowed back.

Clemens was happy not to be quarantined, but not because he had any particular appetite for Naples. His disaf-

[23] *Brooklyn Daily Eagle,* September 19, 1867.

fection for Italy and Italian cities was at its peak. "It may be thought I am prejudiced," he was to write later in *IA*. "perhaps I am. I would be ashamed of myself if I were not" (pp. 312–13). The ignorance, the disease, the general filth conspired to make all the *Quaker City* excursionists relatively unsympathetic to the architectural beauty and the historical significance which surrounded them. "We all have the feeling," wrote Mrs. Severance, "that the Neapolitans themselves are the lowest dregs of humanity we have yet seen. I would not trust any of them with the smallest sum, and as to filth—you simply have no conception of it! Of course you can expect vermin to be plenty, and we all know what fleas are now, if never before." [24] Clemens' animadversions were, therefore, typical. " 'See Naples and die;' " he wrote. "Well, I don't know that one would necessarily die after merely seeing it, but to start in to try to live there might turn out a little differently." [25] He hated the crowding, it brought his latent antipathy to cities surging to the surface. He was particularly offended by the extremes of wealth and poverty which he saw, the pitiful life of the poor, and the unfounded pretensions of the upper class. And there were more "miraculous circuses" to feed his displeasure. In the Cathedral he discovered the vials of the blood of St. Januarius, which was believed to liquify twice a year, and his indignation was rampant. "Every day for eight days, this dismal farce is repeated, while the priests browse around among the crowd of staring asses and collect toll for the exhibition." [26] Shortly after he arrived in Naples he attended the San Carlo Opera House and was shocked by the abuse a famous soprano was given; it reflected, he thought, on the general treatment of women in Italy. And he mistrusted the Neapolitans:

They cheat everybody they can, and they always are expecting to get cheated themselves. They always ask four times as much money as they intend to take, but if you give them what they first

[24] *Journal Letters*, p. 98.

[25] *Alta*, October 6, 1867; *Traveling*, p. 89; cf. *IA*, 315.

[26] *Alta*, October 1, 1867; *Traveling*, p. 86. Clemens toned this down a bit in the book; cf. *IA*, p. 311.

demand, they feel ashamed of themselves for aiming so low, and immediately ask more.[27]

Naples clearly gave him much cause for irritation, but his irascibility was caused as much by physical exhaustion as by what he saw about him. Not only Neapolitans aroused his ire; his fellow passengers were less and less easy for him to abide. When the quarantine ended, the excursionists planned a trip en masse up Vesuvius, and Clemens quickly escaped—alone—to Ischia, the largest of the islands bordering the Bay of Naples, with only a note to Dan saying where he had gone. "Leave Herculaneum and Vesuvius alone till Thursday," he wrote, "We don't want to go with those—." He was evidently unable to find a fitting denunciatory word for his fellow pilgrims and left the message incomplete.[28]

He planned to remain in Ischia for only one day but he stayed two, during which time he rested and probably wrote two letters, one describing Ischia itself and another "concerning the Volcano of Stromboli, the city and Straits of Messina, the land of Sicily, Scylla and Charybdis, etc." which he later mentioned in a letter to his mother.[29] Clemens never went to Sicily and never visited Stromboli or the Straits of Messina (he was to pass both in the night a week hence), but this did not keep him from anticipating his reactions for his readers, though what they were to be we will never know, for both these letters were lost. His rest was, therefore, of a professional kind; as he was to write later, "I . . . tired myself to death 'resting' a couple of days and studying human villainy." [30] He stayed up all night his second night there, perhaps finishing his letters, and sailed for Naples at dawn, planning to sleep on his arrival, but, as might be expected, his garrulity got the better of his exhaustion. He "got to talking," he wrote his family later in the day, "then went to see the King's palace—lost time one way

[27] *Alta*, October 1, 1867; *Traveling*, p. 87; cf. *IA*, p. 312.

[28] Clemens to Dan Slote. From Sale Catalogue, AAA–Anderson Galleries. Item 68, Sale No. 4346, November 11–12, 1937. Present whereabouts unknown.

[29] *Letters*, p. 135.

[30] *Alta*, October 6, 1876; *Traveling*, p. 93; cf. *IA*, 321–22.

or another till now it is night & I learn for the first time that our own party have decided to start for Vesuvius at midnight. I have some little preparation to make." [31] The ascent of Vesuvius was, in Clemens' opinion, well worth the effort. Clemens, Dan, Dr. Jackson, and four or five others took the train to Torre Annunziata. They continued by muleback via Boscotrecase, passing at first through vineyards, then among scrub pine until finally all vegetation ceased and the trail became a zigzag path through the ash cone to the crater itself. By sunrise they were at the summit, and Clemens had a magnificent view of Naples, the

> . . . strong black ribs and seams of lava stretching down to the limitless level campagna—a green carpet that enchants the eye and leads it on and on, past clusters of trees, and isolated houses, and snowy villages, until it shreds out in a fringe of mist and general vagueness far away. It is from the Hermitage, there on the side of Vesuvius, that one should "see Naples and die." [32]

This was the beginning of their last day in Italy and it was to be one of Clemens' busiest: by mid-morning they had retraced their steps and returned to Torre Annunziata, a journey much longer than the four minutes Clemens said it was but much shorter than the ascent had been. A 45-minute carriage ride took them to Pompeii which, as one of his best letters to the *Alta California* suggests, fascinated Clemens and evoked in him a characteristic romantic response to ancient times: his imagination was easily projected back to the time of Pompeii, its vitality enhanced by the tension between historical fact and romantic conjecture.

By early afternoon the party had returned to Naples. Clemens, having now spent two sleepless nights, was no doubt hoping to settle himself on board the *Quaker City* and relax until it sailed, but a group of passengers (Solon Severance at their head) had chartered a steamship for an excursion around the Bay, and they invited Clemens to join them. He did not refuse, for he had not seen Capri and was eager to visit the Blue Grotto. He was not long on the

[31] Clemens to Jane Clemens, ALS, *MTP*.
[32] *Alta*, October 6, 1867; *Traveling*, p. 89; cf. *IA*, p. 315.

island, but long enough to enter that "placid subterranean
lake" which flashed, he wrote later, "like blue theatrical
fires." [33] The excursion returned to Naples by way of Ischia
and Procida, stopping for a short time at Pozzuoli to allow a
visit to the Serapeum, Lake Agnano, newly drained and
supposed to contain a sunken city (it didn't), the nearby
ruins of Baia and the Baths of Nero, and, of course, the
Grotto of the Dog to which Clemens devoted much of a
subsequent *Alta* letter. They arrived "home" on board the
ship before dark, in time to greet Mrs. Fairbanks and Mrs.
Severance who had spent the day in a last minute carriage
tour through Naples with Charlie Langdon gallantly in
attendance.

The *Quaker City* was busy in preparation for its departure the next morning. Supplies were being stowed below
and boatload after boatload of passengers arrived bearing
quantities of packages—the ladies proudly showing the rolls
of silk and velvet they had purchased (they were ever so
much cheaper in Naples than in Paris!), the men their
newly tailored suits and fine linen. Quantities of objets d'art
were trundled aboard, uncrated, unpacked, viewed, and
clucked over. Rev. Quereau arrived in a boat filled with old
masters' copies he had purchased in his travels, and he
insisted on spreading them out on deck for the admiration
of his fellow passengers. The pilgrims returned with jewelry,
too—cameos and mosaic bracelets. Major Denny displayed
an elaborate coral necklace he had purchased—for whom it
was not quite clear—and some of the men wore new Swiss
watches. There were boats full of wine and mosaic tables
and alabaster statues and embroidered shawls. And, hoping
to glean any lire still unspent, many more boats large and
small floated about the ship and from them voluble Italians
hawked their wares—straw work and fruit. One had pictures for sale, another, jewelry. In one an old man played
bagpipes while keeping two dancing dolls in motion on the
seat before him. In another, two beautiful Italian girls
played guitars and sang and smiled when the Americans
threw money at them. A few Italians even managed to
scramble on board, dancing and singing the Garibaldi song

[33] *Alta*, October 6, 1867; *Traveling*, p. 93; cf. *IA*, p. 321.

before they were shooed back overboard. Finally, dark came and with it Captain Duncan. In 36 hours he had managed to tour Rome, Naples, and Vesuvius, "guzzling" everything. He announced that the last mail would be picked up by the American consul at 10:00 P.M., and the ship assumed a sudden calm as passengers rushed to finish letters. These dispatched, the ship settled down for the night, prepared at last for departure.

At 6:00 A.M. the ship's boilers had a head of steam, and the *Quaker City* had begun to wheel about, heading into the Mediterranean, when an alarm went up: a check of the passengers had revealed that Mr. Haldeman was not in his stateroom nor, indeed, anywhere on board. Someone thought they had seen him ashore and, as Mrs. Severance delicately put it, they feared that that "victim of intemperance" would be "unfit to get back." [34] A search party was sent ashore to find him, but just as it passed out of earshot, another boat, four oarsmen rowing, was seen making for the ship with Mr. Haldeman waving frantically from its stern. He had, evidently, seen the *Quaker City* turning and, suddenly sobered, feared he had been left. The departure was delayed two hours while the ship waited the return of the search party. Finally at 8:00 A.M. the *Quaker City's* paddles began to turn and the ship steamed out of Naples Harbor and away from Italy. "There was no lack of cheerfulness on board the *Quaker City*," Clemens wrote later. "For once, her title was a misnomer" (p. 337).

[34] *Journal Letters*, p. 106.

ATHENS
CONSTANTINOPLE
RUSSIA

"We are a handful of private citizens of America . . ."

Captain Duncan's prospectus for the voyage had promised a
stop at Palermo, Sicily, but the excursionists learned in
Leghorn that Palermo was an infected port, and they all
agreed therefore to bypass Sicily and proceed from Naples
directly to Athens. The morning of their departure was clear
and bright, and the pilgrims gathered on deck to watch the
passing of Sorrento and Capri. ("Nothing in sight there
being of particular interest" [1] wrote Duncan somewhat pet-

----

[1] *Log,* pp. 39–40.

ulantly.) At noon they conducted the usual Sabbath services on the quarterdeck, (Rev. Bullard preaching fervently
on "Individual Accountability"), and after lunch the passengers relaxed, reading or gathering in small groups to
gossip away the late afternoon. They had written themselves out the evening before, families and friends had been
informed, and all the pilgrims rested briefly from their
correspondence.

All, that is, except Clemens. In the next three days he was
to write five letters to the *Alta* concerning his sojourn in
Naples.[2] Taking his ascent of Vesuvius, completed barely
twenty-four hours before, as a point of departure, he described his activities of the previous four days in a loose,
burlesque fashion reminiscent of his lecture style. It is a
leisurely account and suggests, perhaps, something of his
own relaxed feeling; he had several days of cool, clear
sailing ahead of him with no trains to catch, no sights to see,
and no Italians to contend with. The writing came easily,
and when his daily stint of composition was completed he
joined the other passengers on deck and watched the passing
scene. "7 P.M." he wrote in his notebook of that Sabbath
evening, "with the western horizon all golden from the
sunken sun and specked with the distant ships the bright
full moon shining like a silver shield high overhead."[3] That
moon was to follow them for nearly a week, making the
nights bright. The first night out the air was cool and fresh,
and Clemens stayed up past midnight smoking and talking.
They passed the volcano Stromboli off to the right. "How
grand it looms up out of the lonely sea," he wrote, "and how
symmetrical. It is beautiful now with its dark blue just
veiled under a pearly mist that half conceals and half
discloses."[4] Stromboli was quiet; only a pale wisp of smoke
suggested it was an active volcano. At two in the morning
the moon was down and the ship passed through the Straits
of Messina, the city itself a "mass of gas lights."

Throughout the morning of the next day the ship skirted
the coast of Calabria, Mt. Etna barely visible far behind

---

[2] Numbered 9 through 13 when printed.
[3] *Notebook*, p. 70.
[4] *Ibid.*

them as they went. By noon they were out of sight of land cutting directly across the Ionian Sea, and by Tuesday morning the *Quaker City* was close to Greece.

Been skirting along the Isles of Greece all day [Clemens wrote in his notebook]—western side—very mountainous—prevailing tints gray & brown approaching to red. Pretty little white villages surrounded by trees nestle in little depressions & roost upon gentle elevations on the lofty table-lands with high perpendicular sea-walls. We see them all as if laid down on a map.

Before evening the coast of Greece was in sight and gilded by what Clemens called a "splendid, rich carmine sunset," much finer, he thought, than any they had had in Italy, and it was the more beautiful for being rare. Southern sunsets "are lovely, often, but their loveliness is soft & rich— elegant, refined—never grand, splendid, gorgeous, like those in our cold Northern States," [5] he wrote.

At noon on Wednesday, without chart or pilot, controlled only by Bursley's skill, the ship passed between two light-houses and entered a tortuous canal two miles long and barely wide enough for passage. It had arrived at the harbor of Piraeus.

Since the *Quaker City* was coming directly from Italy where cholera was reaching epidemic proportions, many on board feared they would not be allowed to land. Slightly more than ten years before the crew of a British ship had broken quarantine in Piraeus and had brought a cholera epidemic which killed ten thousand people, and since that time quarantine had been rigidly enforced in Greece. The pilgrims therefore watched with some trepidation as the Health Officer's boat approached, and they were more angered than surprised when shortly thereafter they learned they could not land for eleven days. Athens was to be denied them. Moses Beach was particularly outraged. Here they were, "a pleasure party of less than seventy souls, occu-pying the whole of a ship calculated to accommodate four times their number—abounding in health and in a clear bill of health from their last port," he wrote; surely they were

[5] "Unpublished Notebook No. 8" (Typescript, pp. 5–6), *MTP;* cf. *IA,* p. 339.

"entitled by all laws of justice and of public welfare, as well as of courtesy to strangers . . . to feast their eyes upon existing remnants of ancient greatness?" [6] No, the Health Officer was adamant—and the American Consulate was closed. "We would call this enforcement of rule a farce," wrote Mrs. Fairbanks, "but people are expected to laugh at a farce, while we can scarcely 'possess our souls with patience.' " [7] The Military Commandant said he would try to obtain their release by order from Athens, but in the meantime the ship was ordered to drop anchor outside the harbor while it took on provisions.

The pilgrims crowded the railings of the ship. In anguish and disgust they searched out the Acropolis, pale in the distance. They watched the white sailboats that seemed to fly past them on the water ("I would like to stay with them a while," Clemens remarked plaintively in his notebook),[8] and wistfully observed the hundreds of bathers who frolicked in the surf or shore. Even the wretched refugees from the war which Greece was waging against the Turks in Crete—even these, huddled in tents among the hills—had more freedom than they. The *Quaker City* slowly took its station outside the harbor and waited the return of the Commandant. A white sheet (the ship had lost its yellow contagion flag) flapped at the mainmast.

They were quarantined, but they were not isolated; Greek trading boats followed them selling grapes and pears, peaches and figs. One came by with a freezer of lemon ice which Dan Slote genially bought for the ladies. A Greek oarsman promised that he had a friend who could release them and would they then hire him for a guide? The crystal afternoon passed slowly. A camaraderie enclosed the ship: they were victims together. The men took turns reading Henry Ward Beecher's *Norwood* aloud to the ladies. Moses Beach remembered the small sailing craft he had brought with him from New York and, with the approval of the *Quaker City*'s guard boat, he took passengers for short trips about the outer harbor. At length the American Vice Consul

[6] *New York Sun*, September 16, 1867.

[7] *Cleveland Herald*, September 30, 1867.

[8] *Notebook*, p. 71.

appeared in a boat alongside and shouted his commisera-
tions to the *Quaker City*. Yes, he had heard from Washington that they were coming, but there was nothing to be
done, for the Consul was visiting a sick friend in Athens.
The passengers got up a petition which, properly fumigated,
was delivered by the Vice Consul to the port authorities. It
was a touching document as Mrs. Fairbanks described it:

We trusted to the hospitality of a people, whose varied fortunes
had enlisted the sympathies of all Americans, and we were sure
they would not withhold from us a welcome to their country.
Much more of the "mutual admiration" style was written down
and forwarded to the municipal authorities, while we waited
hopefully.[9]

To no avail. Some pilgrims, however, were to escape. Late
in the afternoon, under the instigation of Beach and with
the approval of Duncan, many of the passengers went for a
swim on the nearby shore. While they were bathing Beach
noticed other swimmers not far off and concocted a plan:
when the party returned to the *Quaker City*, he and Rev.
Bullard remained on shore hidden behind rocks; the guard
boats did not detect their absence, and when the ship's boats
were back on board the two escapees found the path where
Beach had seen the other bathers and stole into Piraeus;
there they boldly hired a carriage and proceeded to the
Acropolis. This success exacerbated the frustration of others
still on board the *Quaker City*. Clemens could hardly contain his indignation at the thought of missing Athens which
was to have been one of the high points of the excursion.

The Military Commandant returned. Nothing could be
done. Athens had refused to rescind the quarantine. There
was nothing he could do. Of course, if any of the passengers,
under cover of darkness, were to row quietly to the shore
and walk to Athens *he* probably shouldn't be able to see
them, especially not if they were careful and came back by
daylight. But he could not approve such action, of course,
and they should be severely punished who carelessly attempted such an escapade. And what is more, one should not
trust the local boatmen as guides when one got to shore. He

bade them farewell and said he hoped to see them in the morning.

Thus encouraged, Clemens, Dr. Jackson, Colonel Denny, and Dr. Birch put on the red fezzes they had purchased in Tangier ("to look like Greeks," Mrs. Severance explained) and crawled into a boat manned by Quartermaster Pratt. (Solon Severance wanted to go, too, but Emily was "not quite willing" that he should do so.)

"Remember I don't give you any liberty to take that small boat," Captain Duncan told Pratt, and as Pratt was to tell the tale many years later, he "understood what that meant . . . these four men said they would take the chances if [I] would land them on a rocky point of land away from the Old Port and keep a lookout for their return." It was, he said "a close shave to avoid the quarantine boat, which was on the lookout for anyone who would dare to violate their law," and he feared six months in prison.[10]

That night's exploit was to be a memorable experience—the campaign of the Acropolis, an escapade worthy of Tom Sawyer. The letter Clemens wrote concerning it became one of the most engaging parts of *IA*, and subsequently a lecture recounting the event was a great favorite with Clemens' audiences. "We didn't care about Athens particularly," he was to say,

but we wanted to see the famous Acropolis & its ruined temples, & we did. We climbed the steep hill of the Acropolis about 1 in the morning & tried to storm that grand old fortress that had scorned the battles & sieges of 3,000 years.—We had the garrison out, mighty quick—4 Greeks—& we bribed them to betray the citadel and unlock the gates. In a moment we stood in the presence of the noblest ruins we had ever seen—the most elegant, the most graceful, the most imposing. The renowned Parthenon towered above us, and about us were the wreck of what were once the snowy marble Temples of Hercules & a second Minerva, & another whose name I have forgotten.[11]

Their return, punctuated by barking dogs and the rebukes of an awakened citizenry, was hectic but safe, and they

---

[10] Unidentified newspaper clipping in *MTP*.

[11] "Vandals Lecture," manuscript, DeVoto no. 52 (n.d.), *MTP;* cf. the expansion of these remarks in *IA*, pp. 344–52.

Caryatides on the Acropolis of Athens

were back on board the *Quaker City* before daybreak. Emboldened by the success of Clemens' party, other passengers tried to row to shore in the daylight, but they were turned back.

Beach and Bullard had a more casual time of it. Bullard sought out a classmate, a Greek who was doing missionary work, and the two pilgrims spent the night on shore. Shortly before noon they returned to Piraeus Harbor and, ostensibly to take passage on the *Quaker City*, proceeded to the ship. Since anyone could board a quarantined ship—albeit without returning—they were not stopped. The success of Clemens and the others did little to assuage pilgrims who had unsuccessfully waited for release, and few on board were sorry when the *Quaker City* left Piraeus. Their letters home were filled with imprecations: the Greeks should learn that one does not treat good Christian Americans in this way.

"Where, if not in Greece, may we expect that a flag, floating over a party which represents in a peculiar manner the missionary efforts of the civilized world, will receive that special respect to which it is more than entitled?" asked Moses Beach. The Greeks were chided: "How greatly this one act of neglect will lower you and your people in the consideration of those with whom you would stand well!" [12] Bidding good-bye to the "stupid Athenians," Captain Duncan remarked, "we left their port in disgust." [13]

Clemens alone seems to have been jubilant: "We set sail for Constantinople to-day," he wrote, "but some of us don't care a fig for that. We have seen all that there was to see in the old city. . . ." [14] In his notebook he wrote: "We sailed at noon. Of course the passengers are very sorry they could not go to Athens & the Acropolis, but it could not be helped—if many had made our trip some of us would surely have got into trouble." He was Tom Sawyer, satisfied, and immediately set about writing of the escapade in two letters to the *Alta California*.[15]

Writing was difficult, for the ship encountered a sudden violent head wind which ripped across its decks and slowed its progress. The awning amidships was torn from its moorings and three stanchions broken. Nearly all the passengers and crew were seasick, but not Clemens. "Booming through the Grecian Archipelago with a splendid breeze," he wrote in his notebook. "Many passengers sea-sick. Bloody sunset. Splendid full moon—sea white with foamy waves & a hundred white-winged ships." [16] Such uncompromising good humor must have been particularly obnoxious to his seasick companions. The next day, however, was more pleasant, and the sea relatively calm. Clemens was, to judge from his notebooks, reading guidebooks assiduously and putting down anecdotes and names for future reference. They passed the site of Troy, a strong wind behind them. They

---

[12] *Sun,* September 16, 1867.

[13] *Log,* p. 43.

[14] *San Francisco Daily Alta California,* October 18, 1867; *Traveling,* p. 109; cf. *IA,* p. 352.

[15] Published as one, October 18, 1867; *Traveling,* pp. 100–109.

[16] "Unpublished Notebook no. 8" (Typescript, p. 10), *MTP.*

were under full steam now, and making maximum speed; they raced a French steamer and, amid cheers and general self-congratulation, passed it. Just after noon they entered the Hellespont, and through a glass someone spotted a camel train and a white minaret stark against the green landscape. They were in the Orient now, no doubt of it.

At two they dropped anchor in Dardana, the Turkish quarantine station. Captain Duncan went ashore and, to the great relief of all the pilgrims, soon returned with a clean bill of health for the ship. "The 'barbarous' Turks proved better Christians than their more pretentiously wise neighbors, the Greeks," wrote Moses Beach, "and the door of entrance to the Turkish capital was thrown wide open." [17] They immediately continued toward Constantinople, now dipping their colors to the yacht of the Viceroy of Egypt which easily overtook and passed them—no contest there. In the late afternoon they entered the Sea of Marmora, and, since Captain Duncan anticipated some difficulty in maneuvering through Constantinople Harbor, he decided against arriving in the dark and slowed the *Quaker City*'s pace to ensure their arrival by daylight. In the evening, the Quaker City Club was revived; Rev. Bullard spoke authoritatively about Greece, and Clemens followed him with an account of his night in Athens.

Just as day was breaking, the ship arrived in Constantinople Harbor, and all the passengers were awakened. They came on deck, shivering and expectant, to catch their first glimpse of the Golden Horn. It was, said Mrs. Severance, "beautiful beyond any other place we have seen. Gradually ascending from the water's edge were the myriads of dark cypress trees, the slender minarets, the immense domes, intermingled with the houses on either side of the bay. . . . The picture is one of the most spectacular I have seen or even imagined." [18] The pilgrims' expectations were great—the bazaars, the mosques, the very foreignness of the place intrigued them, and they were eager to see it all. The sight had, wrote Clemens, "the quaint Oriental aspect that one dreams of when he reads books of eastern travel. Con-

[17] *Sun*, September 18, 1867.
[18] *Journal Letters*, pp. 117–18.

stantinople makes a noble picture." [19] By ten they were all on shore hurrying to receive, as Duncan put it, "the best attentions of our Consul Mr. Goodenow."

Unfortunately, the city was not what they expected. "I must confess myself wholly unprepared for the utter disappointment experienced in common with nearly every one of my fellow passengers," Beach wrote home.[20] "Sail up into the harbor," they had been told, "go all round it and admire; but, do *not* land or the illusions will be dispelled," [21] and the *Quaker City* passengers to their sorrow, agreed. "Our opinion of Constantinople so much as we saw of it on our way to the Consulate from the boats was most unfavorable," Captain Duncan confided to his log. "The narrow dirty crowded and stinking streets, shockingly paved were utterly disgusting. The ladies walked as far as they could and then Sedan chairs were sent for." [22] "We have spoken of the filth of the Italian cities," wrote Mrs. Severance, "but they were clean compared with this place." [23] Their preconceptions of the Orient were quickly dispelled, and their disappointment was in no way moderated by the American Minister to Turkey—who wasn't even in town. Although there had been much advance notice of their arrival—including a cable from Dardana—the Minister was unaccountably absent, and Consul Goodenow, despite his name, was an insufficient substitute.

Clemens was no more satisfied with the city than his fellow passengers were. His notebooks reveal a generally disgruntled attitude toward the things he saw in Constantinople. But whereas the other correspondents were able to vent their disappointment in angry letters home, Clemens could not. His Constantinople letters clearly reveal what he saw his function to be: not merely to describe the look of things or to relate exactly his own reactions to them (neither one of which could be very pleasurable in the present instance) but to combine the view with the reaction in such

[19] *Alta,* October 20, 1867; *Traveling,* p. 112; cf. *IA,* p. 358.
[20] *Sun,* September 19, 1867.
[21] *Journal Letters,* p. 118.
[22] *Log,* pp. 45–46.
[23] *Journal Letters,* p. 118.

a way as to entertain his reader, to fabricate, by selection
and imaginative presentation, a pleasurable, amusing series
of incidents. The rest of the *Quaker City* excursionists saw
only an apalling reality—the filthy streets, the squalor of
the buildings, the miserable populace—what Beach called
"the do-nothing, be-nothing, get-nothing, have-nothing,
care-nothing, think-nothing, wish-nothing, and worse than
let-alone policy, or rather want of policy on every hand." [24]
Clemens saw all this and shared his fellow passengers' dislike of it, but he wrote of it differently. He selected details
and elaborated them to ridiculous exaggeration. For example, he described the native boats which took them ashore in
hyperbole, implying a contrast to the way boats operate in
"sensible" countries. "This kind of boating is calculated to
drive a nervous man crazy in a week," he wrote. "The
boatmen are the awkwardest, the stupidest, and the most
unscientific on earth, I think." [25] The key word here is
"unscientific" which is in comic contrast to "awkward" and
"stupid." By such modulations of tone Clemens placed his
irritation in an amusing context. Of the filth which was the
most immediate cause of dissatisfaction among his fellow
passengers, Clemens says nothing. Instead, he builds on the
romantic view which his readers would bring to his subject
and turns it to comedy.

Ashore, it was—well, it was an eternal circus. People were thicker
than bees, in those narrow, crowded streets, and the men were
dressed in all the outrageous, outlandish, idolatrous, extravagant,
infernal costumes that ever a tailor with the delirium tremens and
seven devils could conceive of.[26]

"Circus" is precisely the right word—the bizarre presented
for the amusement of the onlooker—and the series of adjec-
tives which combine the outre ("outlandish") with the com-
ically out-of-place ("idolatrous," "infernal") build to the
climax of the tailor and seven devils. One receives an
impression not of disgust but of amusement and mock surprise.

[24] *Sun*, September 19, 1867.
[25] *Alta*, October 20, 1867; *Traveling*, p. 113; cf. *IA*, p. 358.
[26] *Ibid.*, cf. *IA*, pp. 358–9.

Clemens suggests actuality, but turns it, in fact, into romantic overstatement. The pattern can be found in all of the five extant letters he wrote concerning Constantinople. What he did, in fact, was to satirize his own reactions to the scene. This is notable, perhaps, in his treatment of the dogs of Constantinople. Mrs. Severance presented the general reaction:

The very first thing to attract our attention was the dogs. They are to be seen everywhere—surly, dirty and ill-formed. Half-starved, I should say. Some of them had been fighting and were badly torn. . . . The dogs do not even move when you approach, but you must get out of their way to pass them. They will never be still, and the night is made hideous with their noise.[27]

Clemens disliked the dogs, too, but in his *Alta* letters he played the subject for satiric effect and proceeded to make a mock defense of the "sorry beasts":

I am half willing to believe that the celebrated dogs of Constantinople have been misrepresented—slandered. I have always been led to suppose that they were so thick in the streets that they blocked the way; that they moved about in organized companies, platoons and regiments, and took what they wanted by determined and ferocious assault; and that at night they drowned all other sounds with their terrible howlings. The dogs I see here cannot be those I have read of.[28]

Or again, in his treatment of the beggars and cripples who seemed to be everywhere in the city, Clemens suggests not horror and repulsion, but a certain appetite for the bizarre, and he describes particular cripples in a tone which would have been cruel except for the exaggerated style in which he presents the subject and conveys his objectivity. ("Ah, I tell you, a beggar has to have exceedingly good points to make a living in Constantinople.") [29]

But this comic turn was necessary only concerning those subjects which would have been, in themselves, wholly ob-

[27] *Journal Letters*, pp. 118–19.
[28] *Alta*, October 29, 1867; *Traveling*, p. 124; cf. *IA*, p. 370.
[29] *Alta*, October 23, 1867; *Traveling*, p. 116; cf. *IA*, p. 362.

noxious to his audience. Where personal taste might operate, where, for example, one might like or dislike without prejudice, Clemens did not need to raise his persona. Such an instance was that of Santa Sophia. The reaction of Mrs. Severance was, once again, typical of most of the pilgrims:

> I confess I was greatly disappointed in St. Sophia as a whole. . . . Everything seemed old, and though in a good state of preservation, without harmony or much elegance. I was not much impressed with its size. The interior really contains almost nothing.[30]

Clemens' reaction to the mosque was virtually identical with this and neither his notes nor his finished letter makes any attempt to color his dislike or to place it in a comic context:

> I don't think much of the Mosque of St. Sophia. I suppose I lack appreciation. Well, let it go at that. It is the rustiest old barn in heathendom. . . . Everywhere was dirt, and dust, and dinginess, and gloom; everywhere were signs of hoary antiquity, but with nothing touching or beautiful about them.[31]

The comment reveals a significant shift in Clemens' attitude toward antiquity. In Tangier it was enough that what he was viewing was old. Mere antiquity was, at first, enough to make a sharp contrast to the relatively "new" American civilization. But as Clemens became increasingly familiar with the variety which age might have, he became more discriminating. Now it was no longer enough to be merely ancient—most of what he had been viewing for the past two months could justify that adjective. To be worthy of interest, the antique now had to have something "touching or beautiful" about it. In the Holy Land he would find the hoary past qualified by the "touching," and here and there throughout Europe—as on the Acropolis in Athens—he had found it embodying the "beautiful." But when, according to his lights, the antique had neither quality—when it was to

[30] *Journal Letters*, p. 124.
[31] *Alta*, October 23, 1867; *Traveling*, pp. 116–67; cf. *IA*. pp. 362–64.

his mind, merely *old*—he was no longer impressed. He had acquired a certain sophistication, perhaps, but his remarks concerning Santa Sophia suggest that it was not consummate. He was unable to find the touching or the beautiful in the totally unfamiliar. He was still bound by romantic preconceptions of the "exotic" Orient, and all his letters concerning Constantinople reveal this limitation. American culture was derivative enough of Europe that he could accept most European attitudes without denying anything at home which had intrinsic value to him; there seemed no essential contradiction in his past experiences in America and his present ones in Europe. But in Constantinople he sensed for the first time a culture in many ways antithetical to his own, and his response was to reject it. Moslems were, to him, only "fantastic pagans" who were "keeping up their gymnastics till they ought to have been tired, if they were not." [32] One need have no sympathy for such goings-on, he assumed, and to suggest such sympathy was pretense— something got "out of the guide-book." In holding this attitude Clemens was merely typical of his age. These Turks were, after all, heathen, and, although Clemens did not particularly approve the evangelical Christian missionary spirit which was sending thousands of Americans abroad to save these souls, he certainly believed in trying to reform their way of living. He probably would have fully assented to Moses Beach's observation regarding the "proper missionary work of the world":

When the prejudices of an intelligent man are attacked he is attacked in the strongest part, and just that it is to drive or persuade a Heathen out of his own superstitions and beliefs, whatever they are; a score of the best missionaries who ever existed could affect less in a lifetime of effort here in Constantinople than would a couple of christian [sic] mechanics who, coming with a lathe and a few tools of other kinds, should sit quietly down and by practice as well as precept show the Turks how to save nine-tenths of the labor they bestow upon manufactured articles. . . . Lighten his daily task and he becomes your friend.[33]

[32] *Alta,* October 23, 1867; *Traveling,* p. 117; cf. *IA,* p. 364.
[33] *Sun,* September 23, 1867.

The new evangelicalism as well as the old was on board the *Quaker City.*

Clemens' five letters concerning Constantinople derived from only two days of sight-seeing. He had expected to like the city more—had even thought he might stay behind in Constantinople while the *Quaker City* took a side trip into the Black Sea to Russia—but his initial distaste for Turkey grew. In spite of the friendly welcome at Dardana, the pilgrims were soon made to feel uncomfortable by a prevailing anti-American bias. The war against Greece in Crete was raging, and Americans were generally (and rightly) thought to favor the Greek cause. "On account of sympathy with Crete, Americans in bad odor here," Clemens wrote in his notebook the first day he was in Constantinople,[34] and succeeding days gave new support to this impression. Partly in reaction, he cared little for the Turks. His notebooks reveal a disaffection for what he saw in those two days—and he saw most of what there was to see. Just as he did not care for Santa Sophia, neither did he like "another" mosque whose name he could not remember which "had nothing more remarkable to show than several thousand unclean tame pigeons & some frowsy great trees in the open court of the mosque." The women were "rather pretty" but dressed "like the shrouded dead abroad in the earth." [35] Only the bazaars seemed to please him and they but briefly.

By the time the *Quaker City* weighed anchor for Sebastopol, therefore, Clemens was ready to leave. It was a remarkable change of intention, and Constantinople must have been repellent indeed to have encouraged him to make it, for less than a week before, while the ship lay in Athens harbor, Clemens had drafted a petition to Captain Duncan asking that Sebastopol be dropped from the itinerary and that the *Quaker City* make only a short cruise into the Black Sea to allow more time in Turkey and Palestine: *"First*—There is nothing to see at Sebastopol" he wrote,

but a bare & uninteresting battle-field where military fortifications *have been* but no longer exist—and

[34] "Unpublished Notebook no. 8" (Typescript, p. 19), *MTP.*
[35] *Ibid.,* (Typescript, p. 17).

Secondly—Several among us having stood in the midst of scenes of this character of infinitely greater importance in our own country in the smoke & carnage of battle—and—

Thirdly—The remainder of our company having seen a sufficiency of such things after the battles were over—and

Fourthly—Since by leaving Sebastopol out of the excursion we can gain a precious addition of time for travel in Palestine,—

Therefore, Satisfied that if a short trip be taken through the Bosphorus & into the Black Sea, all parties will be willing to forego the extension of it to desolate Sebastopol with its notable pile of porter bottles, we respectfully request that you will alter your programme in accordance with the suggestion contained in this last paragraph.[36]

The forced exclusion of Greece made additional days in Palestine possible without further changes in the itinerary, and his petition was therefore never presented to Duncan—it exists only in draft form in one of the notebooks—but it reveals Clemens' animadversions to the trip into the Black Sea, and the fact that he accompanied the *Quaker City* on that excursion in spite of these arguments suggests the intensity of his dislike for Constantinople.

The journey to the Black Sea was at best an afterthought for many of the passengers. "Most of them had intended remaining here while the ship went to Russia," Duncan wrote, "but now all but six decide to remain by the ship." [37] Actually, eight passengers stayed in Constantinople. Beach, Emma, Solon Severance, and Bullard wanted to take a tour of the hinterland of Turkey—too arduous a journey for Mrs. Severance who preferred to continue with the ship. Mr. Foster and Judge Haldeman were both ill and thought they might recuperate better on shore. Dan Slote and Jack Van Nostrand—alone among the passengers—wanted to search out more of the alleyways of Constantinople, and therefore remained behind. It was to Clemens' advantage that Dan did so. Clemens had mislaid his passport, and, since Russia

[36] *Ibid.,* (Typescript, p. 61).
[37] *Log,* p. 47.

was believed to be as strict as the Papal States regarding visas, Dan lent him his. One wonders how Clemens, slender, of medium height, with light brown hair and eyes, could have passed for Dan Slote who was short, stout, with a round face and dark complexion—but he evidently did.

Departure for the Black Sea was delayed briefly by trouble among the crew. Throughout the voyage all above decks was, at least superficially, decorous, but below, order was only barely maintained. In very nearly every port the crew had distinguished itself by its recklessness: There had been a running brawl in Marseilles and more mayhem in Genoa, and if the crew were relatively subdued in subsequent ports it was only because quarantine restrictions kept them safely secured. Having been closely confined for nearly a month, the crew evidently went on a grand binge in Constantinople, returning to the ship very reluctantly and very drunk. One of the returning sailors discovered he was out of whisky, decided to swim ashore for more, and was swept away by the current and drowned. So separate was the crew from the passengers that the affair had little effect upon the pilgrims. "It was surprising, you may think," wrote Mrs. Severance, "but the passengers had never seen him and it produced little impression on their minds." [38]

The rebellious crew was finally brought to order, and at one on Monday afternoon (August 19) the ship left Constantinople. The voyage through the Bosporus was pleasant: the sea was calm, the weather cool, and the shoreline beautiful, a vista of green hills marked here and there by marble villas which shone in the sun. It was one of those rare times when the ship was a good "writing desk," and during the two-day voyage to Sebastopol Clemens was busy composing his first Constantinople letter.[39] The evening prayer meetings had a new attraction: a Rev. Washburn, a former classmate of Bullard living in Constantinople, was to take Bullard's place as minister to the Pilgrims during the Black Sea voyage. He had been to Palestine several times, and after prayers the Quaker City Club listened to

[38] *Journal Letters*, p. 123.
[39] Dated August 20, printed *Alta*, October 20, 1867; *Traveling*, pp. 110–14; cf. *IA*, 354–61.

him with interest. Disappointed by Turkey they had begun to look forward to Palestine with increasing appetite, and Washburn's "conversational lecture," as Mrs. Severance called it, was a great success.

The bells of Sebastopol woke the excursionists on Wednesday, and they prepared to disembark, apprehensive about their reception, for Consul Goodenow had warned them that the Russians were notoriously reluctant to grant entry permits. They needn't have been worried. Their reception at Sebastopol—a forerunner of even more exciting events to come—was almost embarrassingly cordial. The Admiral in command of the port waived all legal formalities and permitted the passengers to land without even a show of passports (to Clemens great relief!), the port's navy yard was put at the disposal of the *Quaker City* for any needed repairs, and, when this courtesy was declined, the agent of the port insisted on providing the party with an English guide to the battlefields.

But in spite of the official courtesies, the excursion to Sebastopol did not seem worth the effort. There was not, really, much to see, the pilgrims agreed, and they did not see it in much comfort. The carriages which transported them were ill-designed ("a combination of inconveniences for four persons" Mrs. Fairbanks called them") [40] and drawn by horses so emaciated they looked like survivors of the battle itself. Two whole days had been allotted to surveying the Crimean battlegrounds, but one was quite enough to satisfy everyone; in fact, two hours were sufficient—even for the military men who had insisted on keeping Sebastopol on the itinerary. By eleven all the passengers had landed; by two most of them had returned. It was, as Clemens wrote in his notebook (and implied in the letter to the *Alta* he was to write the next day) a "melancholy place, [a] wilderness of battered down houses." [41] After a short visit to the ruins, he walked to Inkerman, a village on the sea a mile or two away, and returned to the *Quaker City* late in the afternoon. In his absence, the friendliness of the Russians had

[40] *Herald,* October 4, 1867.

[41] *Alta,* November 1, 1867; *Traveling,* pp. 132–36; cf. *IA,* pp. 381–86.

become even more demonstrative: three Russian officers and a number of Russian ladies had paid a social call to the ship. It was a bit awkward, for none of them spoke English and only Mrs. Fairbanks could converse in French, but the Russian ladies surprised the Americans by their friendliness, by the style of their clothes, and by their elegant manners. They shocked them, too, by smoking cigarettes, a sensation which was reported with exclamation points to the folks at home.

It was agreed that, rather than remain in Sebastopol as planned, the ship should proceed to Odessa, and at 9:00 P.M. the Russian visitors finally departed, and the ship sailed, reaching that port at four the following afternoon. Although the authorities at Odessa were friendly, they did not waive the landing regulations, and Captain Duncan had to present passports on shore before anyone was allowed to land. When Duncan returned, looking disgruntled and accompanied by two officers, Clemens was sure he had been found out and would not be allowed to disembark. However, the difficulty was that the passports had been visaed for Sebastopol only. At length the authorities allowed them entry, but in the meantime the sun had set, and few passengers went on shore that night. For his part, Clemens had been busy all day writing a long letter to the *Alta* concerning his Sebastopol experience and the ship's arrival at Odessa.[42] There was little to urge him ashore at once. "We consulted the guide-books," Clemens reported, "and were rejoiced to know that there were no sights in Odessa to see"[43]— a fact which did not keep him and his friends from exploring the city the following day. Most of his day in port was spent in "loafing." He "prowled through the markets and criticized the fearful and wonderful costumes [and] . . . examined the populace as far as the eyes could do it."[44] There may have been no sights of guide-book variety—but the "populace" was interesting: "All day ladies bathe naked in full view of the ship," he wrote in his notebook. "They

[42] *Alta*, November 3, 1867; *Traveling*, pp. 137–41; cf. *IA*, pp. 387–89.

[43] *Alta*, November 3, 1867; *Traveling*, p. 138.

[44] *Alta*, November 3, 1867; *Traveling*, p. 139; cf. *IA*, p. 388.

don't consider it any harm, I suppose. At Odessa all ages and sexes bathe together." [45] This note presaged an amusing paragraph to the *Alta* which he later omitted from *IA:*

I have often thought that our style of bathing was rather reserved than otherwise, and lacked many elements of cheerfulness. But you cannot say that of the Russian style. I watched a party of them at it this afternoon in the harbor, and it is really nice. The men and women, and boys and girls, all go in together, along about noon, and the men don't wear anything at all, the boys don't, the little girls don't, and the young women and the old women usually wear a single white thin garment with ruffles around the top of it and short sleeves, (which I have forgotten the name of it, [sic]) but this would be a good apology for a bathing dress, it if would only stay down. But it don't do it. It will float up around their necks in the most scandalous way, and the water is clear, and yet they don't seem to know enough to kick up the mud on the bottom. I never was so outraged in my life. At least a hundred times, in the seven hours I stayed there, I would just have got up and gone away from there disgusted, if I had had any place to go to.[46]

The Americans were rather closely watched themselves. "The American steamer in the bay, and the American people in the streets were quite the sensation of Odessa," Mrs. Fairbanks reported.[47] As in Sebastopol, Russians visited the *Quaker City*. The American Consul came too, and from him the pilgrims learned that the Emperor of All the Russias (as the pilgrims became fond of calling him) was sojourning at Yalta. Why not, someone suggested, cable the Emperor for an audience? The Consul demurred. Scarcely two weeks before, an English party had made a similar request and been denied; it was quite unlikely that Americans would have any better luck. But the pilgrims were not to be so easily put off, and the message was dispatched. They had planned to return to Constantinople the following day, but, aflame with the possibility of being received by royalty, the excursionists ignored that plan, and all day Friday they waited to hear the Emperor's pleasure.

[45] *Notebook,* p. 81.
[46] *Alta,* November 3, 1867; *Traveling,* pp. 139–40.
[47] *Herald,* October 4, 1867.

There was little to attract them in Odessa and many stayed on board, vaguely interested, perhaps, in the mercantile activity around them. They were anchored in the largest wheat port in the world, and all about them lighters pressed in on freighters loading grain in what the Americans concluded was a very primitive manner. (Not nearly so efficient as it would have been done at home, they agreed.) The few who went ashore wandered through the shops, buying little ("everything is exceedingly high," declared Mrs. Severance), satisfied, for once, to be mere onlookers at the purchases of others. They saw soldiers on parade; they lingered briefly in the two small parks of the town. They were bored. "I must acknowledge that I have caught no inspiration from anything I have seen here," said Mrs. Fairbanks.[48]

Friday night and no word from the Emperor. Saturday, still no word. Clemens filled his time by writing two more *Alta* letters about Constantinople,[49] but most of the *Quaker City* excursionists had nothing to do. Sundown Saturday the passengers met to determine their course of action. Had they been rebuffed? Should they return to Constantinople? But then, perhaps their cable had been missent? Perhaps the Emperor's reply had been misdirected? Yes, surely. It was agreed that they should continue to Yalta even though the Emperor's invitation had not come, "trusting to luck for permission to enter," as Captain Duncan put it.[50]

Some of the pilgrims had misgivings, however. The plan called for a visit to the Emperor on *Sunday,* and for some of the excursionists this was quite clearly a sacrilege. "I do not much expect to see him," Emily Severance wrote home, "for the reception will probably be on the Sabbath, and, if so, I shall not go." [51] The Rev. Mr. Washburn, evidently horrified at finding himself suddenly among a host of infidels, actually left the ship at Odessa and took other passage back to Constantinople. He could not, he told some of the passengers, allow his congregation to think he would have contemplated an excursion on the Lord's Day. Captain Duncan,

[48] *Ibid.*
[49] *Alta,* October 23, 27, 1867.
[50] *Log,* p. 55.
[51] *Journal Letters,* p. 132.

apparently already corrupted by his Sabbath journey to see Garibaldi, had no qualms, and the ship sailed for Yalta—the American Consul in Odessa, Mr. Smith, taking Washburn's place. At noon on Sunday (August 25) Captain Duncan recorded that the *Quaker City* "dropped anchor in the beautiful little town of Yalta." [52]

For the next four days the *Quaker City* excursionists were to indulge a typical nineteenth-century American appetite for royalty. For Clemens the fascination was enormous and ambivalent. For monarchy in the abstract he had little use—throughout his career he made comic capital belittling regal pomp. Only five days before, en route to Sebastopol and unaware of the possibility of meeting a reigning monarch, Clemens had amused himself ridiculing royalty: "The Greek throne," he wrote ". . . went begging for a good while. It was offered to one of Victoria's boys, and afterwards to various other younger sons of royalty who had no thrones and were out of business, but they all had the charity to decline the dreary honor." [53] But such criticism was for the institution; a flesh-and-blood monarch—particularly one he had seen—was a different matter. In his Paris letter, Clemens was exuberant in his praise for Napoleon III, and he was to be even more ecstatic in writing about Czar Alexander II. The *Quaker City* excursionists had shamelessly run after the Emperor, and Clemens, not the least enthusiastic in the pursuit, was hesitant to reveal to his *Alta* readers and, indeed, his own family, just how forward they had actually been. To both, he reported that the eagerness had been not American but Russian, that the pilgrims had actually been unwilling to request an audience with the Czar, that the invitation was made not at their own behest but through the intercession of Russian authorities and that the Czar had eagerly seized the opportunity to greet them—that he had answered "promptly" [54] and "signified his perfect willingness" to grant them an audience.[55] All of this was, of course, pure fabrication.

[52] *Log*, p. 56.
[53] *Alta*, October 20, 1867; *Traveling*, p. 115; cf. *IA*, pp. 355–6.
[54] *Letters*, p. 132.
[55] *Alta*, November 3, 1867; *Traveling*, p. 140.

As a matter of fact, for most of Sunday the excursionists thought their trek to Yalta had been in vain. It was only through the intercession of the Governor-General (to whom Duncan made a special visit and a compelling plea) that the Emperor was finally reached, and only after several hours contemplation that he agreed to see the Americans at his summer palace, Lavidia, the next day (Monday) at noon. "Great was the joy and satisfaction on board," wrote Duncan, "when this was announced from the supper table—Great was the preparations and great the expectations for the morrow." [56] "O, geeminy, what a stir there is!" Clemens wrote in his notebook. "What a calling of meetings! What an appointing of committees! What a furbishing up of swallow-tail coats!" [57] One of the preparations, and the most pressing for Clemens, was composing an address to be presented to the Czar. A committee of five was appointed [58] of which Clemens was chairman. "As I fully expected, and as they fully intended," he wrote home, "I had to write the address myself. I didn't mind it, because I have no modesty and would as soon write to an Emperor as to anybody else—but considering that there were 5 on the committee I thought they might have contributed *one* paragraph among them, anyway." [59] It couldn't have been any worse if they had. The address comes close to being the most bathetic Clemens ever wrote:

We are a handful of private citizens of America, traveling simply for recreation—and unostentatiously, as becomes our unofficial state—and, therefore, we have no excuse to tender for presenting ourselves before your Majesty, save the desire of offering our grateful acknowledgments to the lord of a realm, which through good and through evil report, has been the steadfast friend of the land we love so well.[60]

It went on like that for several paragraphs. So much for lack of ostentation! All the pilgrims signed it and they

[56] *Log*, p. 56.
[57] *Notebook*, p. 78.
[58] Messrs. Clemens, Crocker, Gibson, Sanford, and Colonel Kinney.
[59] *Letters*, Vol. 1: 133.
[60] *Alta*, November 6, 1867; *Traveling*, p. 156.

might, therefore, be said to share the blame. Clemens, evidently proud of the piece, sent a copy to each of his three newspapers, but to his credit he omitted it entirely from *IA*. In any case, he begrudged it the time it took. "But for bothering with this matter," he wrote in his notebook, "I would have caught up entirely with my N.Y. Tribune correspondence, and nearly with the San Francisco cor." [61]

There were general preparations, too. Consul Smith spent some time describing court etiquette to the assembled pilgrims: men must be in black and wear white ties and gloves, and women were to be hatless. "The most *recherche* wardrobes must be selected," wrote Mrs. Griswold. "The ladies' purchases through Europe are now brought in requisition. Paris dresses, laces, coiffures and jewelry are to be worn for the first time." [62] It was to be an elegant company—throughout the evening women asiduously practiced curtseying. At 10:30 the next morning rowboats from the two Russian frigates came alongside the *Quaker City*. There was a heavy sea and it was difficult getting to shore but over sixty passengers safely disembarked and entered the carriages the Emperor had ordered for them. There were not enough carriages to go around, however, and even though some of the men were given horses to ride, quite a few were forced to walk the three miles to the Emperor's summer palace. It was not an easy walk, most of it uphill and through rocky terrain, but the morning was clear and pleasant and the view from the road was impressive.

The summer palace itself, approached by a winding path through a beautiful woods, was a square, two-storied building of stuccoed stone, gaily painted in red and brown. Brown awnings hung from each window and about the roof was a white balustrade decorated with pots of aloes. It was a simple house but it evoked awe from the excursionists. ("It is really much larger than it at first appears" wrote Emily Severance." [63] The audience was to be given in a garden alongside the house, and when the pilgrims were assembled there, Consul Smith placed them in a semicircle,

---

[61] *Notebook*, p. 79.
[62] *Woman's Pilgrimage*, p. 180.
[63] *Journal Letters*, p. 140.

arranging them in what Mrs. Fairbanks called "one of the most effective tableaux I have ever witnessed." [64] "We had not long to wait," wrote Captain Duncan later. "In a few minutes he came out or rather seemed to appear among us." [65] The apparition was the Emperor. Unlike his guests, he was dressed comfortably in a white linen suit, and the Empress who joined him with their youngest son and daughter was also dressed casually in a simple morning dress without jewels or gloves. They were, as Mrs. Fairbanks noted, as "unpretentious as the most republican taste could have desired." [66] The same could not be said for their guests. As the Czar approached, the semicircle underwent a paroxysm of gesticulation as the women among the pilgrims attempted to execute a curtsey and the men a low bow. "Really," Mrs. Griswold said later, "the Pilgrims seemed to act as much at home as though they were accustomed to call on Emperors every day!" [67]

As the Emperor and his family came down some steps to the garden, Duncan, Consul Smith, and Mr. Leary came forward. "Good morning," said the Czar, and, then somewhat less certain, "I am glad to see you; I am gratified: I am delighted; I am happy to receive you. Good morning." The pilgrims were stunned into admiration: he was, said Mrs. Fairbanks, "Noble and commanding." [68] "An unbending will is stamped upon his face, and yet when he smiles his blue eyes are as gentle as a woman's," [69] declared Clemens. "I could not realize," gushed Mrs. Griswold, "that we were being entertained by a ruler of more than seventy-five millions of people, and whose word was the supreme law of the most powerful nation on the globe." [70] Consul Smith drew forth the speech Clemens had prepared and, with suitable flourish, began to read it: "We are a handful of private citizens of America. . . ." The Emperor was seen to nod and smile, as the Consul expatiated on how unostentatious

[64] *Herald,* October 8, 1867.

[65] *Log,* pp. 57–58.

[66] *Herald,* October 8, 1867.

[67] *Woman's Pilgrimage,* p. 184.

[68] *Herald,* October 8, 1867.

[69] *New York Tribune,* September 19, 1867; *Traveling,* p. 149.

[70] *Woman's Pilgrimage,* p. 184.

the Pilgrims were and how steadfast a friend the Emperor was:

We could not presume to take a step like this, did we not know well that the words we speak here, and the sentiments wherewith they are freighted, are but the reflex of the thoughts and feelings of all our countrymen, from the green hills of New England to the shore of the far Pacific. We are few in number, but we utter the voice of a nation!

"Very good, very good," the Czar was heard to mutter.

One of the brightest pages that has graced the world's history since written history had its birth was recorded by your Majesty's hand when it loosed the bonds of twenty millions of men; and Americans can but esteem it a privilege to do honor to a ruler who has wrought so great a deed.

The Emperor nodded again, and Consul Smith continued:

The lesson that was taught us then, we have profited by, and are free in truth to-day, even as we were before in name. America owes much to Russia—is indebted to her in many ways, and chiefly for her unwavering friendship in seasons of our greatest need. That that friendship may still be hers in times to come we confidently pray; that she is and will be grateful to Russia and to her sovereign for it, we know full well; that she will never forfeit it by any unpremeditated, unjust act or unfair course, it were treason to believe.

The Czar smiled, nodded, and said "I am very, very grateful." Mr. Smith gave him the document and the Emperor promptly gave it to an unidentified man standing near him "to be filed away among the archives of Russia—in the stove, perhaps" Clemens remarked later.[71]
Apparently no one other than Duncan, Smith, and Leary was actually introduced to the Emperor, but shortly after the presentation Captain Duncan "begged permission" of the Empress to introduce her to the ladies of the party. This done the Emperor smiled again and reentered his palace and

[71] *Alta,* November 6, 1867; *Traveling,* p. 152.

the pilgrims followed. "The rooms were all without carpets," Emily Severance wrote home, "and hung with various kinds of damasks and chintzes. . . . There were some glass-covered courts and enclosed verandahs with lounges temptingly arranged, pretty book-racks holding clocks, etc., but nothing which looked like regal splendor. Of course we could not linger a great while to make observations, nor take out our note books." [72] The party emerged finally at the same door through which they had entered, and once again the Emperor appeared, still smiling, and after a wave of his hand disappeared into the palace for the last time.

The entire audience had taken about fifteen minutes, but as the pilgrims embellished the occasion it grew both in length and intimacy. Clemens in recounting the affair was to expand the interval in his succeeding accounts, from fifteen minutes,[73] to a half-hour,[74] to four hours.[75] And the relative importance of the meeting grew proportionately. "Our little unpretending visit of a few untitled American scrubs, instead of being [of] no consequence, except as a fifteen minutes' bore to the Czar, which was all we expected, begins to assume a national importance," Clemens wrote.[76]

The audience was over, but the Emperor's brother, the Grand Duke Michael, entertained the Americans at his own palace about a twenty minutes' walk distance. "This, by the way, is a finer house than that of the Emperor," Emily Severance confided to her family back home, and, indeed, the pilgrims, flattered by the Grand Duke's attentions, seemed to find him even more impressive than his brother. He was "a rare brick," "the princeliest figure in Russia," declared Clemens, who had now been in Russia for almost a week and seen two princes. "He is even taller than the Czar, as straight as an Indian, and bears himself like one of those gorgeous knights we read about in romances of the Crusades." [77] Of course, the Grand Duke was wearing a Cossack

[72] *Journal Letters*, pp. 141–42.
[73] *Alta*, November 6, 1867; *Traveling*, p. 157.
[74] *Tribune*, September 19, 1867; *Traveling*, p. 145.
[75] Clemens to his family, *Letters*, p. 132.
[76] *Alta*, November 6, 1867; *Traveling*, p. 157.
[77] *Alta*, November 10, 1867; *Traveling*, 158; cf. *IA*, 396.

uniform in full regalia—he *looked* like a Russian prince—which was to his advantage. He wore a high, black astrakhan hat; his long coat glistened with chains and decorations, and his chest was replete with what Mrs. Fairbanks called "a most fanciful arrangement" of gilt cartridge boxes. He looked, she declared, "like he might *cheer*, while he counselled his royal brother." [78] This was what they had expected from Russian royalty. He showed them through his dacha and, to the pilgrims' delight, served them a "breakfast." They were hungry and the food seemed vastly superior to anything they had ever eaten before. It was only a light repast—tea served with crackers and cheese, and meat, but to the pilgrims it was elegance itself. "Not mere tea, but tea, which, by the way, had never crossed the ocean—" Mrs. Severance declared. (Tea was "injured," they were told, if it passed over sea water and *this* tea had been brought overland from China.) "You can scarcely imagine the difference between it and the poor stuff called by the same name on shipboard." And the bread was "the whitest and softest"—a delicacy which their days at sea made them especially hungry for.[79] The Grand Duke was an affable host who visited the tables of his assembled guests, chatting easily with them in excellent English. The pilgrims glowed and became Russian partisans forever. Mr. Griswold remarked to the Duke that he thought, "ere many years would pass away" Russia would control the Bosporus and Dardanelles—and a good thing, too. "A smile played across the countenance of His Highness," Mrs. Griswold was later to comment, "as he nodded assent and intimated that such a thing was not at all improbable." [80] There were many other Russians present and many informal conversations. The Russian military was most impressed with the fact that Colonel Kinney and Colonel Denny had so recently fought against one another in a bloody civil war and yet now could travel together amicably. "What! Both here as friends?" [81] The Russians found it hard to believe. The excursionists

[78] *Herald*, October 8, 1867.
[79] *Journal Letters*, p. 144.
[80] *Woman's Pilgrimage*, p. 187.
[81] *Herald*, October 8, 1867.

were delighted by all. "I can assure you," Mrs. Fairbanks remarked, "it made my heart throb with delight to hear those fine looking Russians say in their broken French or English, 'We love your country,' 'We are glad to meet people from America.' " [82] Rather repeatedly the Russians were invited to visit the *Quaker City* the next day. At four o'clock the pilgrims departed, elated to the point of ascension. "Is it not enough to turn the head of a novice to be escorted by Russian dukes, and to be attended by ladies of the court?" Mrs. Fairbanks asked. That night the *Quaker City* filled the harbor skies with fireworks.

A casual remark from the Emperor had convinced Duncan that Nicholas wanted to visit the ship. It was an unlikely possibility and not to be taken seriously, but the pilgrims' imaginations were boundless—they expected him on board even while they disclaimed any belief that he would actually come. Of course, he didn't. The sea, they decided, kept him away; it was too rough for him to venture out. They had to content themselves with entertaining other Russian dignitaries and with visiting the royal yacht, a warship reconditioned for His Royal Highness largely with machinery and fittings salvaged from the British man-of-war *Tiger* which had been sunk during the Crimea conflict. The Americans privately thought the workmanship less good than American shipbuilders might have made it, but they were impressed with the elegance of the royal suite and the captain's quarters—and they enjoyed the champagne the captain served them on board. They waited the whole day for the Emperor, but he did not come. Perhaps tomorrow the sea would be calmer? And for a second night the harbor night was filled with skyrockets, starbursts, and roman candles.

The next day the sea was calm, and the Emperor eagerly expected. The ship was put in readiness for the royal visit: the velvet sofas were brought on deck and the saloon was decorated with masses of flowers. The pilgrims once again over-dressed with elaborate care. By one o'clock they were all in readiness and waiting. They continued to wait throughout the afternoon—increasingly restive. Mr. James

[82] *Ibid.*

took the occasion of the universal elegance to make stereopticon pictures of the company. Still the Emperor did not arrive. "At 5," Duncan wrote in his log, "we noticed bustle and preparations going on on shore at the landing. The walk to the water carpeted, the state barge drawn up and other indications of approaching greatness. Now the Emperor was coming *sure.*" [83] Excursionists on shore rushed back to the ship.

All was in readiness. But, alas, the barge brought only the Governor-General and a message from the Czar that he could not come, that he was ill. It was a great disappointment, but the Governor-General was given an elaborate salute, the Russian flag was run up the staff and the ship's cannon fired twice. After introductions, all repaired to the grand saloon where, the Governor-General presiding at one table and Consul Smith at the other, an hour was spent in what Mrs. Fairbanks called "social chat and brilliant repartee." This was thought a fitting occasion for champagne and it flowed rather freely throughout the evening. Captain Duncan made a long-winded, florid speech thanking the Emperor through the Governor-General for his *noblesse* in seeing the "handful of private citizens of America," [84] and proposed a toast to his majesty. The Governor-General responded with a toast to the American President. They toasted the Emperor's family, and the Grand Duke Michael and his family, and the Governor-General and his family, and finally "friendship everlasting between Russia and America." When the Governor-General departed, the *Quaker City* pilgrims gave him three tipsy cheers.

By eight in the evening all visitors had left the ship and it was ready to leave Yalta. The sun was nearly set when they weighed anchor and, firing two more salutes, departed. As the ship passed the palace of the Emperor, the crew began to fire cannon salutes once again and, as a special effect, illuminated the *Quaker City* from prow to stern with blue lights. "The sun is setting on our Russian greatness," Mrs. Fairbanks wrote home. "We were announced by no titles, but the proudest court in Europe had laid aside its ermine to

[83] *Log*, pp. 63–64.
[84] *Ibid.*, p. 65.

meet us upon common ground." [85] "We have got so used to
Princes now," Clemens wrote, "that it is going to be hard
work, during the next few days, to get down to the level of
the common herd again." [86] During the two-day trip back to
Constantinople, only Bloodgood Cutter was disconsolate.
Consul Smith had successfully foiled his persistent attempts
personally to address the Czar with a commemorative poem
("While lying at Yalta, with a grateful mind,/I'll thank
you truly for our reception kind . . ."). Cutter was in-
sufferable in his disappointment. "We ought not to be too
hard on him," Clemens suggested. "For aught we know, God
made him. It is even possible that He made him for some
wise purpose. That the poet has failed to fill the bill is a
matter for regret, but not for execration." [87]

All day Thursday (August 29) the passengers were busy
putting away their finery and writing letters home. Clemens
wrote four letters—two to the *Alta*, one to the *New York
Tribune*, and one to the *New York Herald*—about the royal
welcome. He was as delighted and impressed by their reception as any of the pilgrims, but it would not do, he realized,
to project this admiration into his letters without comic
qualification. His awe of the Czar and Czarina who were, he
said, "politeness itself and the genuine article," precluded
that he make them the subject of his comedy. The pilgrims
were a more likely butt for his humor, but, although their
performance was certainly a fit subject for his satire, Clemens apparently did not yet have the perspective to see it in
a comic light. Although he mentioned the elaborate preparation ("the whole ship's company turned out at about
7 o'clock yesterday morning, and dressed from that time
until 11") [88] he said nothing about the exaggerated *noblesse*
the Americans pretended. The comic tone in these letters
was supplied by his personae: he inserted burlesque descriptions of his own "Mark Twain" behavior ("I captured a fine
old gentleman who seemed perfectly willing to be bored
with questions, and bored him good"); [89] he brought on

[85] *Herald,* October 8, 1867.

[86] *Tribune,* September 19, 1867; *Traveling,* p. 150.

[87] *Alta,* November 10, 1867; *Traveling,* p. 161. Omitted from *IA.*

[88] *Alta,* November 6, 1867, *Traveling,* p. 151.

[89] *Traveling,* p. 152.

Brown-Blucher who evinced an exaggerated appreciation of the Czar's "condescension" ("The idea of him trotting them beats through here himself!") ; [90] and he described the Poet Larriat's attempts at some length. The pilgrims' own behavior was not satirized, although there were apparently a number of faux pas made by the Americans during their sojourn which Clemens knew about. These, he wrote in his notebook, "must never be trusted to treacherous paper." [91] In fact, Clemens wrote nothing of the Americans at Yalta which suggested they behaved in any ludicrous or vulgar way, but despite this, a week after the *Quaker City* returned to New York, Moses Beach wrote a column about the meeting with the Emperor which mildly berated Clemens:

> Let me add here [he wrote] the *Tribune* correspondent to the contrary notwithstanding—that our Quaker City company acquitted themselves well. As representatives not only of every part of their country, but of almost every shade of society in every part, they so appeared that the most fastidious need not blush for word or act. . . . The easy politeness manifested by both gentlemen and ladies left little to be wished for by those who are interested in knowing whether or not our appearance created a desirable impression.[92]

The slap at Clemens was gratuitous not only because he had, indeed, said nothing to warrant the criticism but also because Beach himself had not been on board the *Quaker City* when it went to Russia (although he pretended to his readers that he had been).[93] The criticism was unjustified, but Clemens may have borne it in mind when he rewrote the

[90] *Ibid.*, p. 155.

[91] "What happened in the park—and again in the court of the palace, where the fountain was, and the flowers—and above all the occurrence under the porch which has the Caryatides in imitation of the Temple of Erechtheus at Athens—these were rich—they must never be trusted to treacherous paper—memory will do—I guess no one in the world who could appreciate a joke would be likely to forget them." *Notebook*, p. 80.

[92] *Sun*, November 27, 1867.

[93] Beach wrote a number of letters about the voyage after he returned, and they suggest that he used Duncan's log as the basis for his recollections.

letters for the book, for not only did he omit the innocent comments he made about himself, Brown-Blucher, and Cutter, he also made a point of inserting into this manuscript two paragraphs which had originally appeared in a letter to the *Tribune* which praised the pilgrims' behavior. The insertion merely made explicit what was already obvious but it suggests Clemens' concern that he not be faulted for unfairly criticizing his fellow passengers:

Possibly it may be thought that our party tarried too long, or did other improper things, but such was not the case. The company felt that they were occupying an unusually responsible position—they were representing the people of America, not the Government—and therefore they were careful to do their best to perform their high mission with credit.[94]

But if the *Quaker City's* passengers did not think themselves even mildly ridiculous, its crew thought them hilarious and burlesqued the whole excursion to the Czar. "The sailors in the forecastle have had a royal reception" Mrs. Fairbanks informed her *Herald* readers, "the cook delivered the address, and a soiled table-cloth was spread for the imperial feet." [95] Clemens did not recount the incident in his letters, but he remembered it (perhaps after reading Mrs. Fairbanks' correspondence) when he was writing *IA*. The passage of time evidently allowed him to see the whole royal affair in a more comic light and in recounting the crews' behavior he inserted a humorous commentary on his own address to the Emperor. "Oh d--n the Address!—read it to the police," the cook says in Clemens' account. "Chamberlain, take these people over to my brother, the Grand Duke's and give them a square meal. Adieu! I am happy—I am gratified—I am delighted—I am bored. Adieu, adieu—vamos the ranch!" (pp. 404–5). The crew actually did make unmerciful fun of the address and Clemens at length declared that he "never was so tired of any one phrase as the sailors made me of the opening sentence of the Address to the Emperor of Russia" (p. 406).

[94] *Tribune,* September 19, 1867; *Traveling,* p. 148; cf. *IA,* p. 400.

[95] *Herald,* October 8, 1867.

At daylight, Friday, August 30, they arrived back at Constantinople. The five-day excursion to Russia had lengthened to eleven, and the eight pilgrims left in Turkey had been waiting with something less than perfect patience. "I guess Dan is well tired of Contantinople by this time," Clemens had written in his notebook at Odessa, and he was right. Both Jack and Dan had been bored, and their dissatisfaction was not lessened by hearing stories of regal highjinks they had missed. The general anti-American feeling of Constantinople had been increased during the absence of the ship by the American Congressional Declaration in favor of Crete, and the visit of the *Quaker City* to the Russian Emperor also apparently irritated the Turks. The Turkish Sultan disliked being "passed over" in favor of the Czar, and "Americans," Clemens noted "show no disposition to visit him." [96] Having seen Aziz in Paris, they had little inclination to trouble themselves for another look.

Although all the pilgrims desired nothing so much as to leave Turkey at once, the ship remained at Constantinople for another five days. The problem was coal. The extended trip to Russia had made refueling necessary, but, although it was contracted for, the coal was not delivered at once. The Turks had their own ways of showing antipathy. First there was the unexplained delay in beginning the recoaling, and when the actual process itself was begun, it proceeded "at a pace which bred utter despair among all our passengers," according to Duncan. The coaling continued for four more days, "faster, it is said," he wrote sardonically, "than the cook burns it." [97]

On Sunday, coaling continued—despite the Sabbath. "Coaling going on forward & Mr. Bullard preaching aft," Duncan wrote. "It is to be hoped that our devotions will offset our wickedness in breaking the sabbath." [98] The coal dust was even thicker than usual and most of the passengers left the ship during the day. There was nothing they wanted to see in the city; they had nowhere to go but the bazaars, and nothing to do but to buy. "Everybody (but wife) off on shore making purchases" wrote Duncan, "and *such* purchases

[96] "Unpublished Notebook no. 8" (Typescript, p. 28), *MTP*.
[97] *Log*, pp. 67–68.
[98] *Ibid.*, p. 67.

as our party have made!" [99] The booty was bizarre: some pilgrims purchased gravestones with their names carved on them in Arabic script, some bought brightly painted sailors' chests, embroidered slippers, and hookah pipes; even full-sized caiques such as those which took them to shore were bought and stowed in the hold. There was no end to the pilgrims' appetite for exotica—or, apparently, their ability to pay for it. "More bargains are made with the *Osmanlis* for slippers, chibouks, narghilles, turbans, Turkish towels, beads, and a liberal supply of ottar [sic] of roses, which of course is warranted to be genuine," reported Mrs. Griswold. "Some of the Pilgrims now begin to dress in Oriental style." [100] Their boredom seemed to reach new depths. They were diverted one afternoon when the American Minister visited the ship for wine and cake. He invited them for a day's excursion to his home on the Bosporus and then, perhaps deliberately, forgot to tell them how to get there.

The coaling went on. "Here 17 days!" Clemens wrote in his notebook on September 3. It only seemed that long. He took a day's trip to Scutari across the strait and went by horseback to the summit of a nearby mountain where he stopped for refreshments (grapes, candied green English walnuts—a novelty to Clemens—and Turkish coffee which he was beginning to like) and surveyed the panoramic view of Constantinople, the Bosporus Islands, and the Black Sea beyond. On the way down the mountain his prospector's eye saw gold (or so he thought) in the quartz scattered across the trail—not enough evidently to interrupt his journey for, but enough to encourage his notebook speculation about the feasibility of mining it there "where the labor is so cheap." [101] Back on board he wrote a letter to the *Tribune* and sent it off. But despite his intermittent labors, these were essentially wasted days, and he was as anxious as anyone to be gone from Turkey forever. The coaling was still not completed by Tuesday, but Duncan resolved "to 'go on' whether the coal is in or not."

At 6:30 the *Quaker City* weighed anchor and began to steam from the harbor, but the pilgrims' bad luck was not

[99] *Ibid.*
[100] *Woman's Pilgrimage*, p. 195.
[101] *Notebook*, p. 82.

over. The *Quaker City* rammed another ship. The cause of the accident is uncertain. It may have been (as many of the passengers maintained) merely another example of Duncan's incompetence or (as Duncan averred) the unfortunate result of an unexpected and uncontrollable current. In any case, the ship sliced across the bow of another steamer moored to a buoy, ripping its mainsail and snagging the buoy chain with the *Quaker City*'s anchor. The encounter swung the ship about and against the bowsprit of still another ship anchored close by which smashed into one of the *Quaker City*'s lifeboats and cut it in two. "Maybe it is well we bought so many caiques," [102] Clemens remarked—they might be needed if the ship had to be evacuated in a hurry. Fortunately, after the first flurry of panic swept the ship, calm returned, the damage was seen to be slight and the chief difficulty that of disentangling the anchor from the buoy chain. The operation took three hours, and it was ten o'clock before the ship left Constantinople, ending its unhappy sojourn in Turkey.

[102] "Unpublished Notebook no. 8" (Typescript, p. 28), *MTP*.

SMYRNA
EPHESUS
BEIRUT
PALESTINE
JERUSALEM

"A shout in such a solitude . . ."

Clemens relaxed. For the first time since the ship had moored at Fayal eleven weeks before, he spent a day on board feeling no pressure to write. He had, by his careful count, written 37 letters to the *Alta California*—three-quarters of his contract—and the excursion was only half-completed; he still had the Holy Land and Egypt, chief attractions of the trip, ahead of him, and writing about *those* sights would be easy. But despite his satisfaction, a niggling concern troubled him. "Do the *Alta's* come regularly?" he asked his family in a letter from Constantinople. "I wish I knew whether my letters reach them or not." He knew of no reason why they should not have; none of the mail he received at Constantinople suggested that his newspaper correspondence had been interrupted. Still, he was concerned enough to make a check-list of the letters he had written and sent, and with this list as a basis, he had worked out a program for the 13 letters he had still to write. "I hope to write from the Sea of Tiberius, Damascus, Jerusalem, Joppa, and possibly other points in the Holy Land. The letters from Egypt, the Nile and Algiers I will look out for, myself. I will bring them in my pocket." [1] His labor had been enormous and remarkably well-sustained, and as a reward he could contemplate a trip through the Holy Land and Egypt—areas of great fascination for him—with the leisure of a tourist. He would write now at his pleasure, for whatever correspondence remained unfinished at his departure from Egypt would be easy for him to complete while the *Quaker City* recrossed the Atlantic.

All of which was a disastrous misconception, for of the 37 letters he enumerated in his letter home, 14 had already miscarried.[2] Instead of 13 letters he was to write 27. Not one-quarter but one-half of his labor remained ahead of him.[3] But, relaxed for the first time in months, he was blithely unaware of the catastrophe that had befallen him,

---

[1] *Letters*, pp. 134–35.

[2] Of those he enumerates, the following never appeared in the *San Francisco Daily Alta California:* "1 from some little place in Switzerland—have forgotten the name [probably Chiasso], 4 concerning Lecce [sic], Bergamo, Padua, Verona, Battlefield of Marengo, Pestachio, and some other cities in Northern Italy," "2 from Venice. 1 about Bologna . . . 1 from Pisa. . . . 1 from Rome and Civita Vecchia . . . 1 from the island of Ischia. 1 concerning the Volcano of Stromboli, the city and Straits of Messina, the land of Sicily, Scylla and Charybdis, etc. . . . 1 . . . about . . . Scutari." *Letters*, pp. 134–35.

[3] Fifty-one separate letters were published in the *Alta* over Clemens' byline and, in addition, the Naples *Observer* letter was reprinted. However, this number is misleading; Clemens' letters were not numbered in composition and occasionally he sent very long letters which were counted differently by him and by the *Alta*. For example, he sent a long letter concerning Tangier which

and he did not, in fact, discover the truth for over a month, not, that is, until the ship received mail at Alexandria. For a month he was to indulge himself; he had no misgivings when, a little over a week hence, tired and tortured by the overland trek through Palestine, he stopped writing letters altogether.

The voyage from Constantinople to Smyrna was a fast trip of two nights and a day, for the *Quaker City* had a strong wind behind it. The weather was cool and the skies sunny, and the excursionists clustered about the decks conversing and reading. Clemens himself probably spent part of Thursday (September 5) reading biblical history and preparing for the sights of Smyrna where the ship was to land the following day. "The ship is full of books concerning the Holy Land, and holy places, and every other place on earth," he wrote to the *Alta* in a passage later omitted from *IA*, "and you cannot be surprised to know that I have read whole volumes of the far-fetched conclusions of these curious prophecy-fulfillers.[4] The information was to stand him in good stead later on.

The ship seemed to speed along the coastline. Off to the left hills undulated against the sky, their ridges seeming to intertwine like locked fingers. Here and there the excursionists could see villages on shore, groups of scattered houses that looked, Clemens remarked, "like sugar-loaves" through the glasses.[5] In part because they were free of the tiresome delay at Constantinople, in part because they were now, at last, about to enter the Bible lands they had chiefly planned for, the company revived. After dark, long after evening

---

he counted as one in his letter to his family although the *Alta* printed it as two (nos. 3 and 4). On the other hand, he wrote a very long letter concerning Athens and the Grecian Archipelago which he counted as two and the *Alta* printed as one (no. 15). The letter from Odessa and Sebastopol he counted as one, but the *Alta* as two (nos. 20 and 21). By this calculation, 51 "letters" were printed but only 50 installments were sent. The *Alta* numbering was not consistent, there being two gaps (omitting nos. 40, 41, 42, and 49 and 50) which were, evidently, mere oversights made by typesetters.

[4] *Alta*, November 17, 1867; *Traveling*, p. 166.

[5] *Notebook*. p. 83.

devotions were finished, the passengers sat on deck and talked.

At daybreak Friday, the ship passed through the narrow mouth of Smyrna Bay and sailed toward the city six miles away. At ten they entered its harbor, pleased to discover that they were not to be the only American ship at anchor there. They recognized the flags of two American merchant ships in the distance, and shortly thereafter the *Quaker City* passed the American gunboat *Swatara* which, to the delight of the pilgrims, greeted the steamer with a wild salute; the crew of the man-of-war climbed the shrouds of the ship and gave three cheers. The *Quaker City* was barely anchored when the *Swatara* sent a boat with the captain's best wishes and an offer of assistance.

By twelve the excursionists had cleared health inspection and were swarming over the city. It was just as dirty as Constantinople, but it had a difference: it was holy ground; it was mentioned in the Bible; two disciples had visited it! Whatever its present inadequacies, Smyrna had a holy advantage in its past, and the pious pilgrims accepted whatever discomfort was pressed upon them with a kind of religious sufferance. And there were many discomforts. The city had no carriages—one saw it either on foot or from the back of a swaying donkey. It was crowded and filthy. "Superior to everything," wrote Clemens, "and claiming the bulk of attention first, last, and all the time—is a combination of Mohammedan stinks, to which the stench of a Chinese quarter would be as pleasant as the roasting odors of the fatted calf to the nostrils of the returning Prodigal." [6] But it was holy. And it had fresh fruit—grapes for two cents a pound, enormous sweet melons, dates and some varieties new to the pilgrims ("I ate *figs* for the first time," declared Captain Duncan). The excursionists seemed delighted. "We constantly meet the Pilgrims scattered over the city," wrote Mrs. Griswold, "seated around shops, drinking coffee and lemonade, eating figs and dates, and enjoying themselves generally." [7] They ascended Citadel Hill (the Mt. Pagus of Scripture) and visited the great sheds where figs were

---

[6] *Traveling*, p. 164; cf. *IA*, p. 407.

[7] *Woman's Pilgrimage*, p. 196.

packed for shipment around the world. They saw Caravan
Bridge where the camel trains were loaded and saw
camels—real camels (not "the scrawny specimens one sees
in the menagerie" Clemens declared [8])—loaded with dates
and spices, filing through the streets on their way to the
desert countryside. ("I do not wonder that camels are
meek" wrote Mrs. Fairbanks, "for I am sure they have
nothing to be proud of.") [9]

By late afternoon they had "done" the city and were back
on board to entertain the officers of the *Swatara*. They
didn't make a very good impression: "Without a doubt,"
one of the gunboat officers wrote home, "the party of Holy
Land excursionists are a hard, rough-looking set of people;
mostly backwoodsmen and country farmers . . . there are
thirteen ministers, eleven physicians, and as 'Mark Twain'
expresses it, 'thirteen women and two ladies,' besides a
party of fast young men." [10] There can be little question
which of the "fast young men" furnished the officer with this
information, and it would have given Clemens great satisfaction to know how completely he had gulled the officer
and denigrated the pilgrims at the same time. Three
months in the sun must indeed have changed the complex-
ions of that elegant party! Mistaken for backwoodsmen
indeed!

The chief attraction of Smyrna was its proximity to
Ephesus, the virtually deserted ruins of which lay 40 miles
away. These could be visited only by traveling first by train
to a railhead and then by donkey for three miles to the ruins
themselves, and making plans for this excursion occupied
the pilgrims for the rest of the afternoon. The *Swatara*
officers were invited to join the party. Clemens was later to
write in *IA* that the officers came as "guests," but this was
not the case. "The excursionists hired a train to visit Ephesus, and invited us along," the *Swatara* officer wrote home,
"(provided we would pay our own expenses)."

The plans were necessarily elaborate ones, for Ephesus
was virtually isolated and the party had to bring all neces-

[8] *Alta*, November 17, 1867; *Traveling*, p. 167.
[9] *Cleveland Herald*, November 19, 1867.
[10] *Brooklyn Eagle*, October 11, 1867.

sary provisions—not only the noonday lunch but also sixty donkeys to transport the pilgrims to the ruins themselves. Duncan therefore "hired a train," and he evidently drove a good bargain, for Charleton, the general manager of the railroad, agreed to accompany the excursionists and to oversee the journey; they were to have first-class accommodations for second-class fares, and all the donkeys were to be carried without charge. Duncan and his family were also to travel free in what was called "The Sultan's Carriage." By 5:30 they had breakfasted and were prepared to go ashore, but that process proved more difficult than had been expected. The *Swatara* had placed a longboat at their disposal, but other boats too were needed—virtually all the passengers were to visit Ephesus. Disembarking the pilgrims was therefore time-consuming, and Duncan's precisely calculated plans were soon in disarray. The pilgrims were over an hour late for the train, a circumstance which proved unfortunate, for, although Manager Charleton waited for them, he waited with a bottle, and when the pilgrims arrived he was drunk and remained so much of the day. Moreover, the guides had not provided enough donkeys and those they had balked at getting on board the train, causing further delay. The presence of the *Swatara* officers could not have been very comforting; they were, to quote one of them, "not a little amused by the manners and manoeuvres of the party." They were evidently set upon by Miss Chadeyne and the others, and, the officers reported, were "pretty well monopolized by the four unprotected females." [11]

The rail journey was three hours each way following a rather bleak itinerary between barren hills, but it had a few compensations. There were many ruins along the way, among them the historic Church of Smyrna, one of the "Seven Churches of Asia" mentioned in the Bible, and now and again the train passed women in exotic "native costumes." At 10:00 they had reached the railhead, and the lucky ones mounted the donkeys for the hour's trek to the ruins. It was not a comfortable ride. The donkeys were small (Clemens' long legs dragged on the ground) and could not be guided. Their trappings were elaborate. According to

[11] *Ibid.*

Mrs. Fairbanks, "the saddles were stuffed cushions with Persian covers. Fringes and bands of gay colors around the heads of the donkeys, worked in shells and glass beads." [12] She might also have added, they were so shapeless that the

A Street Scene in Smyrna

women had to ride astride rather than sidesaddle, and the journey to Ephesus was regularly punctuated by one or another of the pilgrims being thrown from his mount into the dust.

But the difficulties and irritations did not lessen the en-

[12] *Herald*, November 19, 1867.

thusiasm of the party. This was holy land, and it was worth any amount of inconvenience. "We soon entered the once magnificent city of the Ephesians," wrote Duncan later. "Through the ruins of a gate and down a steep declivity we passed into the 'Theatre' where as we read in Acts 19, Old St. Paul had an 'uproar' about his ears 'for about the space of two hours.' Here we stood on 'scripture ground.' " [13] They had been denied the view of Mars Hill in Athens where Paul had preached, but Ephesus was theirs. They lunched under the broken arch entry to the amphitheater, read their Bibles and gave themselves up to the drama of the place. "One may read the scriptures and believe," Clemens told his *Alta* readers, "but he cannot go and stand yonder in the ruined theatre and in imagination people it again with the vanished multitudes who mobbed Paul's comrades there and shouted, with one voice, 'Great is Diana of the Ephesians!' The idea of a shout in such a solitude as this almost makes one shudder." [14] For the first time they were present in surroundings which were irrefutably those the disciples had seen. The Roman antiquities—even the Mammertine Prison—were of doubtful authenticity compared with these ruins. The pilgrims' awe was profound and they were deeply moved. "To me the satisfaction was not in contemplating any single group of ruins," Mrs. Fairbanks was to write home,

but rather in riding over those open fields through the rough ground, and broken stones, now turning aside from a thorny thicket, breaking and crushing the tall thistles which grew along our way like sun-flowers, looking off upon surrounding hills where Paul had walked in those Bible days, which seemed nearer to me than ever before.[15]

Their awe was sacramental to the point of melodrama (as when Colonel Kinney passed a cup of wine among the pilgrims declaring they would not meet in this place again), and the company assumed heroic poses in the Amphitheater while Mr. James photographed them several times. But it

[13] *Log,* p. 73.
[14] *Alta,* November 24, 1867; *Traveling,* p. 174; cf. *IA,* p. 422.
[15] *Herald,* November 19, 1867.

wasn't long before the need to commemorate the occasion slipped into the grotesque as the pilgrims began to acquire portable mementoes, preferably stones with carving or inscriptions on them. Neither were they content with fallen pieces; some, like Bloodgood Cutter, actually took away parts of the walls and columns themselves. Although Clemens was later to criticize the pilgrims for such relic-hunting, he too acquired souvenirs of Ephesus, as, indeed, he had from the Parthenon and was to do from various places in Palestine.[16] He was later to write in *IA* that a government official met the excursionists at the railhead and made them "disgorge" their relics, but his assertion isn't well supported. Bloodgood Cutter, at least, took his booty home with him, and Duncan implies they all did.

By five in the afternoon the pilgrims had returned to the train and were on their way back to Smyrna. It had been an eminently successful day, and before the pilgrims left the depot to proceed to their waiting ship Duncan gave Manager Charleton—still drunk—what he called a "complimentary speech" and three cheers. By 8:30 they were back on board and ready to steam out of the harbor, but once again a passenger delayed them. This time it was Dan Slote who had remained on shore to find the American Consul and retrieve a letter of credit he had left to be cashed. He had difficulty. Hours passed; the sun went down; the new moon rose. The city lay pale and silent across the water and the ship was quiet.

In this romantic setting, he was to recall later, Clemens first saw a picture of the woman who was to be his wife: "The Cub," Charlie Langdon, emboldened perhaps by his growing friendship with the older man, showed Clemens a miniature portrait of his adored sister, Olivia. Nothing in Clemens notebooks or letters suggests he was smitten, but, as he was to describe the scene many years afterward, he fell in love with her at once and determined to meet her when the ship got back to New York.[17] It was a romantic time in his life and he seemed particularly sensitive to the blandishments of femininity during the voyage. There had

[16] See Webster Collection, list of relics Clemens brought back from the trip, Typescript in *MTP*.

[17] *Autobiography*, Vol. 1: 26.

been not only Lily Hitchcock in Paris but a "beautiful little devil" of a Russian girl he had met at Yalta and a "very beautiful" girl he had met only the day before in Smyrna with whom, he reported, he "got along very well." Romance was around him; his good friend Dr. Jackson was clearly infatuated with Julia Newell, and apparently other couples had become regularly paired too.[18] It is not altogether un-likely that, viewing the delicate features in the miniature, he imagined himself in love with Olivia Langdon.

Dan finally found the Consul and retrieved his letter, but it was after eleven when he returned to the ship. It had been a long day and most of the *Quaker City* passengers were in their berths and sound asleep when the ship departed from Smyrna. By morning they were in the Mediterranean and passing among the Dodecanese Islands. By one they were abreast of Patmos and within half a mile of its shore. The view excited the passengers, for by tradition it was here that John had written Revelations. "Our passengers were all on deck," Duncan reported.

Glasses, Revelations, guide-books and gazetteers were all brought into requisition. And this is really Patmos! Here St. John was banished by Demetrius and there in the Convent on the Hill just now plainly in sight, he received the Revelations! We gaze, and read, and think. How we would like to land and climb that hill and enter that Convent that we might be where John was! [19]

They considered stopping for a brief visit, the harbor was near, but Patmos was not on the itinerary. To add a new port, all passengers would have had to assent, and since reservations for the journey from Beirut to Damascus had already been made, the ship did not dock. As a concession, it was stopped briefly offshore to allow Mr. James to take some views of the island. The day was splendid, with clear skies and a smooth sea. The ship's course wound among the volcanic islands of the archipelago, past Leros, Levithos, Kalimnos, and Kos before nightfall, and after dark, Chalkes and Rhodes. On Sunday they were in open sea again with no land in sight.

Not all the passengers were on deck. Several were ill, none

[18] *Swatara* officer's letter, *Brooklyn Eagle*, October 11, 1867.
[19] *Log*, p. 76.

seriously. Charlie Langdon had come down with a fever which kept him in bed for several days and Judge Haldeman and Mr. Foster were still convalescent. Clemens was in good health, but after the scenic Greek Isles were past he, too, spent a good while below. He labored. He had no pressing need to do so, but the sojourn at Smyrna and Ephesus had stimulated him, and during Sunday and Monday (September 8 and 9) he wrote three letters to the *Alta California*, hoping, perhaps, to have them posted in Beirut before he began his Palestine pilgrimage, a journey he knew would necessarily interrupt the regular transmission of his letters for several weeks.

On Monday they passed Cyprus, green and fertile in the distance with Mount Olympus towering dimly above it. All that day the ship was in a state of excitement, "Such a burrowing in the hold for trunks that had lain buried for weeks, yes for months," Clemens was to write later. "Such a hurrying to and fro above decks and below; such a riotous system of packing and unpacking; such a littering up of the cabins with shirts and skirts, and indescribable and unclassable odds and ends . . . !" (p. 431). The preparations were complicated, for the clothing and equipment needed in an overland trek through Palestine were multifarious: they would need to bring their own saddles, they had been told, for English and Western saddles were virtually unattainable in Syria and Palestine and, the guidebook warned, "To ride day after day on an Arab saddle, with its short stirrups and narrow seat, is absolute torture." [20] The men were cautioned to carry a revolver. "It should be worn in a leather belt so as to be visible," declared the Guide, "especially when the traveller sees fit to indulge in solitary rides or walks. The robbers of Syria are generally amateurs, who take up the profession when favourable opportunity offers." [21] Some foods had to be carried, too: tea for instance, and biscuits—and wine and brandy (for medicinal purposes only, of course). And perhaps a good folding bed. Clothing was a great problem; they would need heavy

[20] Josias Leslie Porter, *A Handbook for Travellers in Syria and Palestine* 2 vols. (London: John Murry, 1858), p. li.
[21] *Ibid.*, liii.

wraps for the cool evenings along the coast but they should wear lighter garments during the hot midday. They would need broad hats with veils, white umbrellas with dark felt linings and green glass spectacles for sun protection, and sturdy boots and strong riding trousers. "Perhaps," the guide delicately suggested, "if the parts next the saddle were covered with soft leather . . . they would be still more comfortable and more durable—an important consideration in a long tour." Their clothing had to be of wool, they were warned. "It is a great mistake to wear linen, or any other thin material. The body is thus exposed to the direct rays of the sun; the skin becomes dry, perspiration is checked, and fever or diarrhoea is the result." [22] Packing for a week's trip overland was, therefore, no small task, and there were other preparations, too—maps to be studied, routes to be chosen, historical data memorized. Everyone assiduously read his Bible and his guidebook.

The *Quaker City* had originally been scheduled to stop twice in the Holy Land: at Beirut, remaining long enough to allow passengers who wished to see Damascus (about seventy miles inland) and subsequently at Joppa (Jaffa), the principal port of Palestine itself from which they would make a fifty-mile journey overland to Jerusalem. Passengers interested in visiting the Sea of Galilee and Nazareth would do so from Joppa. Captain Duncan evidently assumed there would be few who would journey to Nazareth, but almost all the able-bodied pilgrims wanted to see the scenes of Jesus' childhood and early career, and when they consulted their maps of the Holy Land they discovered that traveling to those places from Joppa meant traversing southern Palestine twice to no apparent purpose and unnecessarily reducing the time to be spent in Jerusalem itself. Before the *Quaker City* arrived at Beirut, therefore, a change of itinerary had been proposed and adopted: the ship would make a supplementary stop at Haifa, the port of Mt. Carmel, to allow passengers who so wished, to disembark and journey to Nazareth more expeditiously.

This was a happy alternative for Clemens, for he was determined to see Nazareth. His notebooks indicate that he

[22] *Ibid.*, lvi.

immediately began to plan his itinerary in Syria and Palestine with some particularity and that its chief feature was a five-day overland trip from Haifa to Jerusalem by way of Nazareth. In the pages of a fresh notebook he wrote "Beirut" and "Baalbec" at the top of two blank pages, planning subsequently to write in geographical and historical details when he visited those places. At the top of still another page he wrote "Damascus" and below this he made notes to be used later in composing his newspaper letters about that city.[23] On subsequent pages he wrote notes for his journey overland, making a day-by-day calculation of the places he would visit and appending notes about the more important ones. For example, on the first page he wrote "1st D *Mount Carmel*" and below it a lengthy note about the mountain and its surrounding countryside. His itinerary was to take him from Carmel on the first day, to Nazareth and Mt. Tabor on the second; to the Sea of Tiberias (Galilee), Endor, Nain, Jezreel, Fountain of Jefrell, Shunen, and Mt. Gilboa on the third; to Dothan, Samaria, and Sechem on the fourth; and to Jerusalem via Joseph's Tomb, Shiloh, Gilgal, Bethel, Beroth, Gibeon, Ajalon, Mizpeh, and Gibeah on the fifth. Some of Clemens' notes for these places were elaborate, virtually first drafts of what he clearly intended to be newspaper dispatches.

He had not yet set foot in Palestine, and his notes therefore owed nothing to personal experience. They were derived entirely from the guidebook which was ultimately to be Clemens' chief source of information about the Holy Land, Murray's *Handbook for Syria and Palestine* by Josias Leslie Porter. Although Clemens praised "Murray's invaluable guidebooks" in *IA* (p. 381), he nowhere specifically mentions Porter's work by name. By the time he composed *IA* he had become self-conscious about the detailed use he had made of the Murray Holy Land guide and did not wish to call particular attention to his source, for his debt to Porter was a real one, not only in the notes he made before his

[23] "The oldest city in the world," he wrote. "No time for 4,000 years that there has not been a city here. Never has changed its name. Tangier next. Cadiz or Athens next." ("Unpublished Notebook no. 9" (Typescript, p. 11), *MTP;* cf. *Alta,* December 15, 1867; *Traveling,* p. 193; *IA,* 457.

journey but also, and, as we shall see, far more significantly, in the composition of the letters he was to send to the *Alta* describing Palestine after the excursion itself was finished. Porter was an obvious choice, for of the few guidebooks for Palestine then in print, his was indisputably the best and most readily procurable, and it had a lengthy and detailed index which made it particularly easy for Clemens to use. The index was indispensable, for Porter's suggested itinerary was exactly the reverse of that Clemens was eventually to follow. It was usual for travelers in the Holy Land to begin their travels either in the Sinai Peninsula or Jerusalem, and to proceed north overland to Damascus, Haifa, or Beirut. Porter was therefore of no help in laying out Clemens' itinerary, but his guide was extremely useful nonetheless, for after Clemens had determined his route independently he consulted Porter's work for descriptive details about the places he intended to visit and made extensive notes for his use on the journey itself. Porter's guidebook was, apparently his only source, for a comparison of Clemens' descriptive notes with Porter reveals that, while they ignore the guide's sequence, virtually all of them derive from the book with no qualification from other sources or from personal experience. Some of them are verbatim quotations,[24] while others are brief synoptic restatements of information Porter gives.[25] Clemens' purpose was evidently to have the information in an abbreviated form for use during the journey itself. It is possible that he did not expect to

[24] For example, Clemens quotes the description of Rizpah's protection of the corpses of her sons, *Porter*, p. 326.

[25] Cf. *Notebook*, pp. 108–109, and *Porter*, p. 225 and the section concerning Mizpeh in Clemens' "Unpublished Notebook no. 9" (Typescript, pp. 26–27), *MTP*, and *Porter*, pp. 226–27. Paine published about half these notes in his edition of the Notebooks, calling them "Supplementary Holy Land Notes." He conjectured that they were "made on the vessel, en route for Egypt" (*Notebook*, p. 102). He implies that Clemens made the notes from memory (the notes themselves disprove this) and was setting down his own observations. Since Clemens never visited some of the places he here described in detail, this could not be correct. Furthermore, Paine ignored the marginal indications of an itinerary.

have Porter's *Handbook* with him in Palestine, either because it belonged to another passenger or because, limited in
what he could carry, he intended to leave the bulky books
(the guidebook was in two fat volumes) on board the
Quaker City.

As it happened, the notes Clemens made before Beirut
were to be of little use to him, for his final itinerary was
very different from the one he first planned, and he was to
bypass many of the places he originally intended to visit.
But he had clearly intended to use all of them, for the
factual notes from Porter are interspersed with suggestions
for newspaper elaboration. Two of these suggestive notes,
those concerning Shiloh and Bethel, are long, and virtual
outlines for *Alta* letters, but they were nevertheless to be of
no use to Clemens for on the actual journey he never visited
those places. Only his notes concerning Jezreel and Joseph's
Tomb have any corollaries in his newspaper correspondence.

Perhaps the chief importance of these preliminary notes
lies in what they reveal of Clemens' preconceptions and the
manner in which these were later developed. For example, in
the notes concerning Nazareth he wrote:

Latin Convent & Church—the church covers the ancient home of
Jos & Mary—down 15 steps into a grotto in the hill-side—(the[y]
run a good many grottoes—well, grottos are durable—but an
infernal piece of cheek to &c) in it is a beautiful altar—Mary said
to have stood there & received the Annunciation. Staircase to
Mary's kitchen—the workshop of Joseph transformed into a
chapel—here Christ worked at his trade.

All these details were taken from Porter.[26] The parenthetical interjection suggests how Clemens planned to expand
the notes into a passage for a newspaper letter, a sardonic
undercutting of the presumed authenticity of the monuments, and this predisposition is reinforced by Porter who
also implies a certain disbelief ("In front of the door . . . is
a broad flight of 15 steps leading down to the shrine—a
grotto of course. . . . Such is the *Latin* 'Holy Grotto' of
Nazareth. . . ."[27] Clemens' facts and skeptical tone both

[26] Unpublished Notebook No. 9, Typescript, p. 13; cf. *Porter,*
p. 361.

[27] *Porter,* p. 361.

derived from Porter, and when Clemens came later to write of the Grotto of the Annunciation in his letter concerning Nazareth this preconception was little changed:

They have got the "Grotto" of the Annunciation here;
and just as convenient to it as one's throat is to his mouth, they have got also the Virgin's Kitchen, and even her sitting-room, where she and Joseph watched the infant Savior play with Hebrew toys eighteen hundred years ago. All under one roof, and all clean, spacious, comfortable "grottoes." It seems funny that personages intimately connected with the Holy Family always lived in grottoes—in Nazareth, in Bethlehem, in imperial Ephesus—and yet nobody else in their day and generation thought of doing anything of the kind. . . . It is exceedingly strange that these tremendous events all happened in grottoes—and exceedingly fortunate, likewise, because the strongest houses must crumble to ruin in time, but a grotto in the living rock will last forever. It is a swindle—this grotto stuff— . . .[28]

The critical disbelief which is apparent occasionally in the Holy Land letters derived, then, not from his experience in Palestine itself but from the preconceptions he brought to it. However, this is not to say that Clemens' attitudes were not changed by his trip. For example, he continued his notebook memoranda in a bizarre vein with suggestions which have no counterpart in Porter:

"J. Christ & Co. Son, Carpenter & Builders." Recall infant Christ's pranks on his school-mates—striking boys dead—withering their hands—burning the dyer's cloth &c. "Joseph of Arimathea, Carpenter." "Orders executed with promptness & dispatch.—Particular attention given to thrones &c." [29]

These suggestions, fortunately, were passed over when Clemens came to write his Nazareth letter; there is nothing in his correspondence to match the sacrilegious tone of this note. Sailing toward the Holy Land, he was able to imagine a rather tasteless burlesque which, once having visited the locales, he was unwilling or unable to develop.

[28] *Alta*, February 16, 1867; *Traveling*, pp. 252–53; cf. *IA*, 528.
[29] "Unpublished Notebook no. 9" (Typescript, pp. 13–14), *MTP*.

Monday was filled with preparations, and by daybreak Tuesday the *Quaker City* was riding at anchor among twenty or thirty ships in Beirut Harbor. According to the plans of the excursion, the trip from Beirut to Damascus should have been a relatively comfortable one. No guides or elaborate preparations were needed since a French company, the Continental Stage Coach, had made a good macadam road between the two cities and ran a daily diligence over the route, and from Smyrna Duncan had telegraphed the company to reserve accommodation for thirty-six passengers on the day of their arrival in Beirut. According to this plan, the ship would be in port for five or six days before it continued to Haifa, enough time to allow passengers to travel to Damascus and return. Unfortunately, once again plans went awry. When Duncan arrived at the American Consulate that morning, he learned that only one diligence ran each day and it carried but twelve passengers. To transport all thirty-six pilgrims would require more days in Beirut than they had planned. Furthermore the Company had reserved the diligence for the excursionists for three days and expected them to use their reservation. The altercation which followed this discovery was resolved eventually with the help of the American Consul: the *Quaker City* kept its reservation, but only for twelve; the rest of the party would make new plans. It was an unhappy group which returned to the ship, for there was no easy way to determine which twelve were to proceed to Damascus via diligence, and only after much angry discussion were the invalid and older members of the company given preference. As it happened, the ship was to be delayed an extra day anyway, for when the fortunate twelve were finally agreed upon and transported to the Company offices they were informed that the Tuesday diligence had already departed and that the next coach would not leave before 4:00 A.M. the following morning.

Two dozen passengers therefore had to make new arrangements on short notice. For most of them the journey to Damascus was not possible—the Continental Stage Coach Company allowed no other carriages to use its road, and overland on horseback, the only alternative, would take too long and be very uncomfortable. The ill feelings and disappointment occasioned by this turn of events was in part assuaged by the change in itinerary which had been approved before the *Quaker City* arrived in Beirut. Damascus had been denied them, but the longer overland journey through Palestine was to allow something else in its stead. They were sorry to miss Damascus, but they were far more eager to visit places directly associated with Jesus.

The *Quaker City* remained in Beirut for six days (it left at midnight the following Sunday), and for the majority of the remaining passengers it was an uneventful week of little sight-seeing and much lounging on board the ship waiting for their cohorts to return. The view of Beirut was beautiful (it reminded some of them of Naples), but despite the view and the comfortable weather (Duncan declared it was much finer than New York at that time of year), time passed slowly and the pilgrims quickly tired of the city. Beirut was much cleaner than either Smyrna or Constantinople, but it seemed only to offer more experiences of a kind they were now used to. The bazaars soon bored. They were eager for holy land and Beirut was not that. Their activities were therefore rather commonplace. Forty excursionists visited a missionary orphanage—hardly a sight to come a quarter of the way around the world for! On Wednesday the ship was entertained by William McClure Thomson, whose book about the Holy Land, *The Land and the Book,* published in 1858, had been one of the most popular in the *Quaker City* library. They had plans to make, of course. On the weekend the passengers contracted for dragomen, the Arab guides who were to conduct their parties from Haifa overland to Jerusalem, "men," according to Moses Beach, "who, for a stipulated sum, agree to monopolize the fleecing of travellers, and provide in return at least so much of bodily nourishment as will keep the wolf, 'Hunger,' from the body." [30] It was a quiet week.

Some of the excursionists escaped the dullness of Beirut by traveling in the surrounding countryside. Beach spent three days visiting missionaries in the hills and traveling to Baalbec—a spectacular sight of Roman ruins denied those who took the diligence to Damascus. Emmeline Beach and

[30] *New York Sun,* November 5, 1867.

Mrs. Fairbanks accompanied him along with James and Rev. Bullard. Dr. Jackson and Miss Newell in company with Dr. and Mrs. Payne visited Baalbec, too, while Leary led another group to reconnoiter the Beirut environs, and the Bonds still another. For their part, Solon Severance and Sanford went overland, following the shoreline from Beirut to Haifa, there to meet Mrs. Severance and the Beach party when the ship arrived several days later.

Clemens and Dan Slote, however, made far more ambitious plans. When it was clear they would not be able to proceed to Damascus according to plan, they contracted with a dragoman to take them and six others (Jack Van Nostrand, Julius Moulton, J. W. Davis, Colonel Denny, William Church, and Dr. Birch) across to Damascus and from there south through Palestine to Jerusalem. This, of course, meant that Clemens' former plans—for which he had made his elaborate notes—were completely changed. The new itinerary was well over twice as long as the old and paralleled it only intermittently during the final third of the journey. "We are here, eight of us," he wrote his family from the office of the U.S. Consul in Beirut,

> making a contract with a dragoman to take us to Baalbec, then to Damascus, Nazareth, &c. then to Lake Genassareth (Sea of Tiberias,) then South through all the celebrated Scriptural localities to Jerusalem—then to the Dead Sea, the Cave of Macpelah and up to Joppa where the ship will be. We shall be in the saddle three weeks—we have horses, tents, provisions, arms, a dragoman and two other servants, and we pay five dollars a day a piece, in gold.[31]

It was usual for such agreements to be made through the Consulate; it insured the tourist that his dragoman was honest and the charges fair. For his fee the dragoman furnished all necessaries—tents, bedding, food, riding and baggage animals, saddles (unless, as in the case of Clemens, the tourist brought his own) and all necessary services, subject to the approval of the tourist. The dragoman paid all baksheesh (tips) to secondary guides, bought all "protection" from local shieks, and provided all escorts and general

---

[31] *Letters*, p. 136.

servants. It was expensive accommodation, but, as virtually every *Quaker City* passenger who went overland testified, it was remarkably sumptuous: the tents were spacious, the beds comfortable, the linen spotless, and the servants pleasant and hard working.

Clemens' dragoman, a Maltese Muslim named Abraham, quickly won his admiration. They were told that 24 hours was necessary to get up an entourage for such a long journey across desolate territory, and Clemens informed his family that they could not leave until two Wednesday morning. But Abraham was ready sooner than that, and the party left Beirut at three that very afternoon—a large entourage, Clemens noted, with

26 pack mules Dragoman & 19 serving men. 8 of ourselves—Col. Denny, Church, & Dr. Birch, in one large tent. Jack Van Nostrand, Davis & Moulton in the other. Dan Slote & I in the small one. 5 tents in all—3 for us—one for kitchen & one for eating saloon.[32]

They camped at 6:00 P.M. that evening and the dinner they were served ("roast mutton, roast chicken, roast goose, potatoes, bread, tea, pudding, apples, and delicious grapes") was finer than anything they had eaten for weeks, and the manner of the serving was better than they were used to on board the *Quaker City*. "They call this camping out," Clemens wrote that night in a letter to the *Alta California*. "At this rate it is a glorious privilege to be a pilgrim to the Holy Land." [33]

Clemens' letter exaggerated the length of the journey somewhat. They contracted with the dragoman for only nineteen days and only fourteen of these were actually

[32] "Unpublished Notebook no. 8" (Typescript, p. 31), *MTP*. This note differs slightly from another note which Paine published (*Notebook*, p. 84, cf: Typescript, p. 30), being heavily scratched over in pencil, not, I conjecture, because Clemens rejected its information but because it was made earlier on a blank portion of the notebook. Later, when his notes eventually arrived at this page he wished to avoid any confusion of information. The data it contains is probably more accurate than that printed by Paine, because it is contemporary with Clemens' departure from Beirut.

[33] *Alta*, December 1, 1867; *Traveling*, p. 182; cf. *IA*, p. 437.

spent "in the saddle." But if the trip was shorter than Clemens suggests, the actual traveling was every bit as strenuous as he expected. Some commentators have implied that to travel in Palestine in the heat of September was unusual not to say foolish, but contemporary authorities disagreed; Porter, for example, noted that since winter is wet and summer hot, autumn, "about the beginning of September" was the best time.[34] The heat was surely no worse than Clemens had experienced many times in Nevada and California, but it was nevertheless oppressive, and the terrain, much of it barren, rocky hills, was hard to ride through, particularly on the decrepit horse Clemens had as his mount. What's more, although Clemens' health was remarkably good throughout most of the voyage, he became ill briefly in Damascus.

However, his spirits were high when the trek began. In spite of the deficiencies of his horse, he took great pleasure in the journey. The second day out (Wednesday) the diligence rolled past them bound for Damascus with Clemens' good friend Colonel Foster among the fortunate group, and later in the day Clemens' group passed the Leary party. The scenery was stark but dramatic, with great stretches of desert giving way to craggy hillocks and, far in the distance to their right, snow-capped Mount Hermon. Early in the morning of the third day Clemens' party reached Baalbec where they remained four hours. In the early afternoon they met the Beaches and Mrs. Fairbanks, and later, just before Clemens' party left, Dr. Jackson and Miss Newell arrived on their way back to Beirut.

Abraham and his accouterments continued to please Clemens, but some of his traveling companions did not. For Moult, Jack, and Dan he had real affection which continued throughout the expedition and long after the *Quaker City* returned to New York. But he had no particular liking for Colonel Denny or Dr. Birch, and for Davis and Church he developed a profound distaste. They were necessary annoyances, for the minimum charge in getting up such an excursion was high, and fewer than eight travelers would have made the cost per person prohibitive. It can hardly be

[34] Porter, p. xlix–l.

doubted that Clemens and Dan must have canvassed all likely parties on the ship before they settled for the company of these hide-bound, sanctimonious characters. Earlier in the voyage Clemens had called all the excursionists "pilgrims"; now the term became one of opprobrium for the four older men in his Palestine party, and he, Dan, Jack, and Moult were henceforth happy "sinners." At the start of the Holy Land journey, Clemens didn't care much for the pilgrims. By its end, eleven days later, he loathed them—particularly Church—and he evidently had cause. For example, the pilgrims tried to keep the party from traveling on Sunday and succeeded. The thought of losing two days on a necessarily short journey—to say nothing of remaining piously in some unknown desolate area of Palestine for 24 sabbatical hours—struck Clemens as, at the very least, unnecessary, and the pilgrims knew from the start that the company would be on the road not one but *two* Sundays. Nevertheless, they insisted that the Sabbath be kept; the group had to be in Damascus by Saturday night so that the religious sensibilities of Church and the others would not be offended.

The point, real enough, was to be a part of a larger comic motif Clemens developed throughout *IA:* the personal inconvenience he suffered from the gross, overweening piety of the excursionists on the voyage. He implies that the demand of the pilgrims in Palestine created a pace which was difficult to maintain on non-too-healthy mounts and that the journey was made more difficult by Church's insistence on visiting places which Clemens thought unimportant. Actually, seven or eight hours on the road was not uncommon practice; Clemens' party was not pressing *unusually* hard. Furthermore, while Church evidently prided himself on his knowledge of the Bible and its historical locale and while he was officious and apparently left no stone unturned (or, if we are to believe Clemens, untaken) in his search for memorabilia, their route was a standard one. They visited no site which was not strongly recommended by the guidebook, and undoubtedly Church was a useful source for some of the historical details which Clemens put into his notebooks en route to Jerusalem. Clemens' disaffection derived not from the procedural details of the journey but from the characters of the pilgrims which he was later to think fair game for his satire.

Clemens' intention is made clear in his manner of using his notebook when he wrote *IA*. On the evening of the day they visited Baalbec, he noted:

Rode seven hours, partly through wild, rocky scenery and camped at ten-thirty on the banks of a pretty stream, near a Syrian village. Two horses lame, and the others worn out.[35]

When he used the note in *IA* he distorted it to suggest a dissatisfaction with Church and the others which he apparently did not feel at the time. He suggests that the day was long because not only did "the pilgrims" insist on "doubling the legitimate stages" of the journey to avoid traveling on Sunday but also they made the group visit Figia Fountain that day

because Baalam's ass had drank there once. So we journeyed on, through the terrible hills and deserts and the roasting sun, and then far into the night, seeking the honored pool of Baalam's ass, the patron saint of all pilgrims like us. I find no entry but this in my note-book:

And then he "quotes" the note above:

"Rode to-day, altogether, thirteen hours, through deserts, partly, and partly over barren, unsightly hills, and latterly through wild, rocky scenery, and camped at about eleven o'clock at night on the banks of a limpid stream, near a Syrian village. Do not know its name—do not wish to know it—want to go to bed. Two horses lame (mine and Jack's) and the others worn out. Jack and I walked three or four miles, over the hills, and led the horses. Fun—but of a mild type" [p. 453].

He exaggerates the length of the riding and ignores the praise ("pretty") he had made of the locale, in order to intensify the pretended inconvenience "the pilgrims" had forced on him. Actually, Figia Fountain was not seen until the following day; it *was* visited at Church's insistence and Clemens *did* make a note that "that infernal fountain took

[35] *Notebook*, p. 87.

us at least 2 hours out of our way" but it was extravagantly
praised in Porter's *Handbook* and the detour did not keep
them from arriving at Damascus by late afternoon. By the
time he came to write *IA*, Clemens was so soured by the
cumulative effect of the pilgrims, by their querulousness and
their incessant bickering among themselves, that he deliberately distorted his notes and recollections to suggest dissatisfaction at the time.

But this disaffection was to come only after the journey
across Palestine was completed. Clemens' initial excitement
was strong enough to encourage him to write two *Alta*
letters on the trip itself. One (*Alta* no. 27) detailing his
delight in the dragoman's arrangements was written during
the evening of the first day out; the other (*Alta* no. 28) was
written at the end of the second day and suggests how keen
his appetite for the trip was. These, however, were the only
letters he was to write in Palestine—and they were the last
letters he was to write until the *Quaker City* left Egypt almost four week later. By his count he had now written 42
letters—he thought he need write only eight more to complete his contract—and the journey was beginning to tire
him. But in spite of this he probably would have written
other letters in Palestine had he not become ill.

The last twenty-four hours we staid in Damascus I lay prostrate
with a violent attack of cholera, or cholera morbus, and therefore I
had a good chance and a good excuse to lay there on that wide
divan and take an honest rest. I had nothing to do but listen to the
pattering of the fountains and take medicine and throw it up
again. It was a dangerous recreation, but it was pleasanter than
traveling in Syria.[36]

They were not merely the "last" twenty-four hours in Damascus, they were the *only* twenty-four hours there, but he
could not tell his readers that. Apparently he had an intesti-
nal infection exacerbated by riding in the sun without an
umbrella on the third day out and bathing in the icy waters
of the River Abana at the "infernal fountain." "Abed all
day yesterday," he wrote in his notebook, "—got enough of
Damascus. Don't want to see any more of it." [37]

[36] *Alta*, December 29, 1867; *Traveling*, p. 204; cf. *IA*, p. 465.
[37] *Notebook*, p. 88.

Clemens' illness was something of a crisis, for he was traveling on a very rigorous schedule and any long delay would have meant not merely cutting short the trip through Palestine but possibly missing the *Quaker City* altogether. Throughout that Sunday in Damascus it looked as though he might not be able to travel the following day, and, except for Dan, his fellow travellers were not disposed to wait for him, for that would have meant reducing the time they would spend in Jerusalem. To further complicate the danger, the *Quaker City* was that very night leaving Beirut for Haifa—he could not return to the ship except by continuing overland and that required more strength than, in the depths of his illness, he thought he was likely to have. The eminence of disaster was therefore probably as efficacious in his recovery as the ministrations of Dr. Birch who prescribed the usual draughts for him. In any case, his return to health—or the semblance of it—was speedy, and on the next day he was determined to go on. He even saw a bit of Damascus. On the morning of his departure, although very weak, he "took a jackass and an Arab to drive it" and spent two hours seeing some of the famous sights. Most of what he saw, he concluded, was not "genuine," and he had very little interest in sight-seeing. "Enough of Damascus," he wrote at the end of scarcely 200 words about the city in his notebook. (Some time later these brief notes were to serve as the basis for two long letters describing the city and its history.) [38] His illness interrupted his correspondence. In the evening of the day after he left Damascus, he began another letter (*Alta* no. 29), but he was too exhausted to complete it. Instead of writing letters, he decided to make fuller comments in his notebook and to leave the actual composition to that later time when he would be comfortably on board the *Quaker City*.

[38] In *Notebook*, Paine published an apocryphal story which duplicated these events with Dan the victim and Clemens his outspoken defender and nurse. Like much of Paine's information, this is mere hearsay and is supported by nothing in Clemens' notebooks, newspaper correspondence, letters, or *IA*. Paine's information, derived very indirectly and without documentation of any kind, was presumably from Church—surely the most unlikely source imaginable.

Shortly before noon Monday they left Damascus on what was to be the hottest and most distressing day of the overland excursion. Their next objective was Banias (Caesarea Phillipi), and to save time they elected to take the short, two-day route over near–desert territory rather than the four-day trip through more interesting country along the Sibarany River. The journey was particularly distressing for Clemens because he had no umbrella or sunglasses. The procedure followed by dragomen was to pack the sleeping tents and baggage as soon as possible after the passengers had arisen and to send these accouterments on ahead of the party to the site of the next night's encampment by as fast and direct a route as possible. The tourists, accompanied by their dragoman and such servants as were necessary to prepare and serve lunch, continued by their own route, confident that when they arrived at the encampment for the night their tents would be pitched and ready for their rest before dinner. Clemens had inadvertently packed his umbrella and sunglasses in baggage which did not travel with him during the day, and his cork helmet was not enough protection. As he described that day, "The sun flowed down like the shafts of fire that stream out before a blow-pipe," [39] and, weakened from his illness in Damascus, he found the journey nearly intolerable.

Four hours out of Damascus they passed the traditional place of Paul's conversion near Juneh, pausing only long enough to take a last look at the green oasis of Damascus far behind them. Ahead was only rocky desolate land, and after another three or four hours they were greatly relieved to stop at Kefr Hauwar, a village slightly over half-way to Banias and one so nondescript that when Clemens came to write of it later he couldn't remember its name and called it "Jonesborough." It had slight fame as one of the reputed tombs of Nimrod, an assumption discounted by all the guidebooks but nevertheless used for a comic addition by Clemens when he expanded his letter (which did not mention Nimrod) into *IA*. The journey the next morning was a little more comfortable. By noon they had entered the hills near Banias and after lunch they climbed to the summit of

[39] *Alta*, December 29, 1867; *Traveling*, p. 204; cf. *IA*, 465.

Mount Subeibeh to visit the renowned Castle Subeibeh (Clemens' "Castle of Banias") which commanded a remarkable view of the green and fertile valley of the Banias River—their first glimpse of Palestine itself.

The mountain is in Bashan & is covered with olive groves & the oaks of Bashan. It is crowned with the grandest old ruined castle in the world— . . . all of massive dressed stone masonry with beveled edges—very well preserved—" [40]

This note was later strangely transformed into the long and somewhat melodramatic description of a "crumbling" castle destroyed by the growth of giant trees, a transformation probably derived from a confusion in his memory between the Castle and the ruined Citadel of Banias which he saw later the same day. In the late afternoon they descended to Banias and camped in the middle of a beautiful olive grove near the Banias Fountain, one of the principal sources of the Jordan River. After two hot and dusty days in the saddle they plunged into the pool with relish. It was "so icy that if I did not know this was a main source of the sacred river," he wrote later, "I would expect harm to come of it." [41]

Rested, the group began to revive. "This is the first place we have ever seen whose pavements were trodden by Jesus Christ," Clemens wrote in his notes, and this realization evoked in him an uncharacteristic religious awe which quickly became the basis for ironic commentary, for in Banias he found greater human degradation and suffering than he had seen before. Everywhere they went they were besieged by hungry, crippled, verminous beggars. One of the women who clustered about their breakfast tent the next morning had a child with festered eyes which Dr. Birch treated with an antiseptic solution. "Christ knew how to preach to these simple, childish, ignorant, superstitious, disease-tortured vagabonds," Clemens wrote. *"he healed the sick.* They flocked to our poor human doctor this morning . . . and they worshiped him with their eyes while they did not know as yet whether there was virtue in his simples or

[40] "Unpublished Notebook no. 8" (Typescript, p. 34), *MTP.*
[41] *Alta* December 29, 1867; *Traveling,* p. 207; cf. *IA,* 470.

not." [42] Clemens was in awe of the locales he was visiting, but he was, nevertheless, somewhat cynical when he wrote about them, as the implied analogy between Dr. Birch and Christ suggests. The people evoked ambivalent reactions from him. He cared no more for the Palestinians than he had for the Syrians, or the Turks—or for that matter, the American Indian, to whom he compared them. They were filthy and they were beggars, and to his mind apparently both by choice. They watched his every motion, he said, with "that vile, uncomplaining impoliteness" which he had experienced from Indians. Such a condition and such a manner was shocking to Clemens; it was impossible for him to be sympathetic with it. These people he thought a lower form of life, and he necessarily found the cause of their damnation in some fault inherent in themselves. Even children, for whom Clemens usually had particularly compassionate feelings, were not excused from his judgment. One of those who came to Dr. Birch to have her sick child treated was the daughter of the local sheik. The daughter, wrote Clemens, was the

only Syrian female we have seen yet who was not so sinfully ugly that she couldn't smile after 10 o'clock Saturday night without breaking the Sabbath. Her child was a hard lot, though—there wasn't enough of it to make a pie, and the poor little thing looked so pleadingly up at all who came near it (as if it had an idea that now was its chance or never), that we were filled with compassion which was genuine and not put on.[43]

It is a characteristic observation: the beauty of the mother is remarked, but in the context of the ugliness of Syrian women in general, and sympathy for the child does not cancel the comic impression of it as something essentially animal, too small to be eaten.

Their journey on the previous two days had been too dry; the road away from Banias was too wet. "Jordan road hard to travel," Clemens quoted in his notebooks, and that was to be a remarkably understated description of the following two days' travel. Their next objective was Tiberias, and

[42] *Alta*, November 9, 1867; *Traveling*, p. 212; cf. *IA*, p. 474.
[43] *Alta*, November 9, 1867; *Traveling*, p. 212–13; cf. *IA*, p. 475.

once again they selected the direct route between the cities, which also happened to be the dreariest and least interesting. Had they added only one more day to their itinerary they might have passed through scenery famed as the most beautiful in Palestine: along the verdant mountain plateau which led through Kedesh to Safed (from which the most renown view of the Jordan valley could be had) and down through rich valleys to the Sea of Galilee, a route filled with important historical sights, monumental ruins, and picturesque vistas. Instead Clemens' party traveled a route through barren desert and alongside mosquito-infested swamps for most of the first day, and through rocky passes—now tortuously ascending, now precipitously descending—through most of the second. It was a remarkably bad choice and one which cannot be accounted for: either they were now governed by a neurasthenic desire to have the whole excursion over with, or the haste with which they made their plans before they left Beirut precluded any careful selection of route. From Banias their path was rocky and overrun with water which caused it now and again to merge with the marshes on either side. Their itinerary went west to Tell el Kady (the Dan of biblical literature), the largest of the springs which fed the Jordan river, then south along the River Leddan through lush arable land, only a few acres of which, Clemens noted, were under cultivation. The hills that swept down to the river's edge were dotted now and again with sheep and Bashan bulls and attendant Bedouin shepherds, but despite the water there were few trees. All day they traveled beneath a desert sun, and they were glad to discover their camp that night was at a mill near Ain Mellahah, near the "waters of Merom," the usual resting place for travelers between Banias and Tiberias.

The area was famous for malaria mosquitos and wild swine, both of which found an ideal breeding ground in the surrounding marshes, and it was an uncomfortable night. The area was also notorious for bandits, a profession, Porter had noted, which "if not actually encouraged, is at least tolerated by the modern rulers of Syria." [44] In the middle of the night a group of wandering Arabs stoned their camp and

[44] *Porter,* p. 438.

unsuccessfully tried to stampede the horses. In his letters, Clemens was later to belittle the need for their armed escort, calling it a "plausible lie about the country beyond this being infested by ferocious Arabs," [45] but at the time he must have thought the danger real enough. In the morning the travelers were as glad to leave Ain Mellahah as they had been, the previous evening, to enter it.

Their route now became drearier than ever. It lay through ridges of sheer rock along paths which were as steep as horses could ascend and so precipitous that riders had to dismount to keep their horses from falling. The whole of the way was strewn with huge, rounded boulders of black basalt. Here and there the desolate country gave way to stretches of rich soil—wholly uncultivated—in which thick clumps of stout thistles and grass as high as the horses' bridles choked their path. There was not a village, not even a house along the route, and in the whole day they saw only three other human beings—Bedouin shepherds. They passed a ruined khan called "Joseph's Well," but although Clemens was to use it in his letters as an excuse for a long retelling of the Joseph story, it was, by all accounts, a filthy sty of no historical significance. Their trail led downward, and, passing through a desolate landscape which reminded Clemens of Nevada, they caught occasional glimpses of the Sea of Galilee. In his notes he said they "passed Safed, and close to that Bethsaida" [46] a comment which suggests how confused he was about his actual route since Safed on the summit of a mountain, and Bethsaida, on the shore of Galilee are not "close" and his own route was well away from Safed.

They finally reached the Sea of Galilee (Sea of Tiberias, Lake Gennesaret) at the traditional site of Capernaum, a place marked only by scarcely distinguishable heaps of stones and rubbish. It was a place having many associations with Jesus: "Christ's dwelling place," Clemens wrote in his notes, "where he performed a great many miracles. (Jairus' daughter, I think.)" [47] but it was nevertheless a disappointing place, and after such a trip even the Sea of Galilee failed

[45] *Alta,* January 5, 1868; *Traveling,* p. 217; cf. *IA,* p. 482.

[46] *Notebook,* pp. 91–92.

[47] *Ibid.,* p. 92; Paine omitted the parenthetical phrase; cf: Unpublished notebook no. 8, *MTP.*

to inspire. It was, he wrote, a "solemn, sailless, tintless lake, reposing within its rim of yellow hills and low, steep banks, and looking just as expressionless and unpoetical (when you leave its sublime history out of the question,) as any bath-tub on earth." The scene was, he said, "an exquisitely dismal solitude." [48] They lunched on the shore and afterward bathed in the lake ("a blessed privilege in this roasting climate"), and, as Clemens noted, the group "tried to get a boat, and didn't." Later in an *Alta* letter Clemens was to describe with comic relish how the penny-pinching pilgrims failed to hire a sailboat to take them about the Lake and fell to quarreling among themselves as a result. The pilgrims might not have been as eager to sail as Clemens suggested nor their cupidity as avid as he described, but the incident evidently intensified the bickering among the excursionists which had grown more insistent as the journey became more difficult and tiring. "How the pilgrims abused each other!" he wrote.

Each said it was the other's fault, and each in turn denied it. No word was spoken by the sinners—even the mildest sarcasm might have been dangerous at such a time. Sinners that have been kept down and had examples held up to them, and suffered frequent lectures, and so put upon in a moral way and in the matter of going slow and being serious and bottling up slang, and so crowded in regard to the matter of being proper and always and forever behaving, that their lives have become a burden to them, would not lag behind pilgrims at such a time as this, and wink furtively, and be joyful, and commit other such crimes, because it wouldn't occur to them to do it.[49]

Later in *IA* he added that having put up with much from the pilgrims he enjoyed seeing them quarrel. "We took an unworthy satisfaction in seeing them fall out," (p. 499) he wrote.

They proceeded to Magdala, which Clemens called "the rattiest, rustiest, dirtiest little collection of mud hovels, tattooed women and sore-eyed children in Palestine," [50] and continued to Tiberias following the shoreline along the base

[48] *Alta,* January 19, 1868; *Traveling,* p. 226; cf. *IA,* p. 508.
[49] *Alta,* January 26, 1868; *Traveling,* p. 232.
[50] *Notebook,* p. 92.

of Mount Hattin. Tiberias was unprepossessing. The ruins, which marked the spot of one of the most sacred cities in Palestine, were in a sad state of dilapidation—scarcely a column was left standing—and the modern village was another of the filthy clusters of animal hovels which Clemens had been encountering with distaste for the week past. His cynical dissatisfaction was rapidly becoming complete. "If all the poetry and nonsense that have been discharged upon the fountains and the bland scenery of Palestine were collected in a book," he wrote, "it would make a most valuable volume to burn." [51] Their tents were waiting for them, and after the desolate and discouraging trip of the day they were havens. The party was somewhat refreshed by bathing in the Sea of Galilee before they retired that night and again before breakfast the next morning, but they were eager to leave Tiberias.

Their next stop was to be Nazareth, a six-hour ride away, but before they could proceed they had to pay baksheesh to the Sheik of Tiberias—a rather elaborate procedure which involved hiring one of his servants ("a wretched-looking scalliwag" Clemens called him) as "protection" from the tribesmen (the Sheik's own) along the route to Nazareth. They were now on the main caravan route which stretched from Egypt to Damascus, and the road was a good one. In four hours they reached the summit of Mount Tabor, the traditional site of Christ's transfiguration. "It is mentioned all through the Bible," Clemens wrote in his notebook. "New convent, and ruins of an old one built by the crusaders. Also ruins of Joshua's time." [52] The convent was Greek and welcomed them for lunch. Twelve hundred feet above the Lake, they rested on cushioned benches while monks served them cups of excellent coffee. To the north and east lay a panorama of country they had crossed during the previous four days, from the mountains surrounding Banias to the Sea of Galilee, the whole of which was now visible. In the opposite direction, Clemens could see the route they were to travel for the next two days: Nazareth to the west and, south of Nazareth, the Plain of Esdraelon, Jenin, and

[51] *Alta,* January 26, 1868; *Traveling,* p. 229.
[52] *Notebook,* p. 93.

Shechem. It was the best view he had had thus far on the journey.

After lunch they descended Mount Tabor and continued to Nazareth, two hours away. The villages through which they passed were so undistinguished and contained ruins so nondescript that even the most imaginative traveller was hard pressed to imagine Jesus living and preaching in them, but the geography of the land was unchanged in 2,000 years and Clemens saw in the terrain about him "the hills that were familiar to the eyes of Jesus," and the association excited him. Nazareth was the most thriving village they had encountered since Damascus. "Glass windows,—some 2-story—many shops," Clemens noted. But there were the usual unpleasant sights, too: "—many cone-shaped mud hovels;—camels & fantastic Arabs & dirty children." He spent the afternoon sight-seeing.

Saw the grotto of the Annunciation [he wrote in his notebook]— the pillar miraculously sustained—old columns by Saint Helena, mother of Constantine—Grotto where lived Joseph, Mary & infant Christ—Workshop of Joseph & Jesus. Great Stone on which Jesus & disciples rested after return from Sea of Galilee. Synagogue where Jesus taught & from which Jews took him to throw him down the mountain, when he "passed from their presence." Fountain of the virgin.

—all of which he was later to describe–and to discount–in his letters to the *Alta.* "Imagine Christ's 30 years of life in the slow village of Nazareth" [53] he wrote. It was clearly hard for him to do so. The notes he had made on board ship indicate his essential skepticism about historical monuments, but only the actual experience of travelling the "barbarous" trail from Damascus to Nazareth could have prepared him for what he saw there. "Dirt and rags and squalor; vermin, hunger and wretchedness; savage costumes, savage weapons and looks of hate—" he wrote to the *Alta,* "these are the things that meet one at every step in Nazareth." [54] His reaction against the city was so strong he

---

[53] "Unpublished Notebook no. 8" (Typescript, p. 39), *MTP.*

[54] *Alta,* February 16, 1868; *Traveling,* p. 251. Clemens omitted this remark in *IA.*

had to omit much of his criticism when he wrote *IA*. But his aversion was not unique. Mrs. Fairbanks, who, along with the rest of the Cleveland party had left Nazareth only two days before, was no more impressed with it than Clemens. "A filthy, unattractive spot," she called it.[55] Virtually none of the *Quaker City* passengers was impressed with the place, despite its association with the childhood of Jesus.

The next day, Saturday, September 21, they made their usual early start. "Left Nazareth and its chalk hills at 7:30," Clemens wrote in his notes, "came down a high steep mountain and galloped across the Plain of Esdraelon to Endor, the rustiest of all of them, almost."[56] It was, he thought, a fit place for the witch Saul met there. Nain, an hour farther on, was no more distinguished, "very old and ratty," he called it. They passed the ruins of the mountain fortress "el-Fuleh," the site of a famous victory of Napoleon over Kleber seventy years before, and proceeded to Shunem and Jezreel, the city where, as Clemens noted, "Ahab, King of Judah, lived in splendor with his awful heifer, Jezebel."[57] They continued across the Valley of Jezreel, stopped briefly at the large fountain of Ain Jalud, and then hurried on to their camp at Jenin, a green garden in the midst of an otherwise desolate countryside.

In Jenin they camped near the tents of Dr. Jackson's party. Jackson, Julia Newell, and Dr. and Mrs. Payne had disembarked at Haifa six days before and like Clemens had an eventful and generally unpleasant trip. Julia had been thrown from her horse before they left Haifa, and this had delayed their departure from that port for a day; on their first day out, their caravan was attacked by Bedouins and several of their servants badly injured; Mrs. Payne was quite ill with a bad cold, brought on, Dr. Payne assured everyone who would listen, by her refusal to follow his orders and remain covered during the chilly nights; and "Robin Goodfellow," as Julia called Dr. Jackson, was also ill with a mild sunstroke. "Poor Robin's countenance has turned from fair and ruddy to crimson and purple," she wrote home, "his lips are parched and his eyes, so wont to

[55] *Herald*, November 22, 1867.
[56] *Notebook*, p. 94.
[57] *Ibid.*, pp. 94–5.

gleam with kindly humor, are dull and sad." [58] Jackson's party stayed in Jenin over Sunday to allow him to recover.

The pilgrims in Clemens' party were also determined to remain over Sunday to avoid trespassing the Sabbath with travel. A day's rest should have been attractive to Clemens, but he was in a fever to get to Jerusalem, and the thought of spending a whole day at Jenin, despite its beautiful view and verdant surroundings, filled him with anguish. The "sinners" therefore decided to go on ahead without the tents, and at one A.M. the following morning they left Jenin with a small retinue and two-days' supplies, accompanied by Dr. Birch, who evidently decided that he was willing to risk Hell if he could quit the Palestine desert a day sooner.

Having determined to travel on Sunday, they decided to travel long. They rode until seven that night, stopping seldom, through an uncompromising countryside. Mrs. Severance, who had traveled the same route the day before Clemens' party, described it with disfavor as an uninhabited wasteland where one was in constant danger from Bedouin tribesmen.[59] But neither the terrain nor the fear of bandits appreciably slowed the sinners on their sacrilegious journey. At daybreak they passed Dothan, the traditional site of Joseph's pit, without stopping (so much for Clemens' elaborate preliminary notes on Dothan!). They passed through the terraced hills of Samaria throughout the morning and entered the city of Samaria at noon. It was, Clemens concluded, a "ruin" of a city. He had little interest in it, and what he had was ill-founded—he mistook a church ruin for Jacob's well where Jesus met the woman of Samaria, an error he discovered when he visited the actual well several hours later. The sinners discovered something of the antipathy of the local residents, too, when a small boy threw a stone at Dr. Birch. A day or so earlier when Mr. James had stopped to photograph the view, his party was badly stoned, and Kate Brown injured. If this was, indeed, the home of the Good Samaritan, Clemens thought, he must have been "the only one that ever lived there." [60]

The route from Samaria took them through a beautiful,

[58] *Janesville* (Wis.) *Gazette,* November 23, 1867.

[59] *Journal Letters,* p. 163–64.

[60] *Notebook,* p. 96.

fertile valley, and by three they arrived at Shechem (Nablus) and had lunch near where the Moses Beach party was camped enjoying a Sabbath rest. Shechem was noted for containing what most authorities believed to be the oldest extant Biblical manuscripts, but despite Clemens' suggestion that they stop to see these archives, his party continued on their way immediately after lunch. However, just outside Shechem they paused briefly at Joseph's Tomb and Jacob's Well ("both well authenticated"), and for the first time the notes he had made prior to landing in Beirut were useful to him. At 7:30 they reached Lubban (Libonia of the Bible) and stopped for the night. Except for their short stay in Shechem they had been traveling continuously for nearly nineteen hours.

Mrs. Fairbanks, the Severances, and the rest of the Cleveland party were also at Lubban, having selected that rather desolate spot for *their* sabbatical rest. Rev. Bullard was one of the group and, perhaps as a result, theirs was the most fervent "pilgrimage" being made through Palestine that week. Each night after dinner they held a prayer meeting, and after hymns and thanksgiving Rev. Bullard would read the parts of the Bible appropriate to the locale they had seen that day. Clemens' group did not discover their shipmates' presence until the next morning, however, and they camped out that night. "Slept on the ground in front of an Arab house. Lice, fleas, horses, jackasses, chickens, and, worse than all, Arabs for company all night," Clemens wrote the next day.[61]

They were bone-tired, but they got little rest, and it is not surprising that they broke camp at 2:30 the next morning, determined to make Jerusalem as quickly and as comfortably as possible. Traveling in the early morning was preferable to riding through the baking heat of the afternoon sun. They were on the road about an hour when the Cleveland party caught up with them, and the entire group rode together toward Jerusalem. They made no tourist detours that day but plodded as directly as they could for the Holy City. At daybreak they were near Shiloh, but it was a mile or so out of their way and they shunned it, despite Clemens'

[61] *Ibid.*, p. 97.

earlier interest in that locale. At Beth-el, the site of Jacob's Ladder, they paused for a brief rest. Clemens had written nearly 1,500 words about Beth-el in his preliminary notes but in his haste and state of exhaustion it had little interest for him; "nothing left now but a shapeless mass of ruins," he noted. Prior to his trek, Gibeon (El Gib) had seemed to him important enough to write a long note about, but now he refused to go two miles out of his way to see that village. The terrain was as difficult as any he had yet passed through. "All the way to Jerusalem," he wrote, "rocks—rocks—rocks! Roads infernal. Thought we never *would* get there." [62]

But they did. By noon the party had arrived at Neby Samwil (Mizpeh), a hill rising abruptly 600 feet above the Plain of Gibeon through which they had passed. It was the culminating point of all the hills surrounding the Holy City, and from its summit one had a wider view than from any other point in southern Palestine. To the west, barely visible on the horizon, one could see Joppa nearly 40 miles away, where the *Quaker City* then lay at anchor; to the south, the Frank Mountain with Bethlehem clustered on a projecting ridge near it; and at his feet lay a low ridge of ashen hills, behind which, looking as though it had been pressed into a sunken valley, Jerusalem, its minarets and domes gleaming in the midday sunlight. "We dismounted," Clemens wrote later, "and looked, with very few words of conversation, across the wide intervening valley for an hour or more; and noted those prominent features of the city that pictures make familiar to all men from their school days till their death." [63] The silence was the result less of awe than of exhaustion. "All of us were too tired to feel enthusiastic or the least bit solemn," [64] Mrs. Severance wrote later. They had traveled a great way over difficult ground and in intense heat, and Jerusalem was less a holy destination than a place where they could, in comfort, retire.

The Cleveland party found its tents pitched outside the walls between the Joppa and the Damascus gates. Many of the *Quaker City* passengers were already there. The Gib-

[62] "Unpublished Notebook no. 8" (Typescript, p. 44), *MTP*.
[63] *Alta*, March 1, 1868; *Traveling*, p. 264; cf. *IA*, p. 556.
[64] *Journal Letters*, p. 173.

sons' tent was nearby; so was Dr. Brown's. Those pilgrims who had, like Duncan, come overland from Joppa were camped there, and had been for nearly three days. "The groups of tents with the stars and stripes fluttering above them looked like an American encampment," wrote Mrs. Fairbanks.[65]

Clemens and the other "sinners" were, of course, well in advance of *their* tents, and they entered Jerusalem by Damascus Gate and proceeded at once to the Mediterranean Hotel, the best in the city. Their accommodations were none too good, but they were exhausted, having slept little and ridden much during the three days past, and they spent the rest of Monday as Clemens said, "loafing."

Hurrying ahead to Jerusalem had given Clemens an extra day there, and after a good night's rest he was ready to spend Tuesday seeing all the sights of the city. It did not take him long. The city was smaller than he had expected and remarkably compact. He discovered that "a fast walker could go outside the walls of Jerusalem and walk entirely around the city in an hour,"[66] and he found in this concentration what he had come to believe was the usual "Arab disease"—filth, cripples, and begging. "Rags, wretchedness, poverty and dirt, those signs and symbols that indicate the presence of Moslem rule more surely than the Crescent flag itself, abound. . . . Jerusalem is mournful, and dreary, and lifeless. I would not desire to live here."[67] In his letters he assumed the proper interest and said he "naturally" visited the Church of the Holy Sepulcher first. In fact, his first visit was to the Mosque of Omar, the "Dome of the Rock," which only ten years before had been opened to non-Muslims. He filled his notebook with references to its historical and architectural details, largely discounting all the miraculous associations which his Arab guide assiduously described to him. His tour from the mosque was the traditional one: first to the Pool of Bethesda and then to the Palace of Caiaphas, on to "Pilate's House" and along the Via Dolorosa, the traditional route Christ took carrying the cross to Calvary. Like most of the excursionists, he was skeptical of it all, and

[65] *Herald,* December 5, 1867.

[66] *Alta,* March 8, 1868; *Traveling,* p. 266; cf. *IA,* p. 558.

[67] *Alta,* March 8, 1868; *Traveling,* p. 267; cf. *IA,* 559–60.

when he described the scene to his *Alta* readers he did so sardonically. About the spot where Christ was supposed to have dropped the cross and broken a pillar Clemens suggested mock wonderment: "We might have thought this story the idle invention of priests and guides, but the broken column was still there to show for itself. One cannot go behind the evidences." Later when he came to rewriting the letters into *IA*, however, he expunged the impression of blatant disbelief and for this comment substituted "such was the guide's story when he halted us before the broken column." [68] The change is typical of the general shift in tone which Clemens' comments underwent between the experience in the Holy Land itself and his later description of it in *IA*.

At the end of the Via Dolorosa was, of course, the Church of the Holy Sepulcher which encompassed under a single roof all the significant sites directly associated with the crucifixion—the pillar of flagellation, the hill of Calvary, and the place of Christ's entombment. His notes reveal both what he saw and the attitude with which he remembered it:

Church of the Holy Sepulchre
Organ & chanting of the Monks
Repairing the Dome
Dim Cathedral light of many smoking tapers.
Maximilian's gift.
Place where Helena found the Cross—& her chapel & where she
    sat.
Pillar of Flagellation.
Stocks.
Place where soldier was beheaded who said Truly this was the son
    of God.
Place where John & Mary stood looking at Christ on the X when
    he said Woman, behold thy son—Behold thy mother.
Place where Jesus appeared to Mary in the Garden.
Place where the women came at early dawn & saw the angels at
    the Sepulchre.
The rent rock & the holes where the 3 crosses stood.
Navel of the world in the Greek Chapel, where Adam's dust came
    from.
Russian gift to the Cross.

[68] *Alta*, March 29, 1868; *Traveling*, p. 282; cf. *IA*, p. 574.

Sword & spurs of Godfrey of Bulloigne, first king of Jerusalem
   (genuine) worn by Patriarch of Greek Church at Installation.
Crown of thorns.[69]

The parenthetical remark "(genuine)" indicates that he
discounted most of what he saw, and the three letters he was
to write to the *Alta* describing the church suggest that he
actually accepted only the site of Calvary as historically
verified. The rest he thought just so many "imaginary holy
places created by the monks." [70] It was an impression generally shared by the excursionists. Mrs. Severance for instance
was generally unmoved by the church. "I do not confess to
feelings of solemnity during our visit," she wrote home.
"Priests chanting mass over the Stone of Unction and clouds
of incense do not make holy those places I am sure could
never have been hallowed." [71] And Mrs. Fairbanks was even
more emphatic: "no sacred presence sanctified the place,"
she wrote.[72]

This reaction suggests the larger dissatisfaction which the
Quaker City pilgrims had with the Holy Land. Most of
them were greatly disillusioned by the experiences they had
there. True, they were exhausted by the rapid march across
desolate country, and many were ill in Jerusalem—they
were not in the best state of mind or body to see and
appreciate holy sights. But even had the conditions under
which they traveled been more comfortable and their pace
slower, they would not have been satisfied, they would not
have found what they sought. They came looking for a
Sunday School supplement; they found a near-desert Middle Eastern country, and they preferred the image they
brought to the one they found. "I would rather remember
'that sweet story of old' as I learned it in my childhood,"
Mrs. Fairbanks wrote, "than encumber it with any of the
unlovely associations of modern Palestine." [73]

The guidebooks they had read had done nothing to prepare them for this disappointment. As Clemens wrote:

[69] "Unpublished Notebook no. 8" (Typescript, pp. 47–8), *MTP;*
incompletely printed in *Notebook,* p. 98.

[70] *Alta,* March 22, 1868; *Traveling,* p. 279; cf. *IA,* 570.

[71] *Journal Letters,* p. 177.

[72] *Herald,* December 5, 1867.

[73] *Ibid.*

All these books of travel managed, somehow, to leave us with a sort of vague notion that Palestine was very beautiful—a notion that we were about to enter a modified form of fairy land. And so a bitter disappointment awaited us. The fairy land was modified too much. It was a howling wilderness instead of a garden. This has incensed us against all our Holy Land authors, and inclines us to say intemperate things about the land itself.[74]

It is true that some of the commentaries they read ignored the barren geography of Palestine and instead dwelt with sentimental fervor on its "spiritual associations." William Prime's *Tent Life in the Holy Land* was the most famous of these commentaries, and as such it was singled out for special criticism. " 'Tent Life in the Holy Land,' is a charming book to read in your library," wrote Mrs. Fairbanks, "but when with your finger upon a certain line of glowing description you look around in vain for the original of the picture, a feeling of resentment comes over you as when you have been deceived." [75] Clemens attacked Prime in his letters to the *Alta*, and when he transformed his letters into *IA* that attack became a full-fledged campaign against the sentimentality he found replete in Prime, a man who apparently wept at every major scriptural monument in Palestine. ("He never bored but he struck water," Clemens declared.) But though many of the books they had read were Sunday School auxiliaries, all of them were not. Porter's *Handbook*—which they all thought the most authoritative concerning the region—did not describe Palestine as a "garden." The fault lay not with Prime and his sentiment but with the pilgrims and theirs. They expected a garden in a subtropical, near-desert land not because the books they read had promised them a garden but because the sentimental religious drama they played out in their imaginations demanded such scenery. If Prime was bad, they were not much better. Clemens himself, when he came to write the description of his travels in the Holy Land, toned down his criticism, omitting the worst of his censure (such as the "howling wilderness" comment), and generally saying nothing which would dislodge the romantic preconceptions which

[74] *Alta*, April 5, 1868, *Traveling*, p. 304.
[75] *Herald*, December 5, 1867.

his audience had of the Bible country. He was not to pretend that Palestine was a garden, surely, and he was more honest about what he saw than most of his contemporaries, but he, like Prime, shaped his view to the predilections of his readers. Not the country but the sentimental traveler was to be his chief object for criticism.

But it was not the look of the country alone which fostered the disillusionment of the *Quaker City* excursionists. Their encounter with Christian missionaries had made them somewhat cynical of one of the major tenets of the evangelical protestant ethos they all shared. Christ had charged his followers with preaching the Gospel to the heathen, and among the churches back home no injunction was taken more seriously or supported more vigorously than this. Missionaries were believed to be martyrs who sacrificed home, health, and civilization to bring the heathen to Christ—and the Holy Land missionaries, struggling in a modern Crusade against the infidels who controlled the Holy Land, were not thought to be the least of these. Most of the missionaries they met, however, had been very comfortably ensconced and not so much concerned with saving the souls of the heathen as enjoying the luxury of servants and idle living unattainable at home. "Comparatively speaking," wrote Moses Beach, "our Missionaries live in a palace. In saying this I touch a sore spot with many travellers." He had seen, he wrote, missionaries living in high style wherever he went; at Smyrna the missionaries maintained elaborate summer homes in the hills to which they repaired in the hottest months. The missionary at Baalbec had entertained the Beach party in elegant and expensive style; the missionary families of Beirut spent "the summer out in the mountains, as fully 'up' in the enjoyment of vacations as the most roundly paid and most fashionable pastor in New York." For the vision of self-sacrifice they had entertained (and financially supported) for many years, the pilgrims found a missionary establishment more intent on living off the land than on bringing Christianity to the unenlightened. "There appears to be something amiss," Beach concluded.[76] Coupled with the overwhelming poverty which they saw everywhere

---

[76] *Sun*, November 5, 1867.

around them, such luxurious living was a shock which fed a general cynicism.

But even more significant, the journey attacked the fundamental faith of some of the pilgrims. Far from giving substance to the profound belief in an historical Jesus which most of the excursionists shared, the trip through Palestine had the effect of undermining the supposed "proofs" of His existence. In their journey they could see for themselves that such proofs were impossible—that the country had been ravaged innumerable times since Jesus' day, that the locale as often as not flatly contradicted the scriptural texts, and that the historical associations were almost entirely conjecture and badly founded conjecture at that. Their belief had been grounded on an assumption that the details of the New Testament could be *proved*—that the miracles which Christ and his followers had worked had left evidence in irrefutable fact. They were, finally, rationalists, and what they found did not support reasonable conjecture. Few of the excursionists would, of course, admit to this failure, but it is apparent in the tone of their letters home and in occasional, inadvertent comments, as when Julia Newell, writing of Dr. Payne ("Dr. Hub of Hubsville" she called him) indicated *his* misgivings: "Day by day as we have journeyed along, Father Hubs' faith in holy things has been getting more and more shaky, she wrote, "and now he openly says he thinks the Bible accounts 'queer' and rather a 'mixed up mess.' " [77]

Dr. Payne was not alone. It was this general loss of credulity which blighted the excursionists' sightseeing. They were tired from several months of travel and they had seen more beautiful sights elsewhere, but these circumstances alone could not account for their general lack of interest in visiting those sanctuaries which they had told themselves were the real attraction of the voyage. Mrs. Fairbanks and the Severances had journeyed a quarter of the way around the world to see the holy places associated with Jesus and yet, now, only two hours distant from Bethlehem—and with a dragoman engaged for just such a journey, they did not even trouble to visit the traditional site of Christ's birth.

[77] *Janesville* (Wis.) *Gazette*, November 23, 1867.

Instead, along with the rest of the Cleveland party, they rode to Joppa, arriving on board the *Quaker City* fully three days before it was scheduled to sail. Clemens had come with fewer orthodox assumptions, perhaps, and he was, therefore, less vulnerable to the general disillusionment the rest of the pilgrims felt, but he was not completely free from its effects. A random note made in his notebook after the Palestine trip suggests a certain anguish. "Oh for the ignorance & the confidingness of ignorance that could enable a man to kneel at the Sepulchre & look at the rift in the rock, & the socket of the cross & the tomb of Adam & feel & know & never question that they were genuine," [78] he wrote. Clemens had lost the comfort of a simple "ignorant" faith and had little to take its place.

But he was more tourist than pilgrim. He may have suffered a loss of innocence in his trip through Palestine, but unlike those in the Severance party he did not on that account cut short his tour. Abraham and the rest of Clemens' party arrived in Jerusalem Tuesday evening, and at eight the following morning they left the city for a three-day trip through its environs to the Dead Sea and Bethlehem. The first day they journeyed over the Valley of Kedron to Bethany, where they stopped for lunch, then proceeded to Jericho, where they stayed the night. Bedouin bandits were supposed to be all about them—Abraham had brought extra guards for their protection—but the only disturbance was an argument with the local Arabs of Jericho over where Abraham might pitch their tents, and the guards were more nuisance than protection: "One guard wanted to smouch me," Clemens noted. Jericho, he decided, was desolation itself. "Lizards all emigrating," he wrote in his notebook. It was a "modern (mud) Jericho" he saw, with little to suggest any religious associations.[79]

The next morning they started for the Dead Sea at 2:00 A.M. "as usual" he wrote, "got up 2 hrs. too soon." [80] Abraham was merely trying to get ahead of a rival party. At 4:00 A.M. they had arrived at the River Jordan and had to wait for daylight to see it. Clemens slept on the ground in

[78] "Unpublished Notebook no. 7" (Typescript, pp. 40–1), *MTP.*
[79] "Unpublished Notebook no. 8" (Typescript, p. 49), *MTP.*
[80] *Notebook,* p. 99.

the interim and caught cold. When dawn came they rushed to bathe in the Jordan, the waters of which were nearly frigid. "The main thing accomplished," Clemens later wrote, "the drooping, miserable gang sat down to wait for the sun again, for all wanted to see the water as well as feel it." [81] In broad daylight they proceeded to the Dead Sea and went swimming again. The salt water was as buoyant as it was reputed to be (Clemens took his horse into the water and was quickly upset), and they swam for an hour, blistering their faces and encrusting their hair with salt. It was an enervating bit of exercise and not one to prepare them for the five-and-a-half hour trip they were to make over "the roughest mountain scenery" to the Convent of Marsaba where they arrived at last, "brimming with gratitude." They spent the night there, made comfortable by the monks, and rose at 3:00 A.M. to proceed to Bethlehem. At daybreak they had arrived at the Plain of the Shepherds where tradition said the angels first proclaimed Christ's birth, and about a quarter of an hour later they arrived at the Church of the Nativity itself. They remained in Bethlehem until lunchtime when they left for the two-hour journey back to Jerusalem.

It was now Friday (September 27) and all *Quaker City* passengers were to be on board the ship by Monday in order to prepare for an early sailing Tuesday. Most of the excursionists had already left Jerusalem, but Clemens wished to remain a bit longer, for the officers of the gunboat *Swatara* had arrived while they were away, and after nearly two weeks with the pilgrims, Clemens, Dan, Jack, and Moult were ready for some sport, and they found it. Clemens noted they had "a rather high time . . . for such a slow old camp as the Holy City." [82] During the day Clemens did more sightseeing, too, until he became, as he said, "surfeited completely surfeited with sights." [83] He saw the Valley of Jehosophat and the Hill of Evil Counsel where Judas received his thirty pieces of silver and hanged himself. "We swabbed the sweat from our faces, and glared up into the tree at some imaginary Judas—" he wrote in an *Alta* pas-

[81] *Alta*, May 17, 1868; *Traveling*, p. 297; cf. *IA*, p. 594.

[82] "Unpublished Notebook no. 9" (Typescript, p. 10), *MTP*.

[83] *Alta*, April 12, 1868; *Traveling*, p. 288.

sage later omitted from *IA*, ". . . the first reflection was,
'Why couldn't *you* have hanged yourself in town?' " [84] They
visited Gethsemane and the Mount of Olives and the "convent where Catholics say Jesus ascended to Heaven" as well
as "another hill between Olivet and Bethany where Bible
says he ascended." [85] He went all through the Church of the
Holy Sepulcher again, too, with no significant change in his
skepticism. And he collected various mementos for the folks
back home: a Bible encased in olive wood for his mother, an
olive wood card case, olive beads from Bethlehem for his
sister, two or three paper knives "from Abraham's oak," a
branch which he tore from King Godfrey's tree at Damascus gate, and a bottle of water from the Bethesda pool—to
go along with the bottles he had collected from River Jordan and the Dead Sea.[86]

At 3:00 P.M. Sunday, Clemens passed through Damascus
Gate for the last time and, riding hard, arrived late that
night at Ramleh in the Valley of Ajalon where, "the moon
stood still." The next morning, after a three-hour gallop, the
party arrived at Joppa. Offshore, rocking gently in the
Mediterranean swells, the gleaming *Quaker City* rode at
anchor. It was cool and inviting, and Clemens was soon on
board.

"I have only one pleasant reminiscence of this Palestine
excursion," he wrote in his notebook, "—time I had the
cholera in Damascus." [87] Actually he had had many delights
on the journey, but these would become clear only in retrospect. As he boarded the *Quaker City* his general attitude
toward the weeks just ended were probably accurately
summed up in a note he had made at the Dead Sea: "No
Second Advent—" he wrote. "Christ been here once, will
never come again." [88] Clemens had no plans to return either.

[84] *Alta*, April 12, 1868; *Traveling*, p. 289.
[85] *Notebook*, p. 101.
[86] See list of articles in Webster Collection, *MTP*.
[87] "Unpublished Notebook no. 8" (Typescript, p. 50), *MTP*.
[88] *Notebook*, p. 99 (cf: "Unpublished Notebook no. 8,"
Typescript, p. 50, *MTP*). Clemens was fond of the statement and
repeated it in a later notebook entry (Typescript, p. 59).

ALEXANDRIA
CAIRO
SPAIN
BERMUDA

"Homesickness was abroad in that ship."

So far as his newspaper correspondence was concerned, Clemens' journey ended with Palestine—he wrote nothing to the *Alta* concerning the last six weeks of the cruise; he kept few notes of his travel through Egypt and none of his trip through Spain. The reasons for this uncharacteristic blackout was Clemens' discovery that 14 *Alta* letters had miscarried and his fevered effort to replace them. In the throes of new composition he made almost no attempt to fix the circumstances of the last weeks of his journey—he apparently did not expect to write of them. About a year

later, of course, he tried to reconstruct the experience for
IA, but he had small help from his notebooks. As a result,
the end of the journey was slighted in the book: he devoted
only 22 of *IA*'s 642 pages to Egypt and none at all to Spain.
His recollections long after the fact were, at best, vague, and
the actual circumstances surrounding the rest of the voyage
are primarily to be found in the correspondence of his fellow
travelers.

The journey from Joppa to Alexandria was only two days
and a night, but it seemed longer. Many months later Clemens was to write it was a "pleasant voyage and a good
rest" (p. 610); it wasn't. A strong north wind tore at the
rigging; huge swells buffeted the ship and made virtually
everyone ill, particularly the forty-one new passengers
whom the excursion had taken on board at Joppa and who
huddled like sheep on the spray-swept upper deck. They
were destitute Americans, part of an experiment in commu-
nal living in the Holy Land which had gone wildly wrong. A
year before, an ex-itinerant actor-turned-messiah named
Adams had convinced nearly one hundred and sixty Maine
farmers that he had had a "call" to establish a New Jerusalem in Palestine. Under a divine delusion, the farmers sold
their farms and bought passage for Joppa near which, under
the aegis of "President" Adams, they established a colony
from which the new light was to shine forth. The land was
fertile enough, but Adams, although apparently no charla-
tan, had more evangelical fervor than good sense, and
within a year the colonists were in great need. The few who
still had money went home; most of those who remained
clutched at the hope of a benefactor who might save them.
This hope was almost miraculously fulfilled by the arrival
of the *Quaker City*, and Duncan agreed to transport the
colonists to Alexandria where they would, apparently,
throw themselves on the mercy of others. Of course, charity
had its limits. The colonists were allowed on deck but not
into the half-filled staterooms of the pilgrims. Although
Clemens noted that women with babies were among the
pathetic group, it apparently never occurred to him that
Cabin 10 might have accommodated several for the night.
Woebegone and universally seasick, they were not happy
company from Joppa to Alexandria.

Fortunately the stormy seas were calmer on Wednesday (October 2), and shortly after dark the *Quaker City* sighted a pilot boat and followed it into Alexandria Harbor. Alexandria impressed the excursionists as the most elegant and well-disposed city they had seen since Paris; it was certainly the most cosmopolitan. As the chief port of call for ships going to and from the Middle East it was one of the busiest ports in the Mediterranean. Its harbor was as crowded as New York's and its streets were thronged with travelers, many of whom were English and American. All the *Quaker City* passengers liked Egypt. Of course, they came to it from more primitive places and it gained by comparison. "The contrast between Egypt and Turkey is beyond all description in favor of Egypt," said Moses Beach,[1] and Mrs. Fairbanks noted that "Afric's shores" were "enhanced by contrast with Palestine." [2] Clemens agreed. Although the past three weeks had been grueling ones for him, he evidently revived enough after two days and a night "at home" to regain his appetite for new sights. Almost as soon as the ship obtained health clearance, he and Jack Van Nostrand went ashore, showing an eagerness which disproved his later comment that "after dismal, smileless Palestine, beautiful Egypt had few charms." [3] He and Jack were apparently the only passengers who stayed in Alexandria that night, and they had a lively time.

Early the following morning they were among the twenty-five *Quaker City* passengers who filled a whole compartment of the Cairo express. The trip took most of the day, but the train was comfortable (they noted with pride that the cars had been made in Springfield, Massachusetts) and the scenery, Mrs. Fairbanks declared, "elicited from us most rapturous admiration." [4] They followed the Nile for a time, the embankment of which, here and there, rose high above the level of the train, and later their route went through lush cultivated fields and past date palms heavy with fruit. Now and again the train took on water at mud

[1] *New York Sun*, November 18, 1867.

[2] *Cleveland Herald*, December 11, 1867.

[3] *New York Herald*, November 20, 1867; *Traveling*, p. 318; cf. *IA*, p. 647.

[4] *Herald*, December 11, 1867.

hut villages where beggars and vendors beseiged the cars, offering trays of cucumbers and roasted corn, pomegranates and figs, "good water" and "fresh eggs."

They arrived in Cairo after dark and took residence at what Clemens was to call "Shepheard's [sic] infamous hotel," perhaps the most famous place of lodging in Africa, which had an immense portico facing the square of Esbeki-yeh, the congregating point for dragomen. Their rooms were excellent too, "not equal to those at Fifth Avenue," Mrs. Severance reported, "yet they were more comfortable," and the dragomen seemed better than their Palestine guides. "They are nearly all beautifully dressed," she wrote. "Light blue seems to be the favorite costume, but they wear, some of them, white with velvet jackets, gold chains, and black silk scarves."⁵ There had been no opulence like this in Palestine!

The great excursion, the chief reason for their trip to Cairo, was the tour to Giza and the pyramids. Dragomen had to be hired, for the journey, while not arduous, required mules and a ferry across the mainstream of the Nile and, after several more miles, one of its branches. The road itself was smooth—the "go ahead Vice Roy," as Duncan called him, was building a rail line to Giza and the pilgrims had the advantage of grading most of the way. Their mounts were much superior to the mangy beasts that had taken them through Palestine, and the journey was therefore quite comfortable. "Splendid atmosphere," Clemens wrote in his notebook. "Beautiful Oriental scenery. Naked girls in the streets—finely built."⁶ Getting across the Nile was difficult, and waiting for the mules (transported a few at a time after the excursionists themselves) was so time-consuming most of the party ended up walking the last mile or so to the pyramids, although Miss Newell was borne aloft on the shoulders of two husky guides to her apparent shock and secret delight. "We walked for some little distance," wrote Emily Severance, "though it seemed much farther on account of the difficulty of progression."⁷

⁵ *Journal Letters*, p. 186.

⁶ *Notebook*, p. 11. Paine omitted "finely built"; cf. Unpublished notebook no. 8, *MTP*.

⁷ *Journal Letters*, p. 190.

She was disappointed by the pyramids. They seemed somehow smaller than she had expected. "They grew upon one," she admitted, "and I presume would have seemed much larger, had I attempted their ascent." [8] The great pyramid of Cheops rose over 450 feet to a flat platform; most of the men climbed it, but of the women apparently only Miss Newell made the ascent. The climb was arduous and fraught with the annoyance of "guides" who "assisted" tourists to the top, now boosting, now carrying, now pushing violently from below. It was not the sort of activity most ladies would have thought proper, and on the way up there was a constant demand for baksheesh coupled with the threat both direct and indirect of being thrown from the sides if one did not give enough. Only one couple "gave way" to such ransom, Moses Beach declared, but several were threatened.

The view from the summit was dramatic enough to make the climb worthwhile. On the one side stretching to the horizon was what Clemens called a "mighty sea of yellow sand" and on the other, "The Eden of Egypt . . . a broad green floor, cloven by the sinuous river, dotted with villages, its vast distances measured and marked by the diminishing stature of receding clusters of palms. It lay asleep in an enchanted atmosphere" (p. 623). In spite of the heat—the sun was now directly overhead—the pilgrims were charmed. Bloodgood Cutter had another spontaneous overflow of powerful feelings: "I sat and gazed in thought profound,/ Then looked beneath me on the ground;/ Ruin 'mid ruin strewed the plain,/ Where millions of the dead are lain. . . . Kings did erect this wondrous pile,/ To preserve their name and bodies vile." [9] The guides, in a hurry, perhaps for more baksheesh, would not let them stay long, and they soon returned to the ground. "The descent is more quickly accomplished," wrote Miss Newell, "and is not quite so fatiguing as going up, as you have gravitation in your favor." [10] Once down they were taken inside the pyramid, a claustrophobic experience for most of them, and they were glad to

[8] *Ibid.*
[9] *Cutter,* pp. 115–18.
[10] *Janesville* (Wis.) *Gazette,* December 7, 1867.

leave the darkness of the funeral chambers and to return to the white-hot sunlight of the desert and the lunch which the dragomen had brought from the hotel. It was not a pleasant repast, however. The food was excellent, but they were again besieged by beggars, and the meal was constantly interrupted by cajoling requests, angry refusals, and passionate imprecations.

They escaped to the Sphinx. Clemens description of the Sphinx, written almost a year later when he was half-way around the world, is one of the most famous passages in *IA*. "After years of waiting, it was before me at last," he was to write. "The great face was so sad, so earnest, so longing, so patient. There was a dignity not of earth in its mien, and in its countenance a benignity such as never any thing human wore" (pp. 628–29). In retrospect it may have awakened such possibilities in him, but at the time he seemed little impressed. His notebook gives no indication of rapture and, if, as usual, he shared the feelings of his fellow passengers he was not overwhelmed. Mrs. Fairbanks was quite unmoved: "The fault may be in my uneducated taste—it must be, but it is nevertheless true that I experienced not the least symptom of rhapsody over this wonderful sculpture." [11] "The immense head is all that seems to have any shape," complained Emily Severance. "The sand has been excavated for a considerable distance about the body, but I could not see any form to it." [12] Its chief attraction, Moses Beach declared, was "a mutilated nose on a large scale." [13] Even Bloodgood Cutter was hard pressed to praise it. It was, he concluded after deep thought, very old.

After the pyramids and the Sphinx, there were three great attractions for the tourist, ("the lions of Cairo" Mrs. Fairbanks called them): the citadel, the Mohammed Ali Mosque, and the museum, and on the day after his trip to Giza Clemens saw them all. From the citadel he had a panoramic view of the city and the surrounding desert: to the east loomed the Obelisk of Heliopolis and the tombs of the Mamelukes; to the south, the quarries of Mount Mokattem from which the stone for the pyramids had been cut; south-

[11] *Herald*, December 11, 1867.

[12] *Journal Letters*, pp. 192–93.

[13] *Sun*, November 19, 1867.

west and west he could see the grand aqueduct and the
mosques of the Nile, and his route of the previous day
through the ruins of Old Cairo to the island of Rhoda, to
Giza, hedged by groves of sycamore and fig trees, and
beyond Giza, the great pyramids themselves, gray now in
the distance. Adjacent to the citadel was the new Mosque of
Mohammed Ali which they all agreed was the finest they
had seen—and they had seen many in the months just past.
Clemens was surprised that birds—hundreds of them—flew
freely beneath the great alabaster dome, nesting in corners
and perching occasionally on the chains from which the
many oil lamps were hung. They were all impressed with
the beauty of the tiled calligraphy which decorated the
walls and by the gold-leafed screen separating the mosque
from the tomb of Mohammed Ali. Adjacent to the mosque
was the Palace of the Pasha with a beautiful garden
("splendid avenue of sycamore and acacias" Clemens
noted), his harem, the mint, his council chamber, and his
arsenal—none of which they were allowed to enter. After
the pyramids, the citadel, and the Great Mosque, the
Museum was something of a letdown. The best of the exhibits, they discovered, had been sent to Paris, an ironic circumstance, for many of the pilgrims had omitted the Egyptian display at the Exhibition in expectation of seeing better
in Cairo. The Museum did not detain them long.

The return to Alexandria the next day was uneventful,
but pleasant. "I shall not tell how we feasted on fresh dates
and enjoyed the pleasant landscape all through the flying
journey" Clemens wrote in *IA*, "nor how we thundered into
Alexandria, at last, swarmed out of the cars, rowed aboard
the ship, . . . raised the anchor, and turned our bows homeward finally and forever from the long voyage"
(pp. 632–33). It wasn't quite *that* fast, of course, and there
were several other places to be visited before home was to be
seriously contemplated. Actually they returned on Sunday
(October 6) and the ship didn't leave Alexandria until
Monday afternoon at 5. They therefore had a day in Alexandria for what Duncan called "last purchases." Greenwood, for example, was negotiating to buy two mummies for
Barnum's Museum for $15,000 apiece, a circumstance
which, when Clemens heard about it, caused him to remark

that he wished all his ancestors mummies so that he could sell them at that price—up to the last one that dies! "And I think he would!" Miss Newell remarked.[14]

Whether Greenwood ever bought his mummies is not known, for he left the *Quaker City* at Alexandria. So did several others of the party. Mr. Vail, the Purser who had been such a gracious escort for the unattached ladies throughout the trip, left abruptly for Constantinople where, he announced, he would marry the Turkish sister of the American Vice-Consul—"an alarming case of 'love at first sight,'" Mrs. Fairbanks called it.[15] Beckwith, one of the Cleveland party, in poor health from the beginning, decided to go more directly home. Mr. Jenkins and the Griswolds, although originally planning to continue to Gibraltar with the ship, decided to return to Europe for several months. Clemens was delighted at the departure of the Griswolds, a couple he had disliked almost from the moment they joined the party in Naples. Griswold had, Clemens was to write long afterward, "the real old familiar Plymouth-Church self-complacency. . . . It is the way God looks when He has had a successful season." [16] However, the *Quaker City* left behind a passenger in Alexandria whom Clemens would miss. Dan Slote decided to return to Europe for several more months of touring. The disappointment which his departure provoked was assuaged by the farewell party which the other "fast young men" gave him on their last night in Alexandria and by the knowledge that they would all meet again in New York several months hence.

At five P.M. on Monday (October 7) the *Quaker City* left Alexandria. It was almost four months to the day since they had departed from New York and now, with the Holy Land and Egypt behind them, they sensed their excursion drawing toward its close. They were sailing west, not east, and they would, in six weeks' time, be home. They looked for-

[14] *Janesville* (Wis.) *Gazette*, December 7.

[15] *Herald*, December 11, 1867.

[16] MS note in Clemens' copy of Griswold's *Sixty Years with Plymouth Church* (New York 1907), *MTP*. This was a presentation copy. Three years later, on the occasion of Clemens' death, Griswold had an interview which indicated he cared even less for Clemens. See *Brooklyn Eagle*, June 5, 1910.

ward to that day with pleasure but not with longing, for there were still other places to be visited which they anticipated with pleasure, particularly Spain. They were nevertheless glad for the respite which being on board allowed them before the exertions of traveling began again. Unfortunately, the first days out of Alexandria were stormy ones. "Ship rolling and tumbling about in Old Atlantic Style," Captain Duncan wrote in his log. Everyone was seasick and there was general confusion, even devotions were canceled the first night out in what was to be one of the worst storms of the voyage. "Dishes smash, organ top thrown off, flower basket thrown down," wrote Duncan, "while on deck salt water bathing is done on a large scale at short notice." [17]

The weather must have seemed in pathetic response to Clemens' own inner turmoil, for those first days out of Alexandria were for him the blackest of the whole voyage. His days in Egypt had been pleasant and the last hours with Dan riotous fun, but nothing could abate his gloom. The excitement of the week past was completely overshadowed by the bad news he received in his mail at Alexandria. Clemens saved none of the correspondence he received on the tour, and the letter which evoked his trauma can be known only by inference. Whether it came from the *Alta* agent in New York (which seems most likely) or from his family (whom he had asked to collect his columns and inform him of their number) is uncertain, but from whatever source he learned that nearly a third of his *Alta* letters had been lost in transit—and he had kept no copies.[18] Under

---

[17] *Log,* p. 100.

[18] That he received this information in Alexandria can be ascertained from his subsequent actions on the voyage. The 22 letters he composed before landing in New York contained approximately 44,000 words. The journey from Alexandria to New York took six weeks, five of which he might have devoted to writing (one he spent going overland in Spain where he wrote no letters). To write 44,000 words in five weeks was, in itself, a Herculean task. After Alexandria he received no mail until Gibraltar, and the three-week journey from Gibraltar to New York would not have given him enough time to complete all the correspondence. Furthermore, *something* must have demanded this extra effort: it is not possible that these 22 *San Francisco*

the pressure of time and evidently believing the much-touted claim of safety and dispatch which the transatlantic steamship lines advertised, he had had little inclination to undergo the labor of making duplicates of his letters and no opportunity to have them made.[19] Now a third of them were gone—irretrievably gone. He had thought his work almost at an end, and he had discovered it was only well begun. Fourteen letters had miscarried. He had not eight letters to write but 22, and his contract with the *Alta*—for which he had already received payment—was barely half completed.[20] Since he had already made plans to go to Washington immediately upon his return to the United States,[21] he had to complete this labor before the ship arrived in New York.[22]

Daily Alta California letters were intended to be "extra" ones written in excess of his contract, letters which just happened to make up for unknown losses, for Clemens never completed all the letters he had promised the *New York Tribune*, and he surely would have met that obligation before gratuitously exceeding the other; the *New York Tribune* probably paid him as much as the *Alta* and, in any case, an Eastern reputation would have been of great value in publicizing the book he intended to write.

[19] See letter to his family, January 9, 1868 in which he asks them to send him clippings of his letters from the *Alta* (*Letters*, p. 144).

[20] See the remark to this effect in Noah Brooks' "Mark Twain in California," *Century*, 57, n.s. 35 (November, 1898): 98. In his *Autobiography* Clemens wrote: "I had gone to Washington [on his return] to write *The Innocents Abroad*, but before beginning that book it was necessary to earn some money to live on meanwhile, or borrow it—which would be difficult, or to take it where it reposed unwatched—which would be unlikely" (vol. 1: 323). This implies he was not paid on his return.

[21] See Clemens to Governor Fuller of Nevada, from Naples, August 7, 1867, (Typescript in *MTP*).

[22] In his first letter to Elisha Bliss concerning the publication of *IA* dated December 2, 1867, Clemens said: "I wrote fifty-two (three) letters for the San Francisco 'Alta California' during the Quaker City excursion, about half of which number have been printed, thus far" (*Letters*, p. 141). This implies that by this date, twelve days after his return, he had completed his Quaker City correspondence with the *Alta*. However, in his letter to his family of January 9, 1868, he mentions *Alta* letters, presumably concerning the trip, which he had "not mailed yet" (*Ibid.*, p. 144).

Replacing the lost letters—the mind-wrenching, soul-exhausting effort of writing thousands of words daily under enormous pressure and under the worst of conditions for over five weeks—inevitably affected the kind and quality of Clemens' subsequent work on the newspaper letters themselves and on the book he was to fashion from them. While the *Quaker City* rolled and pitched in its Mediterranean storm Clemens made a significant decision. Instead of attempting to rewrite the lost letters which concerned places and events long since displaced by subsequent experiences, he decided to add new ones about the Holy Land. As a result, his trip through Palestine comprised a much larger part of his correspondence (and therefore of *IA*) than he had originally intended. In his Constantinople letter to his family he had indicated he would write relatively few letters concerning Palestine; only four subjects were certain: "the Sea of Tiberias, Damascus, Jerusalem, and Joppa." He had also made clear that he intended to write letters from "Egypt, the Nile and Algiers"—none of which were forthcoming.[23] The loss of the *Alta* letters therefore forced Clemens from the pattern he had been following with some consistency throughout the voyage. He had been writing his letters more or less as he went, each of them a kind of installment of his developing awareness and each with an immediate and direct stimulus. Furthermore, each had a vitality derived, in part, from the knowledge that there was more to come, that succeeding experience might, in fact, change and qualify what he described in any particular instance; the earlier letters had immediacy and the possibility of surprise, and their substance was shaped directly by what happened to Clemens day by day. He did not need to

---

This suggests that he might have written some of the Holy Land letters after his return, but the number of Washington letters he wrote for the *Alta* and other papers between November 20 and January 9, the new lecture he wrote and delivered, his duties in Washington as a correspondent, and the visits he made to New York argue against any new composition on the Holy Land letters during this six-weeks period. He may have held the letters for revision, but the harried tone of his letters to his family suggests even this is unlikely.

[23] *Letters*, p. 135.

select the larger subjects themselves—these were determined by the stops en route; all he needed to concern himself with was the selection of corroborating detail, and in this he was a master. But with the need to write 22 letters en bloc came a wholly new procedure and one much less compatible to Clemens' style and interest. What he lost was expectation, the sense of the "yet to be discovered" which had stimulated his imagination heretofore. He was no longer writing individual letters, and his "correspondence" lost the rhythm it had acquired from his passage through foreign locales. He had his Palestine itinerary behind him, of course, but it was increasingly conglomerate in his memory. His Palestine notes, full enough for five or six letters, to be sure, were not sufficient to stimulate 22. As a result, he had to fabricate his writing much more directly than would otherwise have been the case, his inspiration had to be stimulated more artificially, and his information had to be more arbitrarily collected and shaped.

As a result, the immediacy of his writing was lost. His narrative became more vague; for example, the datelines he gave his "letters" became arbitrary. Earlier they were accurate: letter 26,[24] from Ephesus (before the Holy Land trek) is dated September 8, 1867; letter 27, from Lebanon, Syria, after his departure from Beirut, is dated September 11; letter 28, from the Valley of Lebanon, is dated September 12; and letter 29, "8 hours beyond Damascus," is dated September 17. These places and dates correspond exactly to Clemens' itinerary as it can be reconstructed from his notebook. However, the continuum is abruptly broken with letter 30, and throughout the rest of the correspondence (through letter 52) the dateline cites only the month with no day, a circumstance which merely highlights the inexactness of the chronology implicit in the "letters" themselves. The text is, in effect, pulled out of the continuum of actually passing time and put into one of recollection. Furthermore, the place names in the datelines of letters after letter 29 are sometimes arbitrary, having little to do with the scenes described (for example, a letter about Damascus datelined "Banias"), and sometimes fictitious ("Williamsburgh, Ca-

[24] The numbering here is that which was given the letters when they appeared in the *Alta;* it is not Clemens'.

naan"). There is, therefore, a certain geographical as well as chronological vagueness which forces the writing into a new framework. Time and space had been clearly (if probably unconsciously) articulated in his writing, and this articulation provided a motive and a sense of progression to the early letters, both of which were to be apparent in those parts of *IA* which derived from them. But with the later letters this motive and progression is diminished, and with this loss there was a corresponding loss of focus, a movement away from particularity to generality, from the specific day-to-day exposition of his earlier travels to what Van Wyck Brooks has called "the 'Sunday School scholar's' romantic dream of the 'land of Egypt.' " [25] In part it is a shift from relating unique personal experience to recounting what might be called universal anecdotes. This change was a marked one even to his contemporary audience. In a note appended to letter 35 in which Clemens recounts the life of Jesus, the *Alta* editors complained, somewhat playfully,

We have received a private letter from our correspondent, in which we expected some explanation of his strange conduct in presenting the above information to the public with such a confident air of furnishing news, but he offers none.[26]

The fact is, Clemens padded his Holy Land letters considerably with Bible stories which were not particularly pertinent to his narrative. The sketch of the life of Jesus was only one of these; there were half a dozen more of varying lengths: of "Nimrod, the Mighty Hunter," of Naaman, Paul, Joseph, the Prodigal Son, Ahab and Jezebel, and others,[27] and these were only the "set pieces"—his text is studded with shorter but no less well-known biblical vignettes. His use of such material was not always judicious or well integrated, and its presence indicates something of the difficulty Clemens had in fulfilling his *Alta* contract and the reasons for the increased lack of control and finish which these last letters show.

[25] Van Wyck Brooks, *The Ordeal of Mark Twain* (New York: E. P. Dutton and Co., 1920), p. 162.

[26] January 19, 1868.

[27] See *Traveling*, pp. 189–90, 196–98, 201–2, 221–24, 246–47, 254–56.

Most significantly, perhaps, Clemens turned directly to Porter's *Handbook* for assistance. As we have seen, he had earlier gleaned details from Porter in preparation for his trip through Palestine, but the use he now made of the guide was of a very different sort: earlier he had used it to alert his imagination on the trip itself; now he used it as a source for composition. Clemens scorned this direct use of guidebooks; even after he had, himself, been guilty of the practice, he added a paragraph in *IA* to indicate his disgust with the procedure—when practiced by others:

Our pilgrims have brought *their* verdicts with them. They have shown it in their conversation ever since we left Beirout. I can almost tell, in set phrase, what they will say when they see Tabor, Nazareth, Jericho and Jerusalem—*because I have the books they will "smouch" their ideas from.* These authors write pictures and frame rhapsodies, and lesser men follow and see with the author's eyes instead of their own, and speak with his tongue (pp. 511–12).

Clemens was not, of course, opposed to using guidebooks; only to copying from them. Throughout the voyage he had used several guidebooks himself—he had to get his facts from somewhere and he tried to find the most authoritative source available. But until the last he used guidebooks with great circumspection: the facts he gleaned from them were always transmuted, they were never more than supplementary details to the general impression he received from his own experience. It is, indeed, this fusion of experience and imagination with fact which is one of the remarkable achievements of both his letters and the book he made from them. But under the pressure of composing those 22 letters in five weeks, his auctorial pride weakened. In his Holy Land letters he several times indicates that he read many authorities on the subject. "I have read all the books on Palestine, nearly, that have been printed," he wrote in a passage later cut from *IA*,[28] and at another point he indicated that he had "culled information concerning Tiberias" from "various authorities."[29] Actually, while he had, no doubt, read many books on Palestine, he used only Porter in

[28] *Alta*, March 1, 1868; *Traveling*, p. 265.
[29] *Alta*, January 26, 1868; *Traveling*, p. 235.

his letters, and it is significant that, whereas he mentions the titles and authors of several books on the Holy Land, he never refers directly to his chief source, although he quoted it verbatim on several occasions and indirectly many times.

One small but significant change reveals Clemens' awareness of his reliance on Porter. In letter "number 27," one of the last letters he wrote on the journey through the Holy Land before his illness in Damascus made him stop composition altogether, he mentioned that among the articles he had brought along on the journey was "a guide-book (the same being a Bible)." [30] This was probably the Bible he purchased just before leaving Constantinople, and there is little doubt that he referred to it regularly while on the Holy Land journey. Sometime later—with Porter's help—he composed the rest of the Palestine letters, and when he put "letter 27" into *IA* he substituted "a guide-book and a Bible" (p. 434) for the earlier phrase, a clear indication that he was sensitive to his debt and wished to state it, however vaguely, in his text. Using Porter without credit was a fault and he knew it. "A certain amount of pride always goes along with a teaspoonful of brains, and . . . this pride protects a man from deliberately stealing other people's ideas," he was to remark later.[31] He had been stolen from himself, and he knew what it meant, but he had, he thought, overwhelming justification in the present circumstances for his borrowing: He needed help and he could not directly acknowledge his source without undermining his reader's confidence in the originality of his composition.

Even so, his source was apparent to many of his readers. One pirated English edition of *IA*, for example, subtitled it "A Companion to Murray's Guide to Palestine," [32] and, given the fame of Porter's guide, many must have recognized the similarities.[33] It was, perhaps, the very reputation of the

[30] *Alta*, December 1, 1867; *Traveling*, p. 180.

[31] "Unconscious Plagiarism," a speech delivered August 29, 1879. Albert B. Paine, ed., *Mark Twain's Speeches*, (New York: Harper and Brothers, 1910), p. 57.

[32] *Mark Twain's Pleasure Trip on the Continent* (London: John Camden Hotten [1873]).

[33] Leon T. Dickinson first noted several similarities between Porter and *IA* in his unpublished dissertation, *Mark Twain's*

guide which made Clemens avoid citing it by name: he did not, for example hesitate to refer to William Prime's *Tent Life in the Holy Land* or Thomson's *The Land and the Book*, and later when he added new information to *IA* he quoted directly with credit from Charles Wyllys Elliott ("C.W.E.") [34] in the section concerning Palestine and, as I have noted earlier, Neligan concerning Rome. But Clemens usually named only sources he could belittle in an amusing way, as his treatment of both Prime and Neligan illustrates. When he used unimpeachable sources which did not lend themselves to his humor, *Galignani's New Paris Guide for 1867*, for example, he did so without credit. In both his newspaper letters and *IA* he had to suggest *unique* experience, and his borrowing from Porter was so extensive that to have admitted his debt would have been tantamount to revealing, rather specifically, just how conglomerate and derivative many of his "letters from the Holy Land" actually were. This could not have been a happy circumstance for a writer as jealous of his own experience as Clemens certainly was.

But while Clemens' debt to Porter was a large one, it should not be assumed to be excessive nor, except for his refusal to credit Porter as he deserved, illegitimate. In fact, an author less jealous of his own experience than Clemens might readily have acknowledged the debt. Clemens' use of Porter is significant only insofar as it reveals pressure of the demand he felt and his manner of meeting it. Most often,

---

Innocents Abroad: Its Origins, Composition, and Popularity (Chicago, 1945), and suggested Porter was a possible source for the book. Dickinson, however, was concerned only with the finished book; a comparison of Porter with the unedited *Alta* letters and the notebooks (published and unpublished) make this suggestion a certainty.

[34] Charles Wyllys Elliott, *Remarkable Characters and Memorable Places of the Holy Land* (Hartford, Conn.: J. B. Burr and Co., 1868). Clemens quotes Elliott twice: the first time concerning the hills of Galilee (cf: Elliott, pp. 455–56 and *IA*, p. 510) with scorn; the second time on Palestine landscape generally (cf: Elliott, p. 353 and *IA*, p. 606) with approval. Significantly, Clemens misquotes the title of the book and does not refer to the author's initials when he approves his quotation.

Clemens' text merely echoes Porter. This sort of indebtedness can be illustrated by many examples: in almost the first sentence of the first post-Alexandria letter, for instance, Clemens wrote "The early history of Damascus is shrouded in the mists of a hoary antiquity," a comment which clearly suggests Porter's "The history of Damascus reaches away back into the misty regions of antiquity." [35] In this instance, the first direct use he made of Porter, he placed the sentence in quotation marks, but thereafter his borrowed words were not specifically set off from the rest of his text.[36]

More important—because more extensive—use of Porter can be found in Clemens' description of the battle of Hattin and of the Church of the Holy Sepulcher. The battle of Hattin would necessarily suggest an historical source, and Clemens refers somewhat casually to "the Guide-Book," but never by name. Although he compressed the guidebook's description, Clemens kept Porter's order of details and used much of his vocabulary.[37] It is, however, in the three letters

---

[35] *Traveling*, p. 193; *Porter*, p. 471.

[36] There are too many of these borrowings to cite them all and an extensive comparison would not be useful, but the analogies are most apparent in Clemens' discussions of Tiberias (*Traveling*, p. 235; *Porter*, 422–23). Joseph's tomb (*Traveling*, p. 261; *Porter* 342–43), Jacob's well (*Traveling*, p. 262; *Porter*, 340–41) and general comments about Jerusalem (*Traveling*, p. 267; *Porter*, 82).

[37] For example, *Porter:*

The immediate cause of the conflict was a gross infraction of a truce by Raynald of Chatillon, lord of Kerak, who plundered a Damascus caravan, and refused to give up either merchants or merchandise on the demand of the Sultan. Saladin was stung to madness alike by the perfidy and insolence of the petty Christian chief; and he swore a solemn oath to put him to death with his own hand should he ever fall into his power [p. 417].

Cf. Clemens:

There had long been a truce between the opposing forces, but . . . Raynauld of Chattilon [sic], Lord of Kerak, broke it by plundering a Damascus caravan, and refusing to give up either the merchants or their goods when Saladin demanded them. This

describing the Church of the Holy Sepulcher that Clemens' debt to Porter is most apparent, and it is, perhaps, significant that here he makes no mention of a guidebook at all. The parallels between Porter and Clemens are so direct as to suggest he wrote these pages with Porter open in front of him. His notes on the church are not lengthy but long enough to indicate that the order in which he describes the holy places within the confines of the church was not that which he himself took when he visited it; it derived instead from Porter. This much-praised section reveals something of Clemens' manner in his use of guidebooks, and a comparison of a small part of it is revealing. Concerning the grave of Jesus, Porter wrote:

In the very centre of the Rotunda stands the Holy Sepulchre, covered by a building 26 ft. long by 18 broad, rounded, or rather pentagonal at the W. end. It is wholly cased in yellow and white stone, ornamented with slender semicolumns and pilasters, and surmounted by a dome somewhat resembling a crown. It is a tasteless, meaningless fabric, reminding one of an overgrown cage. The entrance is on the E., where a low door opens from a small enclosed area, in which natives leave their shoes, into the first apartment, called the Chapel of the Angel, for here the angel sat on the stone that had been rolled away from the door of the sepulchre. In the middle of the floor, on a small pedestal, stands this stone itself, or rather a fragment of it, 18 in. square. Some affirm, however, that the *real* stone was stolen by the Armenians, and is now in the chapel of the palace of Caiaphas, outside the Zion Gate. At the western extremity of this gloomy antechamber is a low narrow door, through which a strong light is shed. Stooping low, we enter, and stand within the *Sepulchre*. It is a quadrangular vault, about 6 ft. by 7, with a dome roof supported on short marble pillars. The sepulchral couch occupies the whole of the rt. side as we enter; it is raised nearly 3 ft. above the floor, and is covered with a slab of white marble, cracked through the centre, and much worn at the edge by the lips of numerous pilgrims. The slab now serves as an altar, and is garnished with a profusion of tasteless, tawdry ornaments, grim-looking pictures,

---

conduct of an insolent petty chieftain stung the proud Sultan to the quick, and he swore that he would slaughter Raynauld with his own hand, no matter how, or when, or where he found him" [*Traveling*, p. 241].

and a bas-relief of the Resurrection. Over it 42 lamps of gold and silver burn continually, shedding a brilliant light; . . .[38]

Following Porter, Clemens wrote:

Entering the great Rotunda, we stand before the most sacred locality in Christendom—the grave of Jesus. It is in the centre [sic] of the church, and immediately under the great dome. It is inclosed in a sort of little temple of yellow and white stone, of fanciful design. Within the little temple is a portion of the very stone which was rolled away from the door of the Sepulchre, and on which the angel was sitting when Mary came thither "at early dawn." The stone *was* there, at any rate, day before yesterday. Our pilgrims have been there since. Stooping low, we enter the vault—the Sepulchre itself. It is only about six feet by seven, and the stone couch on which the dead Savior lay extends from end to end of the apartment and occupies half its width. It is covered with a marble slab which has been much worn by the lips of pilgrims. This slab serves as an altar, now. Over it hang some fifty gold and silver lamps, which are kept always burning, and the place is otherwise scandalized by trumpery gew-gaws and tawdry ornamentation.[39]

The changes Clemens made in Porter suggest his style in *IA* as a whole. Outside the tomb Clemens' tone is casual; Porter's precision is made more commonplace—"Holy Sepulchre" becomes "the grave of Jesus" and his exact description of the tomb becomes "a sort of little temple . . . of fanciful design." As Clemens comes to the entrance, he interrupts the narrative to insert his own comment about the souvenir-hunting pilgrims which was probably suggested by Porter's reference to the Armenians—a satirical point which is effective only in the context of the factual description of the tomb itself; it is the shift of tone which pleases. Inside the tomb, satire is banished by the seriousness of concrete reality, and Clemens adopts Porter's text almost *verbatim*. As already noted, Clemens' iconoclastic tone (here, concerning the "tawdry ornamentation" of the tomb), sometimes remarked as unique in his view of the Holy Land, derives here and elsewhere from a similar tone

[38] *Porter*, p. 162.
[39] *Alta*, March 8, 1868; *Traveling*, p. 268; cf. *IA*, p. 560.

in Porter who, though reverent, is never uncritical of his subjects.

Porter was not Clemens' only aid in writing the last *Alta* letters. Mrs. Fairbanks, too, assisted him. The nature of this assistance has been so misconstrued and its extent so exaggerated that it is difficult to consider in proper perspective. The misconception derives largely from the praise Clemens gave Mrs. Fairbanks in his letters to her after the trip was over. In context these remarks can be seen as the gentle flattery which Clemens was, on occasion, adept at giving. I have already indicated the professional prestige which Clemens brought aboard with him and the awe with which Mrs. Fairbanks viewed him. To be praised as having taught the famous writer was bound to give delight. In a letter to Mrs. Severance two years after their return he made a similar statement: "But for you and Mrs. Fairbanks," he wrote, "it [*IA*] would have been a very sorry affair. I shall always remember both of you gratefully for the training you gave me—you in your mild persuasive way, and she in her efficient, tyrannical, and overbearing fashion." [40] No one has suggested on the basis of this letter that Mrs. Severance was also his mentor. The tone, in fact, is exactly right. His thanks for help cannot be taken any more seriously than his characterization of Mrs. Fairbanks' manner as "tyrannical" and "overbearing"—had she been such a harridan Clemens would have fled from her. Neither can we credit Paine's apocryphal story—told (like his fictitious story of Dan's illness in Syria) at least three removes from authority— that Clemens destroyed manuscripts of which Mrs. Fairbanks disapproved. It is incredible that, pressed for time, he would, in fact, have *destroyed* manuscript for *whatever* cause. There is, morever, evidence that despite her dislike for some of the things he said in his letters he nevertheless included those remarks in *IA*.[41]

The case for the influence of Mrs. Fairbanks rests finally on the rather sentimental view that Clemens was a victim of feminine domination, that he was always influenced by the women in his life, that, as Dixon Wecter has said, "the

[40] *Journal Letters*, p. 217–18.
[41] For example, see *MF*, p. 30.

influence of his own mother, and of decorous 'Mother' Fairbanks and semi-invalid Livy Langdon in the later years,
powerfully re-enforced his conviction that woman, in her
exquisite purity and gentleness, is the born mentor of the
male." [42] However, the point at issue is whether he wholly
accepted their influence in strictly literary affairs. While
one must agree that Clemens was as deferential to his
womenfolk as any nineteenth-century middle-class American, there is very little evidence that this deference extended very far into professional matters. Certainly there is
nothing to indicate that Mrs. Fairbanks' influence on the
Palestine letters was in any way dominant. Of course, we
have none of her correspondence *to* Clemens—a significant
fact in itself—but the critical dicta which we can reconstruct from his reference to her comments seem merely to
support the conventional attitudes which he himself was
born to and lived by.

Yet his letters to Mrs. Fairbanks make clear that she *did*
read his correspondence on the voyage and that she was a
help to him. Faced with an overwhelming demand, Clemens
sought her aid, and on the return voyage from Alexandria to
Gibraltar and from Cadiz to New York (Mrs. Fairbanks
did not travel with him through Spain), she assisted him. It
is also clear that her assistance was confined to letters
written after Alexandria. In his letter to her of February 20,
1868, several months after their return, he notes his dissatisfaction with the letters already printed in the *Alta:* "I don't
like *any* of those letters that have reached me from California so far," he wrote. "I may think better of those you
weeded of slang, though." [43] The implication is that she had
not worked on any of his correspondence prior to the letters
he had seen printed copies of to that date; allowing three
weeks for transit, the usual length of the trip across the
Isthmus,[44] this means no letter printed before January 2,
that is, no letter before "number 32." Since Clemens stopped
writing letters in Palestine during letter "number 29," this
means she probably did not read all the Holy Land letters

[42] Dixon Wecter, *Sam Clemens of Hannibal* (Boston: Houghton
Mifflin Co., 1952), p. 176.

[43] *MF*, pp. 21–22.

[44] *Ibid.*, p. 23.

he wrote after Alexandria—that it was not until he was already immersed in his new composition after leaving that port that he asked her assistance. His reference in his letter of June 17 to "those Holy Land letters which you did not revise" [45] supports this assumption.

The comment further suggests Clemens' interpretation of Mrs. Fairbanks' function: She "weeded" his writing of slang. While composing *IA,* he wished, he wrote, that she could "revise this mountain of MSS. for me," [46] presumably as she had "revised" the earlier letters. *This* statement was the purest flattery and suggests Clemens' evaluation of Mrs. Fairbanks' function on board. Pressed in composition, he turned the job of copyreading over to her. No doubt she suggested changes in diction, but her function was to do to the MSS those editorial chores of proofreading which Clemens had heretofore done for himself and would, had he not been pressed for time, still have done. Perhaps she suggested additional subjects to him,[47] but her function was generally of a much more mundane sort. Her influence may have extended to treatment, but if so, it does not appear to have improved Clemens' writing since there is some agreement that the Palestine letters show a decline—not an improvement—in his taste. Although one might argue they would have been worse without the lady-like hand of Mrs. Fairbanks, one might more easily argue, judging from her own letters, that they might have been better without her criticism. Significantly, Clemens himself did not ascribe to Mrs. Fairbanks the power with which today's critics endow her. He respected her intelligence and, certainly, the judgment it gave her, and this respect increased with their friendship, but he did not, in the celebrated letter to his family quoted earlier,[48] suggest that she was a dominant *literary*

[45] *Ibid.,* p. 29.

[46] *Ibid.,* p. 30.

[47] For example, Clemens wrote of the beauties of Baalbec by moonlight although he saw it only during the day, whereas Mrs. Fairbanks saw it by full moon and wrote home about it. She may have given him the idea for his casual statement which, read with care, does not say *he* saw the ruins by moonlight but only that they are beautiful when seen thus.

[48] See note 26 in chapter I.

mentor. His words suggest not a professional debt but a personal one to a woman of grace and refinement for whom he had great affection. There is nothing to suggest he sought her literary criticism with any tenacity or deferred to her opinions with humility. In later life he encouraged her critical comments, but as often as not he followed his own inclinations.

While Clemens wrestled with his crisis, the *Quaker City* steamed toward Sardinia, a journey of six days from Alexandria. The ship was originally scheduled to stop at Malta, but in Alexandria they learned that Malta was an infected port, and, rather than risk losing their clean bill of health and being denied entrance to Spain, they bypassed the island. Dropping Malta was not a happy choice for some of the passengers, notably Beach, who wanted to see that island "more than any other in the Mediterranean." The decision brought the whole itinerary into question, and three days out Rev. Bullard proposed a major change in plans: omit Sardinia along with Majorca and Valencia, Spain, and for them substitute Malaga and Cadiz. The *Quaker City* was scheduled to stop at Gibraltar to recoal for four days, and during this time most of the excursionists wanted to travel in Spain. Valencia had originally been planned as the starting point for an overland trip to Madrid, down through Andalusia to Granada, Cordova, and Seville, and from thence to Gibraltar where the ship would be waiting for them. But what had seemed an ideal journey in June was thought less desirable in October. The pilgrims were tired after Palestine, and, in any case, the journey across Spain starting so far north seemed, in the cold light of recent experience, virtually impossible in a mere five days. The alternative of stopping at Malaga on the southern coast and going overland to Granada by horseback and then on to Cordova and Seville by railroad was therefore very attractive; they would be able to see all of the most interesting parts of Andalusia and to have more time there as well. Adding Cadiz on the west coast would add another day or two to the itinerary also, for the railroad from Seville went directly to that port and the overland passengers would be saved the necessity of doubling back to Gibraltar, and the *Quaker City* would be sailing past Cadiz out of Gibraltar anyway. A change in itinerary required unanimous consent, and it appeared that everyone would agree to this one. Even so, a meeting was called to ratify the change—conducted in fully proper parliamentary style, of course, with Major Barry presiding as elected Chairman and Dr. Jackson keeping the minutes. In the course of it Dr. Crane unexpectedly made a long speech denouncing the proposal (and along with it, Rev. Bullard). This, under the rule of unanimity, should have doomed the plan, but more parliamentary wrangling ensued—a motion to adjourn was defeated, amendments to the proposal were made and amended again, the amendments were passed and the motion put—and all but Dr. Crane voted "aye." After hours of peevish argument, he still maintained that no change could be made without his consent. The meeting broke up, Duncan reported, *"without prayers,"* and an unpleasant two days followed: "Passengers who are desirous of visiting the Alhambra from Malaga are bringing pressure to bear on Crane," Duncan reported in his log. "Coaxing won't do." Crane was adamant, the other passengers lost patience with him and used other tactics. "Abuse tried and successful," Duncan noted.[49] Subjected to the full-scale abuse of his shipmates, Dr. Crane finally came round, but he insisted that Sardinia not be omitted. The amended itinerary was therefore Sardinia, Algiers, Malaga, and Gibraltar—to which Duncan added, on his own, Cadiz "else of what use would be one day in Malaga?"

As the controversy quieted, the storm outside the ship calmed too. On Thursday there was general toasting as the Severances celebrated a wedding anniversary (their seventh), and on Friday night (October 11) the skies were clear and the moon full. The pilgrims were no longer fretful; they were over their seasickness and everyone was on deck to enjoy the evening. The next day it rained, the first rainfall the ship had had in 117 days, and they were all driven indoors again, the women to their embroidery or their journals, Beach to the "book" he announced he was writing, and Clemens to his correspondence. Sunday was clear and Rev. Quereau preached on a text with ominous

---

[49] *Log,* p. 99.

implications for the unpleasantness of the previous week: "Whatsoever a Man Soweth That Also Shall he Reap."

At 5:00 P.M., Sardinia was sighted and at 9:00 they had anchored in its harbor, but they were not to see Sardinia. Duncan's boat had barely touched the dock when he learned that cholera was epidemic on the island and that the port's Health Officer was not even maintaining duty. They left Sardinia at once, hoping their arrival and departure would go unrecorded, and spent Monday congratulating themselves that a port of no interest had been avoided and reminding Dr. Crane that but for his intransigence they might already be at Algiers. Shortly after noon on Tuesday they arrived at that port. They had been at sea over a week now and were eager to be on land again. Algiers, glittering white and set at the foot of verdant hills, invited them. Alas, they were to be disappointed again. Although the city was free of disease, the countryside was rife with cholera and thus the city too was deemed "infected." They could land, if they chose, but only "foul health" papers could be issued on their departure, and this would certainly prohibit them from landing in Spain. "I begin to understand why Ulysses' voyage was so prolonged!" [50] Mrs. Fairbanks wrote in exasperation. Their food supplies were perilously low—they were out of fresh vegetables and the potatoes were gone—but they were allowed to take on only fresh supplies of fish.

By 5:30 they had steamed out of Algiers Harbor and were headed for Malaga, Spain, trying to convince themselves that omitting Algiers would give them all another day in the Alhambra. They were not entirely convinced; such a string of bad luck depressed them all, and the next two days did little to reassure them. The rough weather had depleted their coal supply, and on Wednesday, when another rain storm and heavy seas pounded the ship, it was necessary to draw up the emergency supplies of coal from the deep hold, an operation which allowed the sailors and firemen to enter the passengers' baggage compartment and gave them the opportunity to break open the cases of wine stored there. Before noon, most of the crew was drunk and fights were breaking out all over the ship. This annoyed Duncan.

[50] *Herald*, November 25, 1867.

Somehow, despite the weather and the irresponsibility of the crew, the *Quaker City* arrived at Malaga at noon on Thursday, and Duncan, Beach, and Clemens went ashore under guard to learn their fate. All ships from Egypt were suspect, but their papers were in excellent order. They carried a perfect bill of health, and they had every reason to expect immediate clearance to proceed to Granada. They were disappointed again. Yes, their papers were in order, they were told, but Malaga quarantined "everything and everybody" for a full seven days, regardless of papers, to keep itself a clean port. The disappointment of the pilgrims was intense. They had denied themselves Malta, Sardinia, and Algiers in order to ensure a trip to the Alhambra and now that too was to be denied them. It seemed grossly unfair, and the Spanish authorities, stupid. They could mail letters at Malaga, they were informed, but the port authorities put mail through so much hocus-pocus, handling them with tongs and smoking them in acid fumes, that Clemens was convinced it would be madness to entrust the precious manuscript he had been laboriously composing for the past two weeks to their ministrations. The ship could not anchor, but they could send a boat to shore farther up the beach to take on badly needed supplies, and the pilgrims were as much amused as chagrined to see the traders dunk the American gold pieces in water, "Lest we," wrote Moses Beach, "who rioted in good health, should communicate some mysterious disease." [51] By four in the afternoon they were off to Gibraltar, where, they knew, the sensible English would take them in. Despite their disappointment, the voyage to Gibraltar was a pleasant one past the delightful scenery of picturesque villages and cultivated fields with snow-capped Sierras towering above them. "Tonight we had the finest sunset of the entire season," wrote Emily Severance, "one of those rare and gorgeous ones." [52] They had been mistreated, they thought, by many foolish ports, but they were nevertheless sorry to be leaving the Mediterranean. At 10:00 they dropped anchor in Gibraltar.

Southern Spain had been cancelled from the *Quaker City*

[51] *Sun*, November 20, 1867.
[52] *Journal Letters*, p. 202.

itinerary, but four of the passengers, Clemens, Jack Van Nostrand, Julia Newell, and Dr. Jackson were not to be gainsaid. They had *planned* to see Andalusia and they were *going* to do so. Six days in Gibraltar would have been useful to Clemens; he could have well spent the time on his correspondence, but he had been working with great intensity for two weeks and he wanted a respite. Accordingly he worked out an elaborate itinerary which would enable them to see the principal cities of Andalusia despite the quarantine: They would leave Gibraltar as soon as the ship docked (11:30 P.M.), take a four-hour horseback ride to Algeciras, across the Bay of Gibraltar. From there they would board a Spanish steamer (which would not be quarantined) back to Malaga, having lost only one day from their original itinerary. It was a good plan, and it might have worked had the Gibraltar authorities not refused to allow any passengers to land until the morning after their arrival. As a result, when Clemens' party got to Algeciras late in the afternoon of the next day they discovered they had just missed a steamer to Malaga and that there would not be another for three days. This was a blow, for now they should have to go overland all the way. They had planned to go from Granada to Cordova to Seville; now they had to start from Seville, go east to the other cities and retrace their steps returning. Such a journey would take more than six days and they had only five: Granada and its Alhambra would have to be omitted. Even visiting Seville and Cordova would be arduous. They would have to ride all Friday night to Bajez, 33 miles distant, there to take a diligence for another five-hour ride to the railroad at San Fernando from which, if they were lucky, they might get an early train to Seville. It was to be a hard-riding journey, but they decided to take it.

Miss Newell proved to have as much stamina as the men. When the Spanish courier they hired to take them to Algeciras engaged them horses for the ride to Bajez he explained to Julia that he had, with some trouble, found a "Spanish Chair" for her. No one seemed to know what that conveyance would look like (although Clemens suggested it might be a curbstone because he saw the Spanish sit on them oftener than on anything else), but the guide assured Julia she would be much more comfortable in the chair. "He evidently expected me to look pleased—she remarked later, "so I looked pleased," but she wasn't. The contraption turned out to be a great wooden frame lashed to the back of a nearly immobilized horse with a cushion or two to protect the lady from bruising. After nine miles she protested and demanded a saddle horse, and since no sidesaddle was available she pulled up her skirts and rode astride. "Under cover of the night I rode the remainder of the thirty-three miles on a gentleman's saddle, and *as* gentlemen do, and I give this style of riding my unqualified approval." [53]

They rode all night and at daybreak arrived in Bajez where, instead of waiting for the diligence, they hired two calèches, two-wheeled buggies which carried two passengers and a driver at a fast clip. The road to San Fernando was a good one and the scenery interesting: "The country is precisely as it was when Don Quixote and Sancho Panza were possible characters," Clemens wrote his family later.[54] They caused something of a stir as they passed, for apparently foreign passengers seldom went overland through Andalusia, and a woman *never*. Happily, they arrived at San Fernando well in advance of the train and spent several hours looking about that city before boarding the cars at 4:00 P.M. ("a small Spanish town of no special interest," Miss Newell called it). They arrived in Seville at midnight.

They were "over the hard part of our trip, and somewhat tired," Clemens wrote his family in a typical understatement.[55] They rested Sunday in Seville, unaware that the bullfights, which they greatly wanted to attend, occurred *only* on the Sabbath, and hence they missed them entirely. On Monday they visited the great cathedral and followed the recommended procedure of climbing the *Giralda,* or bell tower, to view the whole of the city beneath them—the cigar factory, one of the largest in the world, and the Alcazar, the residence of the Moorish kings of Spain, both of which they were to visit, and the bourse and the bull ring, both of which they missed. The *Fabrica de Tabacas* would have had a particular interest for Clemens, whose inveterate

[53] *Janesville* (Wis.) *Gazette,* December 14, 1867.
[54] *Letters,* p. 138.
[55] *Ibid.*

love of cigars was already well established, and seeing five thousand women working the tobacco into snuff, cigarettes, and cigars was a remarkable experience. (No less remarkable was the procedure at closing time when the girls were searched to ensure they stole no tobacco; Clemens might have seen *that* too.) The most famous building in Seville was the tenth-century Alcazar, the palace of the Moorish Catholic kings of Spain, which had been rebuilt by Ferdinand and Isabella. As a superb specimen of Moorish architecture, it was second only to the Alhambra in Granada, and the Grand Patio rivaled any Moorish courtyard anywhere. At the time of Clemens' visit, the palace was inhabited by the Emperor of Morocco who, rumor had it, maintained the tradition of the old Moorish throne of selecting eight young virgins in the Grand Patio each week for his imperial seraglio. The apartments themselves were supposed to be closed, but for a fee the custodian would show the whole of the palace to a willing tourist, and Clemens was charmed. "I see now what the glory of Spain must have been when it was under Moorish domination," he wrote his family. "No, I will not say that, but when one is carried away, infatuated, entranced, with . . . the supernatural beauty of the Alcazar, he is apt to overflow with admiration for the splendid intellects that created them." [56] The gardens, too, were beautiful. They had been reconstructed by Charles V, but the essential outlines were Moorish and the principal walls, fountains, and kiosks were of Moorish origin. Boxwood and myrtle enclosed green lawns, and throughout the gardens roses bloomed among the orange and lemon trees. For a few extra reales Clemens might have had an orange picked surreptitiously from the Emperor's own garden.

From Seville to Cordova was 80 miles farther up the River Guadalquiver by railroad and took five hours. Julia cared little for the city and admired only the cathedral ("almost the only attraction to strangers," she called it); they stayed only a day in Cordova before returning to Seville. It was now Wednesday and they had to meet the *Quaker City* on Friday morning at Cadiz. To avoid any

[56] *Ibid.*

delay which might leave them stranded in Spain, they arrived in Cadiz on Thursday.

They went by way of Jerez and stopped off to visit the vineyards and sherry soleras of Gonzalez, Dubosc & Company—the largest producers of wine in Spain: the cellars seemed as endless as the Roman catacombs, and the tour through them was conducted with a hushed reverence befitting a holy place. The climax of the tour was an enormous room filled with a dozen huge casks called the "Twelve Apostles," each of which held 1600 gallons of wine. In the midst of these was an even larger cask called "Isabel II," in honor of the queen's visit of several years before. The Gonzalez concern was famous for taking tourists through its cellars, explaining the process of making sherry, and giving out liberal samples of the wines themselves. Even Julia liked them. "You will not expect me to descant critically on the flavor of wines," she wrote home, "but I will say that the soft richness of some of these *old* wines, and the absence of all the harshness and pucker which make most wines so unpalatable, filled me with surprise." She tasted several, she said, but stopped before they got to the one-hundred-year-old varieties. The men of the party did not. "The gentlemen went into raptures," Julia wrote succinctly.[57]

Although very old, Cadiz had few historical attractions, but it charmed them nevertheless. Like Gibraltar, it was on the point of a heavily fortified peninsula and along the battlements were garden paths which had beautiful views of the harbor and ocean. The weather continued to be warm and sunny, and after they had shopped a bit they wandered along the famous Alameda, noticing the Gaditan women, famous for their beauty, and the business of the harbor.

At 7:30 Friday morning the *Quaker City* appeared outside the harbor, by 10:30 the four Spanish travelers were on board, and by 11:00 the ship was putting out to sea again. It had been a pleasant week for Clemens—not too hurried and full of novelty. But it was only an interlude for him, virtually "time out of mind," for he apparently took not a scrap of notes on the tour, and except for a brief reference to

[57] *Janesville* (Wis.) *Gazette*, December 14, 1867.

his "cheery week" in "Old Spain" he said nothing of the experience in *IA*. Pleasant though he found it, he was never to visit Spain again.

The rest of the excursionists were no doubt envious of the Spanish travelers. Gibraltar had been rather dull the second time around, and the pilgrims were restive; after elaborate plans for a tour through Spain they had found themselves with six empty days to fill, and the Rock and its apes were no amusement. Some of the passengers seriously thought of leaving the excursion altogether (the Severances for example very nearly decided to travel through Spain to Paris) but none did. Mail diverted them for a time; Mrs. Fairbanks received copies of the *Herald* filled with news the Cleveland party was eager for, her own letters not the least of all. But their correspondence was soon finished, time lay heavy again, and the ladies took to spending their mornings at dressmakers'. Some of the pilgrims went to Tangier, seeking perhaps the excitement Clemens had told them of several months before, and a few, of course, were seeing Gibraltar for the first time. Beach, his daughter Emma and Charlie Langdon, for example, found some delight in the Rock and the English village, but six days finally seemed too long even for them. Coaling the ship was as dirty and as interminable as ever; Duncan had his usual problems buying livestock and chandlery and only after much dickering managed to purchase eight bullocks and a dozen sheep which were tethered on the forward deck amid the lashed crates of fowl. These preparations drove the passengers ashore. In the depths of boredom, all the pilgrims—in violation of their religious principles—spent their afternoons at the races. "I cannot say I was much excited," wrote Emily Severance after her first visit, "and I can see no great good coming out of it, but I can imagine how people become interested, particularly how they are tempted to bet." [58] It had been a very long week.

Perhaps because of their boredom, there was a ferment among the passengers to add yet another stop to their itinerary before saying goodbye to Europe. "We *may* stop at Lisbon," Clemens wrote his family.[59] Some of the pas-

[58] *Journal Letters*, p. 204.

[59] *Letters*, p. 138.

sengers were very eager to see Portugal, particularly Solon
Severance, who shortly after the ship left Cadiz presented
Duncan with a request signed by a majority of the passengers to stop at Lisbon. To omit a previously scheduled
stop required unanimous consent, but to add a port of call
needed only a majority vote, and Severance's petition
evidently had this. Duncan, for reasons of his own did not
wish to stop at Lisbon, however, and, on the technicality
that a "vote" could be had only in a meeting (presumably
with an elected chairman and someone keeping "minutes"),
he said he "could not admit the legality of the document" [60]
and turned the ship toward Madeira. The majority of the
passengers—who had some reason to feel deprived of the
promised Mediterranean ports of call—thought this all very
high-handed of the Captain, and the unpleasantness of
several weeks past flared up again. Mrs. Fairbanks, for her
part, sought out Duncan after devotions that evening and
told him rather precisely what *she* thought of his behavior.

Thus beleaguered, Duncan protected himself by attack
and began to issue "notices touching the better observance
of the regulations" of the ship. There was a rule against
smoking in the cabins, but throughout the voyage many of
the men—Clemens chief among them—had smoked cigars
and pipes in their staterooms and no one had complained.
Now Duncan rather emphatically indicated that he would
see to it this rule was enforced. And he further commanded
that all lights were to be fully extinguished at "lights out."
The happy poker games which had often continued well into
the night were to be no more—or so Duncan threatened. It
was an ill-chosen time to make such dicta, and the passengers thought his manner peevish in the extreme. Of
course, they happily ignored the notices. Clemens continued
to smoke and played cards as he pleased, and it was only
when a steward inadvertently left his porthole open and
seawater ruined his fine Spanish cigars that he finally re-
duced his smoking in bed. Fortunately the imminent arrival
of the *Quaker City* in Madeira precluded any prolonged
debate on the subject, and a rather stolid peace returned to
the ship.

[60] *Log*, p. 112.

At daybreak Monday (October 28), Baleria was in sight, and at noon the ship was anchored in Funchal Harbor. Intermittent rain fell on deck, but the passengers were delighted with the look of the volcanic islands, or at least with the look they were allowed between showers. The coast was "rocky, but beautifully green" Emily Severance noted,[61] and there was a general excitement among many of the passengers eager to visit the locale of fine wine and beautiful handiwork. There was cynicism too. Some of the passengers were sure they would not be allowed to land without quarantine—it was the way of these foreign ports of call!

As it turned out, the official who kept them from landing was an American. The Health Officer of Funchal was Dr. Leas, the American Consul, and an old friend of Judge Haldeman. He was pleasant enough. Yes, they all looked healthy and he believed that they had had no illness on board but they *had* been in Alexandria and that meant they had to be in quarantine three days. Some ships, he suggested darkly, had to stay *seven*. Immediately the gong sounded and the passengers assembled in the "Synagogue" to determine their course of action. Stay or go? It was a difficult decision, for three days' wait in harbor would be deadly, the island might not be worth the delay, and there was a general desire—now that the ship was actually pointed toward home—to get there as quickly as possible. On the other hand, they *had* been denied Portugal by Duncan's high-handedness, and this was to be their last chance to see someplace European. A vote came quickly and by a narrow majority the ship decided to remain for the quarantine. The fires in the boilers were put out and the ship made a permanent anchor.

However, the decision was no sooner made and these actions carried out than the minority began to agitate to change the decision. "Now commenced wire pulling," Duncan remarked, no doubt wearily.[62] Clemens had voted with the majority, probably in deference to the Severances and Mrs. Fairbanks, who were eager to stay, rather than out of

[61] *Journal Letters,* p. 207.
[62] *Log,* p. 114.

any great desire to see Madeira himself. Now he began to have second thoughts. The light rain of the morning became torrential, and the wind rose. The journey from Spain had not been an easy one, but now a real storm seemed to be developing, and as Clemens surveyed the harbor of Funchal it seemed to him to offer no storm protection at all. As a matter of fact, if the wind got any higher they would almost certainly have to seek safer waters where the tides would not throw them against the rocks. In the face of this danger, he decided to change his vote and requested another meeting to reconsider the action of the morning. At four o'clock another gong was sounded, another meeting called, another chairman elected (this time Dr. Gibson had his chance), and another vote taken. Colonel Kinney moved that the ship leave Madeira immediately and sail for Bermuda, and after Duncan made it clear that *he* wanted to *stay* in Madeira, the passengers voted to leave 29 to 21. Bloodgood Cutter, an advocate for remaining, blamed the vote on wives who, he said, forced their husbands to vote with them. "When ladies travel they incline,/ To be by far too masculine," he wrote. "They show by actions, and their say,/ Determined more to have their way." [63] Duncan was rebuffed. It was all "parliamentary chaff" he remarked airly in his logbook,[64] but the decision was nevertheless made. The fires were rekindled, last-minute supplies of fruit were taken on board, and the port informed the ship would leave at 7:00 P.M.

The decision caused consternation in Funchal. They wanted to maintain a clean port, but they were well off the usual steamer lines and apparently they eagerly desired the money the *Quaker City* passengers were equally eager to spend. They had courted the ship—sending it several cases of "sample" wine with best wishes—and had looked forward to the wealthy Americans' disembarkation. Now all was to be lost! In what was apparently a desperate effort, they summarily informed the *Quaker City* that it would not be allowed to leave the harbor until morning, although it was unclear just why this should be necessary or what new

[63] *Cutter,* p. 133.
[64] *Log,* p. 115.

arrangements morning could bring. Thus threatened, even Duncan became an advocate of departure, and he informed the authorities that the ship would leave when *he* and not they determined. They replied that if the ship attempted to leave before morning, the guns at the entrance of the harbor would fire on it. Duncan, every inch the master of his ship at last, answered that at 7:00 P.M. the *Quaker City* would leave port and the authorities could fire "if they thought best." [65] In reply the port sent a bill for the sample wine.

At seven, the *Quaker City* steamed out of the port. "Custom imposed three days of quarantine, and must be obeyed," wrote Moses Beach. "And custom (!) deprived the Funchal people of some hundreds, if not thousands, of dollars, which otherwise would have been expended among them. . . . They lost our custom because we refused their's [sic]." [66] For the next few days the pilgrims—now adamantly anti-Funchal—amused one another by announcing how much money they had been prepared to spend in Madeira and shaking their heads over the shortsightedness of the port authorities. No one mentioned Dr. Leas.

The storm they expected never materialized; the first day out had strong winds but fine weather, and the second day even the winds were pleasant and the sea "like a river." The pilgrims were all on deck enjoying brief bonhomie disturbed only by the Duncan boys who, evidently at their father's behest, peddled fruit among the passengers. The third day, heavy weather returned, and most of the bonhomie departed. The ship rolled and pitched and the passengers began to wonder if these were the "trade winds" and would they continue like this for the two weeks journey to Bermuda? For the next three days, there was no letup. "Seasickness and chicken soup" Duncan summed up in his log. [67]

Those who were not seasick were bored. "Every one was busy only in 'killing time,' " wrote Beach. "This they accomplished by eating, drinking (water almost exclusively, and far from good water at that) sleeping and enjoying by turns a little sea-sickness." [68] When the weather cleared, the

[65] *Ibid.*, p. 116.

[66] *Sun,* November 20, 1867.

[67] *Log,* p. 117.

[68] *Sun.* November 20, 1867.

tedium became, if possible, worse. They listlessly played charades and dominoes and chess and draughts and back-gammon. They were far enough off the usual shipping lanes that they saw no ships for a week, and they soon *longed* for a storm to break the monotony. Clemens was enervated for other reasons, of course. He was now writing steadily all day and passing his correspondence to Mrs. Fairbanks for correction. It was tiring labor, and he had no high regard for the letters he was composing. He was increasingly irritable, and Duncan increasingly the object of his ire. One day about half way to Bermuda, his anger could no longer be controlled. The food on board, he complained, was inedible and the arrangements generally mismanged. The coffee in particular had been pretty bad throughout the voyage, but on this morning Clemens was served a cup he thought too weak and tasteless to be allowed, and he marched to Duncan's table demanding coffee as good as that he claimed was served the Captain. As Moses Beach was later to report the incident:

It was now the captain's turn for surprise, but instead of cutting capers with the steward, he contented himself for the moment by requesting Apostle Mark to produce a cup of the noxious preparation that the two might be compared. Away went Mark for his cup, and the Twain returned in seeming triumph. Down went this cup by the side of that, the motions accompanied by an almost shout of exultation. "There, didn't I tell you so! and you wouldn't believe me! It's too bad we should be put off so, when your table is well served." etc., etc., etc. How long the outburst might have continued it is impossible to say, for Captain Duncan's eye twinkled and . . . the Apostle was compelled to abate his words and gain breath to annihilate the wretch who thus made merry with his misfortune. When the pause came Captain Duncan filled it to the uttermost with an explosion, the only distinguishable and the only relevant part being the words, "Why, this is tea!" During the uproar which followed Mark disappeared, and since then has not been known to complain of food or drink, nor even of the cook.[69]

Clemens was later to report the incident in *IA* and to try to turn it to comedy—with only middling success. "He had

[69] *Ibid.*

made an egregious ass of himself before the whole ship," he was to write. "He did it no more. After that he took things as they came. That was me" (p. 639).

Alone among the passengers, Clemens had work to do. His fellow excursionists were indolence itself. "We kept very busy, writing and reading," Emily Severance remarked in a monumental self-contradiction. The passengers tried reading aloud: *The Pickwick Papers* and *The Lady of the Lake* and *The Lay of the Last Minstrel.* "Also I hemmed some handkerchiefs," Emily wrote. In such boredom the tensions of the voyage reached their height. The two weeks from Madeira to Bermuda were as unpleasant as any on the voyage. For the month past they had been barred from ports which were to have been the crowning pleasures of the excursion; all through the hot dry months in the middle east they had looked forward to the lush green lands they would be visiting thereafter—Malta, Sardinia, Majorca, Spain, Madeira—and all had been denied them. The minor dissensions among the passengers had become regular and increasingly unpleasant; shipboard manners had long since worn thin and become frayed; Duncan seemed less and less in control of the crew; the weather had been repeatedly bad; and, above all, exacerbating all and, perhaps, if one knew, causing all, they were homesick. "Homesickness was abroad in the ship," Clemens was later to report to the *New York Herald.* "It was epidemic. If the authorities of New York had known how badly we had it, they would have quarantined us here." [70]

It was not a happy ship, then, which sighted the Bermuda light in the early morning hours of November 11. They expected nothing from the islands, which were notorious as a Confederate gun-running station during the war and famous for little else, and they planned to stay only long enough to take on fresh water and a few provisions before they continued to where they really wanted to be. They were, therefore, ill-prepared for what they found. Twenty miles off Bermuda, Duncan slowed the engines to ensure they would not come in sight of land—and shoals—before his signal for a pilot could be seen, but scarcely had the

[70] November 20, 1867; *Traveling,* p. 318.

engines been shut down when a boat of five Negro pilots appeared alongside offering to steer the ship to harbor. With some hesitation Duncan took one of them on board and gave him the wheel. "The skill of the negro pilot was a study to some of our unaccustomed passenger eyes," wrote Moses Beach later.[71] The path to the harbor was treacherous with shoals and reefs and its entrance lay between two rocky outcroppings which seemed impossible to sail through. But they arrived safely and dropped anchor at sunrise in St. George's harbor. The view that lay before them was an almost incredible sight to the pilgrims. "What a harbor! What a sunrise!" Moses Beach exclaimed ecstatically. Their dismal preconceptions of Bermuda only made their surprise the greater and their delight the more intense. "We expected nothing but a sand pile," Duncan reported, "and found high ground, green foliage & fine scenery." [72] The harbor was surrounded by a beach glittering in the early sun, and behind it were gleaming houses which seemed set like precious stones in the dark green vegetation. They could hardly believe their good fortune. They had missed their paradise in the Mediterranean only to find it here, close to home.

After the disappointments of the previous six weeks, they hardly dared to think of quarantine again, but they needn't have feared. The Bermudan port authorities didn't even ask for papers but accepted the Captain's word that the ship was free of disease. "You, who dwell where so little is known of red tape, can but dimly appreciate the free welcome which to us seemed so precious!" Beach wrote. "We felt at home again!" [73] After breakfast they hurried to shore and engaged carriages to take them to Hamilton. "I wish I could describe the entire ride," Emily Severance wrote home,

the charming glimpses out to sea, the naval harbor on Ireland Island, the water with its many colors, the coral reefs, the negro women with their broad straw hats, the woods and wild flowers, the bananas and fields of arrowroot, and finally, the entrance into the pretty town of Hamilton.[74]

[71] *Sun,* November 21, 1867.
[72] *Log,* p. 120.
[73] *Sun,* November 20, 1867.
[74] *Journal Letters,* p. 209.

Everything they saw increased their pleasure. They had become so accustomed to filth in foreign places they could scarcely believe the cleanliness they found about them. The hotel they declared the most comfortable they had found anywhere. They had spectacular views from their rooms, and "the table," Emily Severance wrote, "was one of the best we experienced on the trip." [75] The day was gloriously

"Our Friends, the Bermudians"

clear and their spirits could not have been higher. They explored St. George's island with an enthusiasm which must have been the equal of that they felt at Fayal those many months before. They discovered the shops and Government House, and a few found a Wesleyan chapel just before a wedding took place before their delighted view. In the evening after dinner they walked along the beaches and through the oleanders and palmetto trees. It was a full moon night. "One of the loveliest nights that I *ever* saw!" Mrs. Severance declared. "There was a perfect flood of light resting on the bay and the white roofs." [76]

[75] *Ibid.*
[76] *Ibid.*, p. 211.

They had intended to stay only one day in St. George. They remained five. Pleasure accounted for the first three days; a storm for the last two, but they were not, surprisingly, unhappy to be delayed by bad weather. The island made them wholly welcome. One of its permanent residents, W. C. J. Hyland, was a British businessman who had married a woman from Brooklyn, and he took special interest in showing the island to the excursionists. On the second night after their arrival in St. George, the Hylands invited a few of the excursionists to dine. "We feared we had been so long at sea that we had forgotten drawing-room etiquette," Mrs. Fairbanks wrote later, but "we ventured to accept." [77] The company was more formally dressed than at any time since they left Yalta, and the evening, Emily Severance declared, was a "sumptuous affair." The next day they toured the island and inspected the lighthouse point from which they had an excellent view of all the islands. "If England would give us these coral reefs, I am sure we would make of them one of the most charming resorts in the world," [78] Mrs. Fairbanks asserted. Some of the islands' inhabitants would have been happy to oblige her. At a gala party the Hylands gave the following evening, some of the British officers stationed on the island said they were tired of exile even in such a paradise and wished England would let the islands go to the United States.

It was a lively party, probably the best they had had on the voyage and certainly the longest lasting, for it was in the early morning hours that the passengers returned to the *Quaker City*—intent on sailing the next day. The wind was up and a storm coming in fast, and the voyage to the ship was a perilous one. Clemens steered the boat which carried the Severances and Mrs. Fairbanks back to the ship, and Mrs. Severance, for one, was badly frightened—"the worst storm in which I was ever out in a small boat," she declared. Clemens, tired from a long convivial evening, steered. "Our oarsmen tugged manfully," Mrs. Fairbanks reported, "and 'Mark Twain' held the rudder with a strong hand, while the spray dashed over his Parisian broadcloth and almost ex-

[77] *Herald,* December 14, 1867.
[78] *Ibid.*

tinguished his inevitable cigar. For a time it seemed as if the longer we sailed, the farther we drifted from the lights of the *Quaker City*." [79]

What they were not to learn until later was that the winds which lashed Bermuda were part of a much larger winter storm which struck the east coast of the United States. For two days it raged and they thought it unwise to venture out of their safe harbor. Some of the pilgrims recalled that had they been allowed to land at Madeira they would almost certainly have met the storm en route to Bermuda, with what disastrous results they dared not think. However, by 8:00 A.M. Friday (November 15) the storm had abated enough for the ship to leave the harbor and continue on the last bit of their journey home. Bermuda had softened their feelings toward one another and the imminence of family and friendly surroundings made the atmosphere on board a much happier one than it had been. For Clemens it was a time of celebration, too, for he could see he was going to finish his *Alta* contract before they landed, and he looked forward to his Washington assignment with pleasure. But the voyage was not an easy one, and the *Quaker City* encountered weather which was by all reports the most tumultuous of the entire trip. The end of the storm was still sweeping the middle Atlantic states when they started out, and the ship battled mountainous waves and severe winds. In the storm the first real mishap of the voyage occurred: Judge Haldeman, unsteady throughout the voyage, at last fell and broke his ankle. After four days the storm abated and on the fifth day the ship sailed into New York in a relatively quiet sea and under a calmer sky.

After the balmy weather of Bermuda the air seemed cold as they sighted Sandy Hook, but that scarcely diminished their excitement. "The entrance to New York, incomparably finer than that to any port with which I am acquainted, seemed never finer than in this clear wintry air." wrote Moses Beach in the *Sun* the following Friday.

"Welcome home" glittered in every sunbeam, and as we sped through the Narrows was reflected, flashing back, again and again,

[79] *Ibid.*

in windows of purest crystal, along the shores of Staten Island and New Jersey. . . . Altogether we were as happy and jovial a company as ever entered port.[80]

Not quite, perhaps, but for the moment the dissension of the weeks past was forgotten. They stood together at the rail for the last time and watched New York arrive. The Clevelanders huddled together against the wind, Solon Severance scolding Emily for coming up on deck despite a bad cold which had kept her in her berth since Bermuda, Mrs. Fairbanks wondering perhaps if they should be met and how they should survive customs inspection. And Bloodgood Cutter braced his tiny frame against the wind and searched, in all likelihood, for a rhyme to finish the poem extolling the *Quaker City* which he would write on the morrow ("Long will I think of this good ship,/That conveyed me on this grand trip;/For comfort will her recommend./To all around, both foe and friend." [81] Julia Newell and Dr. Jackson together watched the harbor pass. It was, as Julia later was to state in her matter-of-fact way, "About as pleasant a sight to most of the passengers, I dare say, as any that had met their eyes in all the months past, for were we not Home Again?" [82] Duncan in the wheelhouse was perhaps too busy to give it much thought at the time, but he might have believed the journey worth the effort and the price.

And perhaps Clemens, too, was thoughtful and even for a moment sentimental. Perhaps he remembered that other winter's entry into New York harbor not quite a year before. How much had happened since! How much was yet to happen! But his reverie was interrupted by the start he felt, "the shiver of the decks that told that ship and pier had joined hands again and the long, strange cruise was over" (p. 642).

[80] *Sun*, November 22, 1867.
[81] *Cutter*, p. 137.
[82] *Janesville* (Wis.) *Gazette*, December 14, 1867.

EPILOGUE

The excursion was over but a controversy had begun which was not to end in Clemens' lifetime. It was largely of his own making, for, all his protestations to the contrary, the book he fashioned from his newspaper correspondence was a comic lambasting of his fellow passengers and the excursion they took together. When *IA* appeared on July 20, 1869,[1] most of his impious newspaper comments about the Holy

[1] Frances M. Edwards, ed., *Twainian Notes from the Annotations of Walter Bliss,* (Hartford, Conn., n.d.) p. 6. For accounts of its reception, see Leon T. Dickinson, "Marketing A Best Seller: Mark Twain's *Innocents Abroad,*" *Papers of the Bibliographical Society of America,* 41 (June, 1947); 107–22.

Land had been omitted, much of his provincial irascibility was also cut, but his caricature of the other pilgrims not only remained, it became, if anything, more pointed and sardonic. Most of his fellow excursionists were incensed by the book and some remained so; over 40 years later at least two of them took the occasion of his death to answer him, bitterly, in print.[2] They had been forewarned, perhaps. They knew Clemens was a newspaper humorist and they must have known he was unlikely to ignore them as a subject.

The *Quaker City* was scarcely tied to its Wall Street pier before Clemens had written an hilarious burlesque of the excursion and given it to the *New York Herald*. He wrote the letter largely out of guilt: he had sent the *Herald* only three short dispatches on the voyage[3] although he had promised them more than three times that many,[4] and the letter was an attempt to make up for his silence. But there can be little doubt that it expressed a sincere initial dissatisfaction with the voyage, for he was later to print most of it in the last chapter of *IA*.

Is any man insane enough to imagine that this picnic of patriarchs sang, made love, danced, laughed, told anecdotes, dealt in ungodly levity? In my experience they sinned little in these matters. . . . The pleasure ship was a synagogue, and the pleasure trip was a funeral excursion without a corpse. (There is nothing exhilarating about a funeral excursion without a corpse.) A free, hearty laugh was a sound that was not heard oftener than once in seven days about those decks or in those cabins; and when it was heard it met with precious little sympathy.

. . . When they were not seasick they were uncommonly prompt when the dinner gong sounded. Such was our daily life on board the ship—solemnity, decorum, dinner, dominoes, prayer, slander. It was not lively enough for a pleasure trip; but if we had only had a corpse it would have made a gorgeous funeral excursion. It is all over now; but when I look back, the idea of these venerable fossils skipping forth on a six months' picnic, seems exquisitely

[2] Nina Larrowe in the *Portland Morning Oregonian*, April 22, 1910, and Stephen Griswold in the *Brooklyn Eagle*, June 5, 1910.
[3] See Dewey Ganzel, "Samuel Clemens, Sub Rosa Correspondent," *English Language Notes*, Vol. 1: 270–73.
[4] *BM*, p. 95.

ludicrous. The advertised title of the expedition—"The Grand
Holy Land Pleasure Excursion"—was a ghastly misnomer. "The
Grand Holy Land Funeral Procession" would have been
better—much better.[5]

The "venerable fossils" were not slow to react to his criticism. Through an error Clemens' name was left off the
letter (he insisted that the paper identify him the following
day), but none of his recent shipmates would have had
trouble recognizing him as its author. Few of them, however, could have been prepared for his valedictory. They
had not, of course, read the correspondence he had been
sending home all along, and it must have been something of
a shock to return prepared to bask in the glamor of a
famous six-months' cruise only to watch it made a laughing-
stock by a professional humorist almost as they disembarked. It was apparent, too, that Clemens' criticism was,
at bottom, serious. He really *didn't* care much for most of
his fellow pilgrims and his humor was in part a weapon
against them. In a burlesque *pax vobiscum* he concluded his
letter:

The grand pilgrimage is over. Goodby to it, and a pleasant
memory to it, I am able to say in all kindness. I bear no malice, no
ill will towards any individual that was connected with it, either as
passenger or officer. Such persons as I did not like at all yesterday
I like very well to-day, now that I am home, and always hereafter
I shall be able to poke fun at the whole gang if the spirit so moves
me to do, without ever saying a malicious word. The expedition
accomplished all that its programme promised that it should
accomplish, and we ought all to be satisfied with the management
of the matter, certainly.

When he reprinted the letter in *IA* he concluded his quotation at this point and remarked:

I call that complimentary. It *is* complimentary; and yet I never
have received a word of thanks for it from the Hadjis; on the
contrary I speak nothing but the serious truth when I say that
many of them even took exceptions to the article [p. 647].

---

[5] *New York Herald*, November 20, 1867; *Traveling*, pp. 314–15.

Perhaps if he had reprinted the rest of the letter in *IA*, their discomfort would have been better understood, for his *Herald* letter ended with comic condemnation:

But that such pleasure excursions as this are calculated to be suffocated with pleasure, I deny; and that a party more ill-fitted, by age and awful solemnity, for skurrying around the world on a giddy picnic, ever went to sea in a ship since the world began, I deny also, most fervently.[6]

He intended his letter to make the pilgrims "skip," as he called it, and he succeeded; the shock waves of indignation caused tremors for months afterward. But not all of his fellow passengers took him quite so seriously. Mrs. Fairbanks gently disagreed with him. "I have read all the 'squibs' and the 'flings,' at the 'Pilgrims' and the 'Quaker City,' " she wrote in her final letter to the *Cleveland Herald*.

I have listened to more, but notwithstanding all I still aver that the agreeable features of the voyage far outweigh the disagreeable. In every community there are some elements of discord. Seventy passengers have not always been of one mind. There have been some errors in the 'administration of affairs,' but they have been oftener errors of the head than the heart.[7]

And Moses Beach also disagreed with Clemens' judgment of the excursion. But even these replies from Clemens' friends could not quiet the controversy, for there was a widespread dissatisfaction with the excursion and Clemens was by no means its only critic. Dr. Jackson, for example, wrote the *New York Herald* the day after Clemens, and his letter (signed "A Passenger") criticized the voyage with less humor than Clemens, and with more specific condemnation—particularly respecting Duncan whom he charged with "incompetency and irresponsibility." [8] He was even more severe in criticizing the backbiting gossip among the passenger "cliques," and his final judgment of the voyage was far more condemnatory than Clemens':

From all these things, it will be seen that this great pleasure party, as such, has been a failure. It is true that we have visited a

[6] *New York Herald*, November 20, 1867; *Traveling*, p. 319.

[7] *Cleveland Herald*, December 14, 1867.

[8] A few of the passengers thought Clemens wrote this letter, too.

number of interesting places, but we have done so in the most hurried and unsatisfactory manner, while the expense has been much greater than if the travel had been made upon the regular lines.

. . . The experience of this trip has shown how dangerous to the comfort and pleasure of travel it is to bring together persons from parts of the country widely separated, unknown to each other, and who, by reason of disparity of age, disposition and interest, have but few feelings in common, and compel them to live together in one house, as it were, for many months. It seems probable, therefore, that this great Mediterranean excursion will be the last of its kind.[9]

It was not the last of its kind, of course, and in large part because Clemens, despite his disaffection, made the trip seem fun. There may have been anger in his heart when he first got home: "To this day," he wrote Mrs. Fairbanks two weeks after landing, "I have a strong desire, whenever I think of some of the events of that trip with that menagerie, to print the savagest kind of history of the excursion." [10] He even started a play (printed in the Appendix to this book) full of heavy-handed humor which was meant to lampoon Duncan and the pilgrims on the voyage, but he found he couldn't finish it. By the time he came to write *IA* some months later, his anger had, in large part disappeared and in its place was a kind of amused toleration, encouraged, perhaps, by his continuing success. The pilgrims returned in November; by January he had signed a "tip-top contract" for *IA* with The American Publishing Company, and he was sure (and rightly so) that he would make a lot of money from his book; he had had happy days in Washington, and his newspaper correspondence was getting a larger and larger circulation as his commercial value soared—and he had met Olivia Langdon, Charlie's lovely sister, and fallen in love with her. It would have been hard

---

However, Jackson is identified as its author in a letter Clemens wrote to Emeline Beach quoted in Bradford A. Booth, "Mark Twain's Friendship With Emeline Beach," *AL,* 19 (November, 1947): 222.

[9] *New York Herald,* November 21, 1867.

[10] *MF,* p. 4.

indeed for him to have maintained any bitterness in the midst of such good fortune. The new sections he composed for *IA* are closer to the tone and exuberant manner of his early letters to the *Alta* than they are to the nose-thumbing wit of the *Herald* letter, and the book's popularity was no doubt enhanced by this circumstance. "This book," he wrote in his Preface, "is the record of a pleasure trip," and his readers believed him.

Although some of the pilgrims remained bitter toward Clemens, others with the passage of time softened their attitude. As the fame of *IA* spread, many of the passengers took special pride in having been one of the "pilgrims"—Bloodgood Cutter, for example, actually advertised himself in later years as "Mark Twain's 'Larriat' in 'Innocents Abroad.' " [11]

For most of the passengers, this tenuous association with Clemens was to be as close as they would come to historically memorable experience; when they left the ship they returned to their former anonymity. But Clemens' was not the only success to grow out of the trip. Others, in their own way, found what they were looking for on the voyage. Mr. James, for example, had a great success publishing his stereopticon slides of the Holy Land, and Mr. Parsons was successful in his search for new agricultural specimens—as a direct result of the cruise, he imported the first valencia orange trees ever seen in the United States, and when he planted them in Florida he founded an industry. John Greenwood shipped back a hold full of exhibits for Barnum's Museum; no room was set aside for the excursion in the Museum—too few of the pilgrims wanted to give up their collections—but Greenwood's specimens were an important part of the Museum's exhibits until it burned several years later. Even Dr. Jackson—despite his harsh criticism of the trip—apparently found a new impetus for his life on the voyage. To the surprise of no one, he married Julia Newell (although he continued to court her for three years!). Shortly after his return he left Stroudsburg, moved to Chicago, and began a new career in medicine, eventually becoming one of America's first eminent gynecologists.

One way and another the cruise brought notice to a few of

[11] See title page of *Cutter*.

its passengers. Many of the pilgrims returned to their home towns and found, with the advent of *IA*, that they were "notabilities" through their association with Clemens. Typical of these was William Gibson who, despite his sharp disagreements with Clemens and Clemens' scathing burlesque of his pretensions in *IA*, flaunted their relationship among his Jamestown, Pennsylvania, peers.[12] Two other pilgrims wrote memoirs of the journey. In 1871, two years after the publication of *IA*, Mrs. Griswold published her account, *A Woman's Pilgrimage to the Holy Land; or, Pleasant Days Abroad,* hoping, perhaps, that Clemens' success would be repeated by one of her own. (It wasn't.) And Bloodgood Cutter brought out a flossy private edition of his epic poetry of the voyage (*Lines Written on the "Quaker City" Excursion to Palestine, and Other Poems*) and died a quarter of a century later apparently content in his presumed immortality, piously leaving his fortune to the American Bible Society.

But for a few of Clemens' fellow excursionists, the journey seemed the last important act of their careers. Moses Beach, for example, sold his interest in the *Sun* to Charles Dana a month after he returned from the cruise and left newspaper publishing for good. His career before the voyage had been highly successful, but, although he lived for another twenty-five years, his life after the cruise was undistinguished. Solon Severance returned to Cleveland with even less direction than he had left with. His neurasthenia made it impossible for him to continue in his position at the bank and within a year he sold his interest, to retire—at thirty-three. Although he was later to be associated with various mercantile and philanthropic endeavors, he spent most of the remainder of his eighty-one years traveling and giving lantern-slide lectures concerning his journeys.

The ship and its captain came to more dramatic ends. Shortly after the *Quaker City* returned from the Mediterranean, Leary sold her and she became, for a time, a Cuban gunrunner, an object of suspicion and intrigue. In 1869 she was sold again to the provisional government of Haiti, then

[12] See Henry F. Pommer, "Mark Twain's 'Commissioner of the United States' ", *AL*, 34 (November, 1962): 385–92.

undergoing one of its periodic revolutions. Fitted up as a man-of-war and renamed the *Republic,* she was used primarily as a blockader and had a number of successful fighting encounters with insurrectionist ships. When peace came she was sold yet again, repaired and fitted up for trade between Haiti and New York. She was making her first voyage back to New York when, on February 22, 1871, her boilers blew up at sea and she sank off the coast of Bermuda.[13]

The cruise marked the beginning of Duncan's professional decline, and Clemens had something to do with it. In an attempt to recoup some of the cost of the cruise, Duncan toured the lecture circuit as the "Captain of the Quaker City" and evidently was successful in capitalizing on both *IA* and Clemens' own lectures concerning the voyage. In his lecture Duncan returned some of Clemens' insults: Clemens was, he told his audiences "full of whiskey, or something" and pretending to be a Baptist minister when he applied for his passage on the voyage. Duncan's action so infuriated Clemens that ten years after the voyage, when Duncan, then a functionary in the Port of New York, was accused by the Ship-owners' Association of misappropriating fees and other corruption, Clemens gave a vituperative interview to the *New York World,* which brought on a lawsuit against both Clemens and the paper. Clemens evidently settled the case out of court, but his anger was unabated, and five years later, in 1883, when U.S. District Attorney Root charged Duncan with taking graft from seamen wishing to ship out of New York, Clemens gave another interview to the press, this time to the *New York Times,* which was even more denunciatory and brought on an even larger lawsuit. Clemens claimed he was misquoted and extricated himself from the case, but Duncan pressed against the *Times.* Although Duncan was never to be convicted of fraud, the case against him was such that the court awarded him damages of only 12 cents, and his career came to an ignominious end.[14]

[13] See *New York Times,* February 25, 1871, p. 4.

[14] See Henry Nash Smith and William Gibson, eds., *Mark Twain-Howells Letters* 2 vols. (Cambridge, Mass.: Harvard University Press, 1960) p. 865–67.

Duncan's quarrel with Clemens was the most notable controversy to grow out of the voyage, but it was not the only one. The four "fast young men" did not continue close friends for long. Jack Van Nostrand and Julius Moulton remained visible for a time—companions along with Dan Slote on one or two gay reunions when Clemens passed through New York—but they soon went different ways and disappeared. Dan's friendship with Clemens was longer but ultimately much more unhappy. Two years after he returned from the cruise Dan married, and the Clemens and Slote families were intimately acquainted. Clemens invested money in Slote, Woodman & Company, and his friendship with Dan acquired business associations of some complexity. For instance, Dan was in charge of producing Clemens' "self-paste" scrapbook, one of many inventions Clemens was to patent (and almost the only one which made money). And still later Clemens put him in charge of developing kaolatype, a German process of engraving, which Clemens wanted to adapt to printed bookbindings. It was over this undertaking that they eventually fell out. The exact nature of their quarrel is unknown, but Clemens became convinced that Slote was cheating him and in 1881 their fourteen-year friendship ended in great bitterness.[15] When Dan died of typhoid fever six months later, Clemens was still unforgiving:

If Dan had died thirteen months earlier [he wrote angrily to Mrs. Fairbanks], I should have been at the funeral, and squandered many tears; but as it is, I did not go and saved my tears. Dan . . . was not a robber. There is a sort of robust dignity about robbing. He was only a pick-pocke[t], more base than ordinary pick-pockets, who merely filches [sic] from strangers. . . . I came very near sending him to the penitentiary.[16]

It was a pathetic end to a long and rewarding friendship.

Charlie Langdon, of course, became Clemens' brother-in-law on February 2, 1870, seven months after *IA* ap-

---

[15] In her anger, Slote's wife Sarah burned the voluminous correspondence from Clemens which Dan had kept, thus destroying the most valuable source of details of their friendship.

[16] *MF,* p. 247.

peared. Less than a year later, he himself married, and when his father died shortly thereafter Charlie, then twenty-one, assumed control of the family lumber and coal business and most of the family fortune. By all accounts he handled it well and lived a blameless and unremarkable life as a community leader (police commissioner and town councilman for Elmira) and life-long Republican (he was a Grant delegate to the Chicago convention of 1880).

Only Clemens' friendship with Mary Mason Fairbanks seemed ultimately to flourish. In fact, they became closer friends on shore than they had been on shipboard—at one point shortly after his marriage Clemens very nearly became her husband's partner in the *Cleveland Herald*. For nearly thirty years, until her death in 1898, she was Clemens' confidante, and their voluminous correspondence was to reveal that she saw in him qualities of spirit and mind which many of his more famous—and influential—friends did not. She was his defender from the first:

" 'Mark Twain' may have ridiculed our prayer-meetings and our psalm-singing—" she wrote in the *Cleveland Herald* shortly after Clemens had stirred up the *Quaker City* controversy,

that is his profession—and his newspapers expected it of him; but the better man, Samuel L. Clemens, I believe in his heart reverences the sacred mission of prayer, and will, I am sure, often recall with satisfaction the evening hours when his voice blended with others in the hymns of the "Plymouth Collection." [17]

He would. But not alone the pious circumstances Mrs. Fairbanks described. Throughout his life his thoughts would return with pleasure—or consternation—to the events of the Holy Land Excursion of 1867 among the "godless" and godly pilgrims. He would come finally to see it as a formative time in his life and *IA* as a chronicle of self-discovery and initiation. It was, he wrote long after, a "book of a youth on his first travels." This was a poetic overstatement, of course; at thirty-one Clemens was no longer young when he went abroad, but as metaphor it is significant, for it suggests his final attitude toward the cruise and the book he

[17] *Herald*, December 14, 1867.

wrote about it. *IA* was a product of his "youth" and like his youth it was immutable. In later life he recognized its faults and wished them gone, but he could not, be realized, revise the book any more than he could recapture the experience which gave it birth or reshape the man who wrote it.

I should simply knock out a compact brick of ignorance here and there, and insert an ineffectual clod of unsure learning; I should knock out the boy's chipper confidence, and insert the man's chilly caution; I should knock out the boy's giddy enthusiasms all away, and insert the man's shorn and subjugated impulses and wary speech.[18]

The Innocents Abroad was of a piece with the past which made it.

[18] Introduction to *The Innocents Abroad* (Leipzig: Tauchnitz, 1879), pp. 7–8.

THE QUAKER CITY HOLY LAND EXCURSION

Fragments of an unfinished play by Samuel Clemens

Shortly after returning from the *Quaker City* cruise, Clemens began a drama satirizing its events. The genesis of the play is uncertain. Apparently his friend Charles Henry Webb, who had recently published *The Celebrated Jumping Frog of Calaveras County and Other Sketches*, suggested that the excursion would be a likely subject for a successful drama. The possibility of a profitable return from small labors may have encouraged Clemens to make the attempt, but the fragment which follows suggests the idea did not develop easily. He had never written a play before, and he seems to have been bewildered as to how one shaped such disparate material into an organic whole. The experience of the cruise lent itself directly to the kind of personalized narrative he was to make of it in *Innocents Abroad*, but it was not so easily adapted to the dramatic form which demanded greater consistency in character, motivation and story line.

He soon abandoned his attempt, and on November 25 he wrote Webb from Washington that he had the "will" to write the play but not the time:

I am enrolled as an "occasional" on the Tribune staff, have received a letter from the Herald offering me the same position in that paper, (shall accept if it don't interfere with the Tribune arrangement) & must keep up a Pacific coast correspondence. If you were *here* to stir me up, we could do this play, sure. As it is, I don't think I will accomplish anything but my correspondence.[1]

His decision was a wise one, for as his later experience in writing drama was to prove, he lacked the theatrical bent which would have made his project successful. The ambition died hard, however. On at least four later occasions, he was to try his hand at writing for the stage. Of these attempts, only *Ah Sin!* had anything which might be called a success, and that of a very minor and unprofitable kind.[2]

The fragments of *The Quaker City Holy Land Excursion* are, therefore, of little interest in themselves, but they are useful as a comparison with Clemens' later development of the same subject in *IA*. In particular, his treatment of Captain Duncan in the play is much more pointed—not to say vicious—than it was later to appear in the book. In the play, Duncan is called Captain Dusenberry—a name Clemens had used earlier for comic effect in a letter to the

---

[1] Clemens to Webb, November 25, 1867; from a photostat reproduced in the unpublished play cited hereafter.

[2] For the details of Clemens' later career as dramatist, see "Introduction," *"Ah Sin," a Dramatic Work by Mark Twain and Bret Harte*, ed. Frederick Anderson (San Francisco: Book Club of California, 1961).

Alta [3]—and Duncan-Dusenberry has no redeeming qualities of mind or manner. His is an angry portrait made when Clemens was still smarting from his experience with the original. In particular, Clemens' treatment of the Committee on Credentials suggests a dishonesty in Duncan of which there is no suggestion in *IA*. The "pilgrims" come in for heavier handling, too: their general crassness and provincialism is out of keeping with their character as Clemens was to suggest it in *IA*. The "deacons" and "sisters" are a thoroughly unpleasant lot and broadly caricatured. The character Stiggers was evidently going to embody most of the mannerisms of Brown-Blucher. Significantly, however, Stiggers is introduced as a "newspaperman," and the satire which was likely to develop here was therefore of a slightly different kind from that associated with Brown in *IA*, although the instance of his trouble with the passage of time was taken directly from a Brown incident in the letters. Significantly, Dan Slote (here thinly veiled beneath the name Sproat) appears as a sidekick to "Mark Twain," a suggestion that these were to be the two "straight" characters against whom the rest of the mélange would play. The fact that "Mark Twain" alone among the *Quaker City* passengers appears without apparent disguise suggests that Clemens, his interest whetted, perhaps, by experience on the lecture platform, may have planned to play this part himself. For that reason alone one might wish that the play had been finished. Finally, the notebook fragment introduces another character which has no counterpart in either *IA* or the other play fragment. The character, designated solely by "Buttrw," was evidently designed to be a burlesque stereotype. His interest here derives from his drunkenness—a subject which Clemens carefully avoided in *IA*. The fragment suggests that "Buttrw" was pretty well worked out in Clemens' mind and that the comedy he intended was to be of a rather obvious sort.

A comparison of the tone and treatment of the play with that of *IA* suggests that Clemens rather consciously tempered his burlesque sensibilities when he came to write the book, that he deliberately avoided ascribing dishonest intentions to Duncan, and that he just as deliberately

[3] See *Alta*, April 5, 1868; *Traveling*, p. 305.

avoided characterizing the "pilgrims" as pious, empty-headed provincials. The play fragments may have served as a release for the anger Clemens revealed in the *Herald* letter, allowing him thereafter to treat his subject with greater objectivity and control.

The text which follows embodies two loosely related fragments. The first and longer of the two derives from a manuscript now in the Lilly Collection, Indiana University Library, which was privately printed in 1927.[4] The copy of this edition in the Berg Collection of the New York Public Library has a note indicating that its publication was suppressed. I reprint the Lilly manuscript from photostats in the Mark Twain Papers.

The second fragment is found on two pages of Clemens' "Unpublished Notebook No. 9." It is very brief, but clearly related to the drama. For the sake of completeness, I reprint it here.

ACT I.   SCENE I.

Capt. Dusenberry's Office in Wall Street
> (Enter six old maids, in obsolete costumes, & a dozen veterans of both sexes in all stages of sickness, mutilation & dilapidation. With cats, parrots, poodles, etc.)

1st Maid—(with youthful diffidence) Good morning sir is this the office of the Grand Pleasure Excursion all over the Habitable Globe & the Holy Land in Five Months?

Capt—It is, Madam—or Miss, no doubt, judging by appearances—pray be seated. James—(to the clerk) bring chairs—be seated, ladies & gentlemen.

1st Maid—We have seen by the published programme that none but persons of the highest respectability & the most stainless morality—

Capt—You will be safe ladies, I assure you that *you* need not have any fears if you go with us, of the snares of designing men. *Aside*—Your faces are security for *that*, anyway.

---

[4] The title page gives no particulars of publication.

1st M—We are very, *very* glad to hear you say that. It lifts a *load* of apprehension from our hearts. And we see, also, that Mr. Beecher is going with you—is that true?

Capt—Entirely so.

M—Oh, Joy! And Gen. Sherman?

Capt—Yes—

M—And the Drummer Boy & Maggie Mitchell?

Capt—Both.

M—Rapture!—what a delightful variety!—And it is published in the programme that the $1250 fare must be paid in advance & the recommendations of all applicants for passage submitted to the Committee on Credentials. We have brought our money (they pass it in) & some letters endorsing our characters (they hand over a voluminous mass of manuscripts) & now Captain, if we should be so fortunate as to meet with favor in the eyes of the Committee,—

Capt (pretending to glance over the recommendations)—No danger in the world, my dear Miss—encomiums like these could never be slighted by any committee.

M—You see, we are poor unprotected young things—

All Maids—Silly unsophisticated creatures—

M—Just of an age to fall into the pitfalls that line the paths of thoughtless youth—

All—Gay, & foolish & giddy—

1st M—Just in that budding spring of life when innocence & beauty are too apt to prove the sources of bitterest sorrow to their possessors—

All—Sad, sad lot—(snuffling)

1st M—And—and—Will you—will you be our dear guardian & friend & shield us from harm with your manly breast? Speak!

All—Oh, be our guardian angel!

Capt—This hand shall defend you from all peril—this breast shall shield you—this heart shall be your refuge! All the ship's company shall know my fatherly care, but unto you I will be father, mother, brother, uncle, sister-in-law (Excuse these tears)

All—Heaven bless you, Sire! (Exit.)

Capt D—(*Aside*)—Well, a few more old cats like that

would make a unique excursion of it, *I* should say.
(To the others.)—Ah, ladies & gentlemen—

1st Cripple—Wher[e] do you stop at first, Capt?

Capt—At the Azores.

1st Cr—Is that a tribe, or is it a mountain or something?

Capt—Oh—neither. It is a group of islands.

1 Cr—Jes so—Jes so.—Where next?

Capt—At Gibraltar.

Cr—Tribe? Or maybe—maybe, mountain?

Capt—(Cursed old fool)—No, Oh, no—Kind of a mountain—great rock on a peninsula of Southern Spain.

Cr—That's good. That's powerful good. Wher[e] next?

Capt—Marseilles.

1 Cr—I-yi—where they make the white vests & sing March
on March on ye brave, the 'venging sword unsheath
& so on. That's very good. Marseilles—that's very
good—only place in Ireland that's *worth* a d--n.

Cap—I should be glad to converse with you at some length,
Mr.—Mr.—for I perceive that you are of an observ-
ing turn of mind & endowed with a fund of interesting information which cannot fail to make your conversation entertaining to any man in the world
who—who—would be likely to be entertained by
it—(No—no—no thanks)—but time presses, &—did
you wish to say anything in particular?

1 Cr—Nothing, only here is my money.

The Others—And mine—

1 Cr—And my recommendations—

The Others—And mine, also—

1 Cr—And I guess we're all in the same boat together—
leastways, we want to be. (They pass the compliments & exit.)

Capt—(Throwing the stacks of recommendations in the
fire) Committee on Credentials! Humph!—Twelve
Hundred & Fifty Dollars—*paid!*—(ironically—well,
I guess you'll all pass the Committee without running
aground. And here's another stack of recommendations come by mail from Arkansas, & Jersey & other
out of the way places. Let's see what *they* say.
(Reads.)

Whangwhang, Minn.

Jan 67.

"This is to certify that we have known the inclosed
Deacon Pendergrass for 62 year[s], & always found
him a stunner at awakening, & hark from the tomb!
when it comes to giving 'experience.' A square man &
not knowing of his own gifts.

Jno Smith—Jno W. Smith

Jno H. Smith—Jno Peter Smith &c, &.

$1250 Enclosed.

Cap—Pendergrass will do. Reads—

Alligator Terrace

Indiana &c

"This is to signify that the within named Jno
Butterfield has retired from business and does not
keep corner grocery any more. He has the soap. He
comes from the first families of this place & his uncle
was postmaster once & his grandfather was a Home
Guard in the Revolutionary War. He knowed the
nigger that was body-servant to Genl Washington.
Notwithstanding that that nigger in a bogus form
keeps turning up every year & dying in the newspapers at the most cussedest unearthly ages that ever
even Methusalem heard of, but not genuine & not to
be relied on. He is 57 years old—Butterfield, not the
nigger—& is poorly as to health but handy with a
knife & fork.

Jno Jones, J. B. Jones

Wm. H. Jones, Geor[g]e Washington Jones &c

$1250 Enclosed)

Cap D—Well, I suppose this dazzling acquisition must be
added to the ship's list, too. The last recommendation
is a good one.

Rondout, N. Y. Jan. & c.

The young gentleman whose father sends a note
with this requesting that his name may be placed
before your Committee on Credentials, is of stainless
reputation & exalted principles. He is a graduate of
Yale College, & although he will necessarily have to
remain in the modest & retiring position proper to

him in the midst of such a constellation of intellect &
learning as will illuminate your ship, he will still feel
only too grateful if allowed to mingle, though ever so
little, with these great lights, & borrow of the radi-
ance that falls, unnoted of themselves upon all who
come within their orbits. Mr. Livingston's father
commanded a brigade in the late war, his uncle was a
class mate of Gen. Grant at West Point, & another
uncle has served in the Senate of the United States
for 16 years. Another member of the family was for
many years our Minister at the Court of France, &c,
&c, &c.—

Cap D—No use to read it all—a man could get passage in
an Emperor's State barge with half such a recommendation as that. I don't propose to take the young
man to *Heaven*. His money is received—that is of
more consequence to me than it is to know what his
respectable old grandfather did. I'll take the money
out of the balance of these letters & burn them. I
guess I can risk the Com. on Credentials. Oh, that
Com. on Cre. was a rare dodge! (laughs exhaustingly
or otherwise) (Exit)

ACT II

Scene I—Quarter Deck of a Steamer
Enter 2 Newspaper Correspondents. They look dejected.
A pause.

Mark Twain—Ah, me!

Stiggers—The remark I was about to make.

M. T.—Well, how does it strike *you?*

S.—Don't mention it.

M. T. (quoting from programme) Splendid Ship.

S.—Eight miles an hour.

M. T.—Plenty of instrumental music.

S.—Three wheezy melodeons & a clarinet.

M. T.—Vocal ditto.

S.—Plymouth Collection of Hymns!

M. T.—Excessively select company.

S.—Selected out of a camp meeting & a hospital—some of

them sick, some of them crippled & the balance reading sermons & back biting each other all day long.

M. T.—Passengers will be lively, young & happy.

S.—Rustiest gang of old fossils since Methuselah's time.
There ain't 14 out of the 60 but are over 60 years old.

M. T.—No passenger accepted without a spotless reputation.

Both.—How did *you* get here?

M. T.—Committee on Credentials.

S.—Bah! Twelve hundred & Fifty Dollars in greenbacks!
Could have brought Sing-Sing along if they had the
money.

M. T.—Beecher!

S.—Backed water—they advertised him to death.

M. T.—Sherman!

S.—They made him sick, too. They made him a medium for
advertising the Grand Holy Land Funeral Excursion
for Pleasure till he got so distressed at last that he
fled to the savages of the plains—preferring a merci-
ful swift death by the tomahawk to the lingering
torture of wearing out his life carrying a bulletin
board on his back.

M. T.—Maggie Mitchell.

S.—*She* died of advertising, too. Human nature couldn't
stand this infernal advertising!

(A Pause.)

M. T.—Well, did you bring your share of the programme
list of books for the ship's library?

S.—What is *that?*

M. T.—Tent Life in the Holy Land, Pilgrim's Progress &
Other Travels, Shepherd of Salisbury Plain, Thomp-
son's Whole Duty of Man, Mother Goose's Melo-
dies.—

S.—*I* brought four reams of quarto post, thirty gross of steel
pens & a barrel of gin!

M. T.—Stiggers, I *love* you. (They embrace.)

S.—Well, we've been out ten days, now, and—here comes
the whitest man in the ship!

(Enter Dan Sproat
low, fat & chunky.)

Dan—Boys, it's awful. Them venerable old pilgrims are going to run the prayer meeting *every* night, now that the most of them are not seasick anymore, instead of every *other* night. And they're going to have two sermons every Sunday. Ain't it a gay pleasure trip, I don't reckon? I wish we had brought along a corpse, & then we could have a bully funeral every now & then—anything to be cheerful. We'll die with the dry rot if this sort of thing goes on. And don't you know, they have been just howling about the little claret & stuff we take in our room occasionally. They are down on No. 10 you know. It's on your account Mark, not mine. And I say, Stiggers—I—by George there goes that old gong!—here, get behind the booby-hatch!—Or them old pilgrims will rope you in for the prayer meeting. Look at old Homily, now, with his nose in the air. He hasn't got his sea-legs, yet—*I* wouldn't laugh if one of them heavy seas was to fetch him. Wouldn't *care* a d--n, either. (They hide.)

(Enter Patriarchs, male & female, in procession.)

Elder Homily—(with a sigh)—How wonderful is prophecy! Here we are, brethren & sisters, far on the briny deep. We are not trusting in our own might, yet are we marvellously upheld. Such protection—such love as this, ought to warm our hearts toward all our fellow creatures & fill them with charity for all their short comings, & sinful, sinful conduct. Ah yes, it ought. Let us be lenient with the failings of those who are in the ways of iniquity, & the paths of e-*ter*-nal destruction! Ah, me, there is that abandoned Sproat, for instance. (Pantomime by Sproat & Co.)—& that Twain (More pantomime) & that ridiculous Stiggers (Extravagant by-play.) They drink & drink & drink, in that No. 10 till it is horrible—perfectly *horrible!* And they smoke there—which is against the ship's rules—& they have bribed the cabin crew & the porter & they burn safety lanterns there all night (which is against the rules, too) & they say they are writing to the newspapers—which is a *lie,* brethren & sisters—they're playing sinful 7-up. That's what they're doing. Ain't it so, Sister Whistler?

Sis. S. (fine voice)—Yes, bless goodness, it *is*. It ain't no longer ago than last night that the sea give one of them wretched heaves which it pretty nigh fetches my very insides out of me every time it does it, & goodness knows glad am I we don't have 'em on the farm or sure I am that never *I* should survive, *I* know—Glory be to God! And when that sea give that heave I stumbled, sorter, & accidentally fell up agin the keyhole & lo & behold you I hear Dan Sproat say "I played the tray for low"—& Twain says "Seventeen for game," & that sinful Stiggers he said he guessed he'd take a drink. And the way them heathens was a carrying on!—I never hear the beat of it in *my* life, bless you. Much *they* care whether the ship goes down or not.

Elder H—Much use it is to wrestle with the Lord for quiet weather with such as these on board. But it is our duty to wrestle—Brother Bascom is over his long hypocritical prayer by this time—*Sis. S*—Which it never gets no higher than the fore-spanker-gaff-tops'l-jib-boom, *I* don't think—as them bejiggered sailors calls it, nobody being able to understand them but a born lunatic.

Elder S—And so *we* will wrestle if Providence be willing. (Exit.)

Stiggers—Now the blamed old bag of bogus piety is going down to pray up another nor-wester. The first time these people get a settled stomach in them they get out their Plymouth Collections & start another storm that sets them to heaving again. If they'd only let up once, we could have some fair weather. But didn't they give it to us! Out of whole cloth, too! I'd like to catch old Whistler at that keyhole once. Here comes *Bascom's* flock, now—stand back. [The Lilly manuscript ends here.]

[The following fragment is found in Clemens' "Unpublished Notebook no. 9" (Typescript, p. 28), *MTP*.]

[unidentified speaker—] 7—Bells—All hands on deck to pump ship!

Buttrw—You'll excuse *me*—(goes below.)

Gent & 1st Maid—Oh, how lovely, how serene the night
  is!—The sea is like a mirror it is so smooth!
  Enter Buttrw
[*Buttrw*] (Drunk [)]—Hic! Heavy Sea again!—Plymouth
  Collection—ain't they never going to let up!
  Gent & 1 Maid converse & he comments.
  6—Bells—
Buttr—By geminy it ain't been forty minutes since that
  blame clock struck 5—I never.
[new page]
Butrw [sic]—How does she head, shipmet [sic]
[Wh—] E. N. E. & by Nothe 3/4 nothe—
Buttrw—Well she's crooked I should think—Humph! ain't
  trying to get the ship along at all—no sails up—
Wh—Sails, you d'd fool & the wind dead ahead. [Fragment
  ends]

APPENDIX B

PASSENGERS AND CREW
ON THE QUAKER CITY

The following list derives from contemporary accounts of
the voyage and is intended to correct and supplement
Paine's list in *Mark Twain: A Biography* (pp. 1609–10).
Names marked with a single asterisk were listed as leaving
on the *Quaker City* but not as returning with it; those
marked with a double asterisk joined the ship en route.

Anthony Bezenet Allen,   Dr. Edward Andrews,
    New York, N.Y.   Albany, N.Y.

Major James G. Barry, St. Louis, Mo.

Moses Sperry Beach, Brooklyn, N.Y.

Miss Emeline Beach, Brooklyn, N.Y.

Thomas S. Beckwith,* Cleveland, Ohio

Mr. and Mrs. R. A. H. Bell, Portsmouth, Ohio

Dr. G. B. Birch, Hannibal, Mo.

Mr. and Mrs. John W. Bond, St. Paul, Minn.

Miss Ada Bond, St. Paul, Minn.

Miss Mary E. Bond, Plaquemine, La.

Dr. M. Brown, Circleville, Ohio

Miss Kate L. Brown, Circleville, Ohio

John Brynam,* Philadelphia, Pa.

Rev. Henry Bullard, Wayland, Mass.

Miss Carrie D. Chadeyne, Jersey City, N.J.

William F. Church, Cincinnati, Ohio

Samuel Langhorne Clemens ("Mark Twain"), San Francisco, Cal.

Dr. Albert Crane, New Orleans, La.

Albert Crane, Jr., New Orleans, La.

Mr. and Mrs. T. D. Crocker, Cleveland, Ohio

Bloodgood Haviland Cutter, Little Neck, L.I.

J. W. Davis, New York, N.Y.

Nathan Decan,* Long Island

Col. W. R. Denny, Winchester, Va.

Mr. and Mrs. Fred Dimon, Norwalk, Conn.

Mrs. Charles C. Duncan, Brooklyn, N.Y.

George Duncan, Brooklyn, N.Y.

Henry E. Duncan, Brooklyn, N.Y.

P. A. Elliott,* Columbus, Ohio

Mary Mason (Mrs. Abel W.) Fairbanks, Cleveland, Ohio

Col. J. Herron Foster, Pittsburgh, Pa.

Dr. and Mrs. William Gibson, Jamestown, Pa.

Mrs. J. O. Green, Washington, D.C.

John Greenwood, Jr.,* New York, N.Y.

F. H. Greer, Boston, Mass.

Mr. and Mrs. Stephen M. Griswold,** Brooklyn, N.Y.

Gen. B. B. Grubb,* Burlington, N.J.

Hon. Jacob S. Haldeman, Harrisburg, Pa.

Goddard Heiss,** Philadelphia, Pa.

Capt. W. R. Hoel, Cincinnati, Ohio

Rev. E. Carter Hutchinson, St. Louis, Mo.

Hon. James K. Hyde, Hydeville, Vt.

John G. Isham, Cincinnati, Ohio

Dr. Abraham Reeves Jackson, Stroudsburgh, Pa.

William E. James, Brooklyn, N.Y.

Frederick P. Jenkins,* Boston, Mass.

Col. Peter Kinney, Portsmouth, Ohio

George W. Krauss, Harrisburg, Pa.

Charles Jervis Langdon, Elmira, N.Y.

Miss Nina Larrowe, San Francisco, Cal.

Daniel D. Leary, New York, N.Y.

Mrs. S. G. Lee, Brooklyn, N.Y.

Mr. and Mrs. E. K. Lockwood, Norwalk, Conn.

J. M. May,* Janesville, Wisconsin

Louis McDonald,** Bristol, England

Capt. Lucius Moody, Canton, N.Y.

Julius Moulton, St. Louis, Mo.

Arba Nelson, Alton, Ill.

Dr. B. B. Nesbit,** Louisville, Ky.

Thomas B. Nesbit, Fulton, Mo.

Miss Julia Newell, Janesville, Wis.

W. A. Otis,* Cleveland, Ohio

C. C. Paine,* Pennsylvania

Rev. A. L. Park,* Boston, Mass.

Miss Park,* Boston, Mass.

Samuel B. Parsons, New York, N.Y.

Dr. and Mrs. J. H. Payne, Boston, Mass.

Rev. G. W. Quereau, Aurora, Ill.

S. N. Sanford, Cleveland, Ohio

M. A. Serfaty,** Gibraltar

Solon Severance, Cleveland, Ohio

Emily (Mrs. Solon) Severance, Cleveland, Ohio

Nicholas Sexton,** New York, N.Y.

Daniel Slote,* New York, N.Y.

S. Willets,* Long Island

John A. Van Nostrand, Greenville, N.J.

CAPTAIN: Charles C. Duncan
SAILING MASTER AND EXECUTIVE OFFICER: Ira Bursley
SECOND OFFICER: William Jones
STEWARD: Benjamin Burdick
CHIEF ENGINEER: John Harris
PURSER: Robert Vail *
QUARTERMASTER: Mr. Pratt

A hitherto unnoticed item in the *New York Sun* for November 20, 1867, states that the passenger list had a "total of 74, or, with the addition of Miss Langdon who joined them at Bermuda, a total of 75." This addition suggests the possibility that Olivia Langdon joined the Excursion in Bermuda and that Clemens may, therefore, have met his future wife in person on the voyage rather than at the St. Nicholas Hotel in late December, 1867, as he states in his *Autobiography* (II, 103). Clemens' memory as reflected in the *Autobiography* is not to be trusted absolutely, and the facts of their first meeting are uncertain at best. The *Sun* article is a good contemporary authority because its information derived from Moses Beach who was on the trip from Bermuda. "Miss Langdon" may have been Susan Langdon, Charlie and Olivia's step-sister, but it appears that she was already Mrs. Theodore Crane in November, 1867. It is not impossible that Olivia, a semi-invalid, journeyed to Bermuda for her health and planned there to meet Charlie and return to New York with him.

INDEX